WORRIES OF THE HEART

WORRIES OF THE HEART

Widows, Family, and Community in Kenya

KENDA MUTONGI

THE UNIVERSITY OF CHICAGO PRESS

CHICAGO AND LONDON

KENDA MUTONGI is associate professor of history at Williams College.

The University of Chicago Press, Chicago 60637
The University of Chicago Press, Ltd., London
© 2007 by The University of Chicago
All rights reserved. Published 2007
Printed in the United States of America

16 15 14 13 12 11 10 09 08 07   1 2 3 4 5

ISBN-13: 978-0-226-55419-8 (cloth)
ISBN-13: 978-0-226-55420-4 (paper)
ISBN-10: 0-226-55419-8 (cloth)
ISBN-10: 0-226-55420-1 (paper)

Library of Congress Cataloging-in-Publication Data

Mutongi, Kenda Beatrice.
  Worries of the heart : widows, family, and community in Kenya / Kenda Mutongi.
    p. cm.
  Includes bibliographical references and index.
  ISBN-13: 978-0-226-55419-8 (cloth : alk. paper)
  ISBN-10: 0-226-55419-8 (cloth : alk. paper)
  ISBN-13: 978-0-226-55420-4 (pbk. : alk. paper)
  ISBN-10: 0-226-55420-1 (pbk. : alk. paper)
    1. Widows—Kenya—Maragoli—Social conditions.   2. Women—Kenya—
Maragoli—Social conditions.   3. Family—Kenya—Maragoli.   4. Kenya—Colonial
influence.   I. Title.
  HQ1058.5.K4M88 2007
  306.88'30967628—dc22

                                                              2006038721

For my mother, husband, and children,
with love and gratitude

CONTENTS

Acknowledgments	*ix*
Abbreviations	*xiii*
Maps of Kenya	*xiv*
Introduction	*1*

Part I: Everyday Life

1.	Western Kenya, 1880–1902	*15*
2.	Feeble Little Lads Looking for Food	*23*
3.	"What Harm Can an Old Dry Bone Do?"	*34*
4.	Lessons in Practical Christianity	*45*
5.	Living "in Line"	*56*
6.	The Impact of Gold Mining	*69*
7.	Land Conflicts in the 1930s	*82*

Part II: Family Life

8.	Educating "Progressive" Sons	*97*
9.	The Burden of "Progressive" Sons	*107*
10.	Cash, Cows, and Bridewealth	*118*
11.	Domestic Education at the Girls Boarding School	*128*
12.	Moral Panic	*139*
13.	Wife Beating	*149*

Part III: Postcolonial Promises

14. Citizenship and Land Rights in Postcolonial Kenya   *163*

15. Rural Widows, City Widows, and the Fight for Inheritance   *178*

Conclusion   *193*

Glossary   *199*

Notes   *201*

Bibliography   *227*

Index   *247*

ACKNOWLEDGMENTS

I have been working on this project long enough that nearly everybody I know has helped me in some way or other. In the early 1990s, when I was a graduate student at the University of Virginia, Joseph C. Miller introduced me to the study of African history. His approach to history was and remains entirely humane. He urged me not to focus on judging the various historical actors but instead to try to understand why people in Africa did the things they did and said the things they said. I have tried to follow his advice, but of course Joe does not bear blame for any interpretational or conceptual errors that one might find in this book. Joe has been a terrific mentor, and I was lucky to have been one of his students. At Virginia, I also learned a great deal from the following friends and colleagues: Wendy Bearns, Lenard Berlanstein, Edward Ayers, Julia Clancy-Smith, Richard Handler, Cynthia Hochler-Fatton, Jim La Fleur, Adria La Violate, Jeanne Maddox Toungara, John Mason, Kelly Mulroney, Becky Popenoe, and the late Armstead Robinson.

The Rockefeller Foundation and the Social Science Research Council provided funds that enabled me to do the dissertation research in Kenya and England that became the foundation of this book. A Newcombe Fellowship from the Woodrow Wilson Foundation, Princeton, allowed me the time to write the dissertation.

I consulted several archives and libraries to gather information for the book. In particular, I would like to thank Michelle Riggs and Professor Thomas Hamm for assisting me at the Friends Collection and Archives at Earlham College in Richmond, Indiana. I also owe many thanks to the staff members at the Kakamega Provincial Record Center; the Kenya National Archives; Rhodes House, Oxford; and the Public Record Office, Kew Gardens, London.

Maseno University was my host institution in western Kenya. I would like to extend my gratitude to Professors William Ochieng and B. A. Ogot for graciously agreeing to accommodate me. More important, though, I would like to thank the Maragoli men and women who took the time to speak with me and who encouraged me to "write our history." They welcomed me into their homes and shared with me whatever little food and water they had, and this gave me the energy that I needed to walk up and down the numerous hills scattered all over Maragoli.

∽

After spending a couple of years figuring out ways to revise my dissertation for publication, I decided that the dissertation needed to be tossed away, chopped into small pieces, and recycled to generate new paper on which I could write a new book from scratch. It was not an easy decision. But generous grants from Williams College allowed me the opportunity to make several trips to Kenya and Indiana to gather more information for the book. I would especially like to thank D. L. Smith, then dean of faculty, and his assistant, Sally Bird, for making this possible. I wrote the first draft of the book while a fellow at Radcliffe Institute for Advanced Study, Harvard University. My special thanks go to Cathy Silber, Denise Buell, and Sue Miller, all fellows at the institute, for reading draft chapters of the book. Cathy, in particular, has continued to follow the evolution of the book and its long history with keen interest and has consistently given me invaluable editorial and conceptual advice. Viviane Jaffe, Jane Taylor, and Anna Battigelli also offered useful editorial comments on earlier drafts. I made final revisions to the book while a member at the Institute for Advanced Study, Princeton. The institute was a marvelous home for me during that year, and I would especially like to thank Adam Ashforth, Sarah Igo, Krishan Kumar, Bruce Grant, Helen Tilley, Paulla Ebron, Julia Adeney Thomas, Donne Petito, Rama Ramakrishna, and Charu Chakravarty for their friendship and support.

Among Africanists, my gratitude goes to E. S. Atieno Odhiambo, David Anderson, Charles Ambler, Lisa Lindsay, Simon Gikandi, Tom Spear, Timothy Burke, Sue O'Brien, Emmanuel Akyeampong, Lynn Thomas, Nancy Rose Hunt, and Luise White, friends and colleagues who have taught me a great deal about African history and culture. In particular, this book has benefited from my sustained conversations with Lynn Thomas, whom I first met in Kenya in 1994. Lynn is a great friend and a terrific researcher, and her passion for Kenyan history is truly infectious. Since then, Lynn and I have often synchronized our visits to Kenya, and I have been extremely lucky to be in her company throughout my fieldwork years in Kenya. Lynn also read each and every word of this book in its many incarnations.

Support from colleagues and friends at Williams College has also en-
riched this book. Special thanks go to Charles Dew, Robb Forman Dew, Bob
Dalzell, Frank Oakley, Jim Wood, Regina Kunzel, Karen Merrill, Roger Kit-
tleson, Tom Kohut, Chris Waters, K. Scott Wong, Bill Wagner, Cheryl Hicks,
Shanti Singham, Caroline Reeves, Dan Goodwin, Vivian Cooke-Buckhoy,
and Magnus Bernhardsson. Friends from elsewhere have also talked through
the material for this book with me. They are Bill Amundson, Dennis Dicker-
son, Tony Eprile, Craig Wilder, Peter Frost, Kim Springer, Rachana Kamtekar,
Yaseen Noorani, Miki Makihara, Jonathan Conning, Pat Tracy, Binyavanga
Wainaina, Jane Poncia, Johan Thor, and Paul Johnston.

Last but not least, I thank my editor, T. David Brent, for his support,
patience, and, above all, his great sense of humor, which has sustained me
throughout and kept me writing. His confidence in me and in the project
has been invaluable. David is a brilliant editor, and my respect for and gratitude to him are great. My immense gratitude also goes to Elizabeth Branch
Dyson and Ruth Goring, who carefully and patiently guided me through the
intricate technical processes entailed in the production of this book.

This book has also benefited from tremendous support from my family.
My niece Sandra Opanga accompanied my two-month-old daughter and me
to Earlham College for several days and assisted me with research. My brother
Vincent Jumba read the whole manuscript and commented thoroughly, vig-
orously, and, at times, ruthlessly—but always with a great deal of love and
laughter. His insights into Kenyan history and culture are truly remarkable.
Numerous conversations with family members and friends from western
Kenya have been invaluable. Special thanks go to Margareth Opanga, Eric
Opanga, Chrispo Opanga, Eunice Oyungi, Reba Mudavadi, Edith Mmbone,
Jane Mukiri, Patrick Mutongi, Anne Mutongi, Yvonne Mutongi, Florence
Otiende, Reba Mudavadi, and Linet Mutongi.

My most heartfelt gratitude, however, goes to my mother, Rose Mutongi. She has been the greatest source of inspiration throughout my life. In
particular, she has made me think over and over again about the importance
of supporting one another as family and community members. She is one of
the most generous people I know. My deepest gratitude goes to my husband,
Alan de Gooyer. Alan has given me the priceless gifts of patience, love, laughter, and courage. He has asked penetrating conceptual and editorial questions
and read every word. He is, I am sure, happy to see this book leave my
study and enter the bigger and, I hope, a better world out there. Lastly, my
children, Ada and Stefan, have added a great deal of joy to my life, and
this has made writing this book more enjoyable. I dedicate this book to my
mother, husband, and children.

ABBREVIATIONS

AF	*American Friend*
AR	*African Report*
DC	district commissioner
EC	Earlham College
FMA	*Friends Missionary Advocate*
GBS	Girls Boarding School
IBEAC	Imperial British East African Company
KAR	King's African Rifle
KNA	Kenya National Archives
KPRC	Kakamega Provincial Record Center
LNC	Local Native Council
MP	member of Parliament
NKCA	North Kavirondo Central Association
PC	provincial commissioner

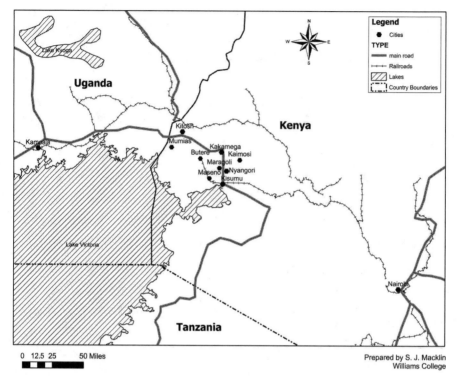

Western Kenya

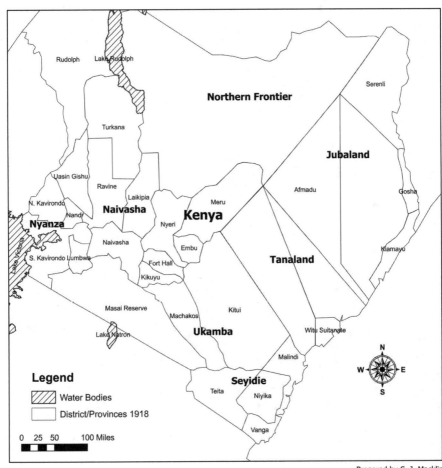

Kenya's administrative units, 1918–61

꧁꧂

INTRODUCTION

Approaching Maragoli from Lake Victoria requires a sharp northwest climb to 4,800 feet until you cross the equator. On the hills in the near distance sit boulders the size of cars and houses, strewn randomly as if dropped from the sky by some careless god; occasionally you run across haphazard markets crowded with goats, chickens, and cows and with people in every state of dress (or undress) hawking fruits, grain, vegetables, earthen pots, pans, and secondhand clothing. Behind and between the markets are small plots of land, rarely more than an acre, in which tea bushes, maize, cassava, potatoes, or beans grow timidly between the larger clusters of banana, mango, guava, and eucalyptus trees. Near the gardens stand resolute mud huts with thatched roofs or, at the well-off homesteads, with corrugated iron roofs. Occasionally you will pass the brick house of a professional man, a lawyer or an accountant, who works in one of the major Kenyan cities and keeps a "home house" that he visits a few times a year and where he plans to be buried. Only ninety-five square miles in size, Maragoli is a land of peasants, a heavily settled land whose soils are, unfortunately, rapidly becoming depleted of nutrients; it is, in other words, a land where people, animals, and plants struggle to survive.[1] It is, in fact, a fairly typical rural community in Africa today.

Maragoli is also my home, and the setting for this book. I grew up there right after Kenya's independence, in the late 1960s and 1970s, in one of the brick houses with a corrugated iron roof, in a fairly well-off peasant household, surrounded by goats, chickens, and cows and a few acres of tea bushes. My father, who died when I was five years old, had been a teacher at a local primary school. In those days, teachers were respected men who earned enough money to build brick houses that were almost but not quite as grand as the "home houses" of the professionals. Though I grew up without a father,

A typical household, 1995 (photo by author)

I was surrounded by relatives and family friends, all of whom had lived under colonial rule, and all of whom sang the praises of white men and women.
Again and again I heard my mother, uncles, aunts, and their friends com-
mend the departed missionaries and colonialists for bringing them "civilization." They were sincere and convincing. "Mrs. Spoon was a very nice
person; she taught us how to read and write," my mother remarked of her
white missionary teacher at Kaimosi Girls School. Our neighbor Matayo
Kavaya had worked as a clerk for the district commissioner in the late 1940s
and praised his honesty and punctuality: "Mr. Williams was a very honest
man; he kept his word and never deceived you." Kavaya himself became
known as the most organized and punctual man in the village—no doubt
emulating his former boss.

I also listened to compelling complaints about black rule. According to
my parents' generation, once "our people" took over after independence they
"ruined our schools and hospitals." "That Kaimosi hospital where you were
born," my mother would say, pointing at me, "used to be a first-class mater-
nity hospital; now there is nothing, not even gloves. When our black people
took over, they stole everything." My mother and her friends rarely—if
ever—talked about the cruelty of colonial rule. To them, the missionaries,
and by extension all white people, including colonists, were good people who

had brought them all the benefits of the civilized world. For me, then, and perhaps for many other Kenyans of my generation, the colonial era was presented as a time of prosperity and advancement. If your parents were closely tied to missionary and colonial institutions (my father had six and my mother three years of missionary schooling), the inevitability of postcolonial decline was drummed into you. The loss of colonial rule was lamented, the good old days were gone, and as a young person, you could expect to face worse times ahead.

This rosy picture of the colonial era changed once I entered Butere Girls High School, an Anglican boarding school in western Kenya, to study for my A-level diploma. Here, many of my teachers were highly politicized Ugandan exiles who had fled their country to escape Idi Amin. Almost all of them had, at the height of the independence movements in the 1960s, attended Makerere University, the first and most prestigious university in East Africa. My teachers were certainly aware of the fact that they had reached the pinnacle of black education in East Africa. Even in exile these men (there were hardly any women) walked about confidently and aired their opinions so strongly that their enthusiasm sometimes compensated for their rootlessness. They spent a great deal of time teaching us about the inherent evils of colonialism, avidly undermining the strict A-level syllabus that required us to memorize which European had discovered what mountain or lake in Africa, the details of lumbering in British Columbia, the advancement brought about by the Tennessee Valley Authority in the U.S. South, or how the Swiss had promoted winter tourism in the Alps. Instead, our teachers urged us to take pride in things African, to love our culture, our people. My literature teacher, who defiantly sported a long beard despite our headmistress's insistence that he shave, sent us back to our villages to record oral traditions, talk to our elders, and reconnect with our culture. He insisted that we write essays about our family histories, our genealogies, and our African leaders, our kings and queens. He also made us read black writers like Ngugi wa Thiongo, Ezekiel Mphalele, Sembene Ousmane, Okot p'Bitek, and George Lamming, all authors who railed against the wickedness of colonialism.

Both realities, the benevolent colonialism presented by my relatives and the earnest anticolonialism promoted at school, seemed equally true—and equally wrong. Somehow I had to resolve the conflict. Perhaps it is no surprise, then, that I have chosen to examine the colonial and postcolonial periods in an attempt to understand these conflicting views. I am also returning to my own past—or, perhaps I should say, to my mother's past. My mother spent the first half of her life under colonial rule and the second half under black rule, and she has strong opinions about both. Moreover, the fact that she is a widow makes her experience especially instructive—though her life as a widow was not unique. Quite the contrary. Families headed by widows constitute a large proportion of families in Africa: nearly 30 percent of adult women in Africa today are widows.[2] And, for fairly clear reasons, Maragoli has suffered some of the highest rates of widowhood in Kenya. Because of its large population and limited land, Maragoli men were often forced to migrate to the urban areas of East Africa to find work, and there they faced a host of dangers—car accidents, industrial accidents, unheard-of diseases, even world wars—all of which increased their rate of mortality. Of course, many of these deaths left behind a widow and, often, several children. To make matters worse, in recent years AIDS has led to an increase in widow-headed households, a development that is rapidly changing the nature of family relations in western Kenya, as elsewhere in Kenya and Africa.

Although widowhood hardly represents an exceptional circumstance, the situation of widows is especially enlightening. In fact, widows and their families serve as an ideal barometer of the impact of colonial and postcolonial rule in western Kenya. As marginal yet familiar figures, widows have always been acutely sensitive to changes in village life; any change in the economy or in social or familial structures and any change brought about by colonial or postcolonial rule usually had a disproportionate effect on them. Moreover, their sensitivity to change certainly increased during the twentieth century as the policies of colonial and postcolonial rulers altered the nature of interactions among family and community members. At the turn of the twentieth century, for example, much of western Kenya was devastated by disease and by local wars of conquest that killed men and left widows and children behind. Hungry and ailing, these children were the first to join the Quaker missionaries, who had come to the area in 1902. As newly minted Christians, the children were able to attend missionary schools and later become clerks and teachers; they were thus able to work closely with the colonial government and eventually become leaders of their communities. So even though widows were often the first to suffer, they were sometimes the first to benefit from many of the reforms contrived by the colonizers; struggling at the edges of their communities, they often found themselves at the center of the colonial enterprise. In other words, the widows' hardships were exacerbated by unheralded changes, and yet, paradoxically, their circumstances were sometimes improved by the new opportunities presented to them by the colonizers (and, of course, their own power to adapt to them). Even this brief example demonstrates, I hope, how the ambiguous experience of widows and their families provides a particularly revealing perspective through which to view some of the contradictions of colonial rule.

Widows' experience also offers a vivid commentary on the fraught promises and seemingly irredeemable dilemmas of postcolonial Kenya. At independence, the new black leaders promised to provide for ordinary people and especially to protect the interests of vulnerable citizens like widows. In the euphoric atmosphere of self-rule, widows, like other ordinary Kenyans, trusted the black leaders to fulfill their promises. Yet all too often, the leaders proved incompetent or merely looked out for their own interests. To give but one example, the new leaders instituted haphazard new laws of succession and land reform that threatened to disinherit widows of their deceased husbands' land and property; the immediate effect was to jeopardize the livelihood of widows and their children. Such miscalculations were common—and for this, and many other perceived betrayals, widows felt disappointed and frustrated, and their experience points directly to the disappointments and conflicts in postcolonial Kenya.

⌒∞⌒

The lives of Maragoli families and communities in the twentieth century, and especially the families and communities of widows, are the subject of this book. For practical reasons, the first part of the book (chapters 1–7) primarily focuses on the general social, economic, and political changes brought about in Maragoli as the missionaries and colonialists interacted with Maragoli men and women (and particularly widows) during the first three decades of the century. Drawing on colonial archival materials, ethnographies, photographs, obituaries, lamentations, folktales, local idioms and sayings, interviews with Maragoli men and women, and missionaries' diaries, letters, and memoirs, I offer a few glimpses of the ways things looked and felt in western Kenya in the early decades of the twentieth century. Precisely because there are very few written sources by the Maragoli themselves, I rely heavily on interviews to reveal the more intimate experiences of widows and their families and communities. Part of what I do is to immerse myself in local stories, gossip, and rumors. We all know what people in small communities talk about—who is sleeping with whom, who is bewitching whom, who is jealous of whom, who has more money, who is eating what, who is wearing what, whose kids are doing what, who has what disease, whose marriage is in crisis, and so on. This is partly what this book is about. It is in many ways a historical ethnography.[3]

All this talk—or gossip—is probably interesting in and of itself, but it also helps bring out the intimate nuances in intra-African relations in their own terms. This is more important than it may seem. Colonizers and missionaries were not writing on a blank slate; the Maragoli had their own way of understanding things, and they predictably generated rumors and hearsay of their own that fed into their perceptions of the white newcomers. These perceptions certainly influenced the way they acted. In other words, the stories and gossip of the village shaped the ways in which the Maragoli understood the missionaries and the colonizers whom they had so suddenly found in their midst, and these stories and gossip no doubt helped determine the ways they responded. And this is the point. If we can better understand how the colonizers and the missionaries were imagined by local gossips and storytellers, we can then better understand the actions of the Maragoli community. In other words, if we want a fuller picture, if we want to know why the Maragoli thought what they thought and did what they did, we need to know how they talked among themselves—villager to villager, Maragoli to Maragoli.

Not surprisingly, we find that many of the ideas and actions of the whites were entirely alien to them. We also learn, moreover, that many people in Maragoli did not necessarily understand their lives in terms of one long struggle under colonial rule. In fact, we find, as we should expect, that their actions were not always driven by self-interest or in reaction to the attitudes of colonizers or missionaries. Despite the intrusive colonial policies, despite the problems widows encountered raising their children, despite the sometimes-malicious gossiping by their neighbors and relatives, despite the jealousies people sometimes felt about their neighbors' good fortune, they still enjoyed sharing their daily experiences. The newly converted Christians, for example, were happy to wear their Sunday best to attend church, where they delighted in singing hymns and praying together. Young boys enjoyed herding cattle together and telling hunting stories late into the night, and young girls also liked the time they spent together in their village dormitories, where they chatted and laughed until they fell asleep. Men and women enjoyed browsing the colorful new wares that were displayed in the local markets in the 1930s. All of them took pleasure in celebrating Christmas and attending marriage and circumcision ceremonies. In short, the families and communities of Maragoli—like most families we know—had good times as well as bad times, even under the shadow of colonial rule. Widows as well.

But it was never easy. Existence was often quite grim. More than others, widows and their families suffered during famines and droughts; they suffered and sometimes died of diseases like smallpox, malaria, and typhoid; and, above all they suffered, often quite severely, the consequences of harsh and ill-conceived colonial policies. It is these policies and their consequences that I describe in the first part of the book.

The second part (chapters 8–13) focuses on the period between the 1930s and 1950s and takes on the topic of widowhood in greater detail by discussing the ways in which widows and their families interacted with each other, the members of their communities, the missionaries, and the colonialists. More specifically, this part examines the sometimes-troubled relationship between widows and their children as the children confronted new colonial policies that made it hard for them to meet their mothers' needs and expectations. During World War II, for example, the colonial government, afraid that the wives of the Kenyan men serving in the war might stray into infidelity, instituted stringent laws to restrict the movement of young women. This intensified surveillance gave rise to malicious rumors and moral panics throughout Kenya. Familial trust broke down. When the men returned from the war, some of them severely beat their wives—some of whom were widows' daughters—for their supposed infidelities. Such problems were all too typical of the familial conflicts of the period.

How families resolved problems such as these is one of my major concerns. In particular, I examine a strategy called *kehenda mwoyo,* or "worries of the heart," used by widows to get help from male members of their families and communities. Maragoli widows referred to their practical problems—problems that they faced precisely because they were widows, because they were women without husbands to "protect" them—as *kehenda mwoyo.* To them the term *kehenda mwoyo* designated their worries about how to take care of oneself: how one will eat, take care of one's children, and who will protect one.[4] (It was distinct from the emotional grief suffered at the loss of a loved one, for which they used the term *ovovereli.*) *Kehenda mwoyo* concerned a widow's social, political, economic, and emotional needs and her ability (or lack of ability) to meet them. *Kehenda mwoyo* explicitly expressed the threat to a widow's survival.

How, then, did widows counter the threats to their livelihood signified by *kehenda mwoyo?* One of the ways was for widows to stage their grief publicly so that those better off were compelled to help them. Or, as one widow told me, "You looked for different ways to help yourself and also publicly informed men in your community of your *kehenda mwoyo* and hoped that they would show *tsimbavasi* [sympathy] and help you."[5] Given the gender expectations of their patriarchal communities, this strategy was often effective. By publicly expressing their "worries of the heart" to the male

A court meeting in which a widow is expressing her "worries of the heart" before a group of male elders (from Friends Collection and Archives, Earlham College)

members of their communities, widows put men on the spot. The men could not afford to ignore a widow's plight without risking ridicule from other community members for deficiencies of masculinity. They had to respond because traditional gender roles stipulated that men be "strong," "powerful," and "paternalistic" and demanded that they assist widows with the tasks once performed by their husbands. Women, on the other hand, and widows in particular, were regarded as dependents, as people who were expected to become helpless at the death of their husbands. And so men, afraid to be humiliated in public, afraid to be seen as lesser men in front of their peers, were often forced in this indirect way to give assistance. And widows, by invoking the very gender roles that were designed to control them, by, in other words, turning the language of patriarchy into one of entitlement, were able to get what they needed and at the same time enforce gender roles upon men. To put it bluntly, widows sometimes found ways to use patriarchy to their own advantage.

Widows' relationships with members of their communities were, however, not just about gender politics. Many people in Maragoli—men, women, daughters, and sons—helped out widows simply because they wanted to, simply because it was the right thing to do and not because they expected some kind of credit. So while people gossiped about others and sometimes caused them to suffer, at other times they were genuinely concerned about the welfare of their neighbors. For example, in the 1930s, neighbors and widows' children stepped in to help widows with their agricultural work. When, in the 1940s, moral panic over promiscuity threatened to ruin the lives of young girls, some of whom were widows' daughters, the mothers of these girls came together to support one another. And when locusts invaded crops, as they seemed to do so frequently in the 1930s and 1940s, village members took up sticks, pots, pans, or whatever other weapon they found at hand and helped one another wage a counterattack. More often than not, Maragoli community members treated one another the way they would have liked to be treated, regardless of their gender, age, status, or lineage affiliation. The specific negotiations among widows, their families, and their communities are the focus of the book's second part. In general, these negotiations serve to illustrate more forcibly the conflicts described in the book's opening chapters.

Finally, the last part of the book (chapters 14–15) focuses on the years immediately after Kenya gained independence and examines the ways in which widows increasingly turned to a new language of citizenship to demand their rights. Right after independence, the new black leaders, in order to get elected to public office, claimed that all Kenyans were now citizens and not the subjects they had been under colonial rule. As citizens, they had rights and obligations. One of the obligations was that peasants carry out land reform by registering their land and acquiring title deeds in order to secure their land rights and then grow lucrative cash crops like coffee and tea. Such crops, leaders claimed, would enhance the economic status of peasants and also boost the economic development of the new nation. But this process was marred by some of the worst forms of corruption and nepotism, as widows' brothers-in-law and wealthy neighbors bribed the new leaders to give them access to widows' land. To voice their grievances and to get their rights recognized, Maragoli widows increasingly invoked the new language of citizenship, just as they had once used the discourse of the worries of the heart to get men in their communities to help them. They demanded, often unsuccessfully, that the new leaders recognize their rights as *wanainchi* (citizens) of the new nation of Kenya. Thus, the book ends by examining some of the frustrations the widows felt after independence.

I would like to make one last point. Because the book is a study of the everyday socioeconomic and political lives of widows and their families, I have chosen *not* to focus on the levirate/widow remarriage rituals that have dominated so many previous studies of widowhood in Africa.[6] Although the Maragoli practiced several forms of widow remarriage, and I will discuss them as they come up, there was more to widows' lives than remarriage issues.[7]

Colonial and postcolonial governments' practices affected widows just as much as—if not more than—the leviratic traditions that have intrigued many scholars. By examining closely the widows' lived experiences, I hope I can better discern why, for example, people like my mother and her friends felt that life was better under colonialism than under African rule, while my teachers felt that the colonizers were oppressive and degrading. In other words, I hope to understand some of the contradictions of colonial rule as experienced by the colonized, to understand the unsettling gains and unresolved dilemmas faced by Kenyans in postcolonial Kenya, to understand the complexities of life and relationships in Maragoli, and, more generally, to understand how and why the Maragoli came to think and act as they did. Of course, I cannot come to terms with all these issues. But by exploring some of them I can at least provide a detailed historical case study that helps clarify the contradictory nature of the colonial experience—its paradoxical muddle of opportunity and oppression—and I can at least shed a little more light on the issue of postcolonial disillusionment. These topics have been eloquently explored, from the vantage point of political science and philosophy, by Mahmood Mamdani, Kwame Anthony Appiah, Achille Mbembe, and others.[8] I only wish to enrich the now-ongoing discussion of Africans' perspectives on colonial and postcolonial rule.[9]

⌾

I began the research for this book in the mid-1990s, when I spent over a year in western Kenya talking with members of the Maragoli community. Over the course of a year, I had detailed conversations with some fifty widows of varying ages and members of their families. Male assistants assigned to me by chiefs of the six major Maragoli locations chose the first of these women. My assistants knew many of the women in some capacity (usually as friends or relatives); some of the women, in turn, introduced me to their widowed relatives and friends. The fifty or so widows with whom I developed relationships seemed to reflect the different socioeconomic, religious, and political affiliations of Maragoli society. I visited the women at least once every other week for a year, and we got to know each other fairly well. I also spoke with widows' male and female relatives, who provided information about widows they knew as great-grandmothers, grandmothers, aunts, mothers, sisters, and so on.

On an average day I spoke with at least eight people. Our conversations were not always structured, and they took place in various venues: at roadsides or markets, in *shambas* (gardens), in *dukas* (small shops), on homesteads, and occasionally in formal living rooms. Our topics were just as varied. While widowhood was often our focus, we talked about current topics in the news and perennial socioeconomic problems such as teenage pregnancy, crime, the high price of goods, and unemployment rates. We also talked about health, and I often heard elaborate stories of my informants' ailments, among them high blood pressure, diabetes, typhoid, and malaria. At times, I intentionally provoked heated discussions and arguments with my hosts. I discovered that arguments often provided one of the best ways to learn how people really felt about the issues we discussed; it was always intriguing to watch the extent to which people would go to defend a view that they cared about deeply.

Usually I took notes during our conversations; however, I regularly used a tape recorder, especially in more formal conversations. I asked everyone I spoke with for permission to use his or her name. Few objected to my request, and if they did, or showed any reservations, I offered to use pseudonyms, which they agreed to. I also kept a diary in which I wrote my personal reflections on what I observed and felt. As a child who had grown up in one of the Maragoli villages, I was constantly confronted not only with the ways in which I had changed in the ten years since my relocation to America but also with the ways in which the villages had changed—or not changed. In the diary, I recorded my own thoughts on Maragoli perceptions of me both as their "daughter" and also as a researcher who, in their eyes, was almost a *mzungu*, a "white person."

PART ONE

Everyday Life

CHAPTER ONE

Western Kenya, 1880–1902

Roughly seven thousand square miles, western Kenya stretches north-east from Lake Victoria to Mount Elgon. The first Europeans to visit the area referred to its inhabitants as Bantu Kavirondo, a name they had heard from the "coast people."[1] While "Bantu" refers to a group of languages spoken in many areas of eastern and southern Africa, no one seems to know what "Kavirondo" means—not even the coastal people who came up with the name.[2] Yet Europeans continued to use the term throughout much of the colonial period; indeed, this area of western Kenya was officially known as North Kavirondo District until 1961, when the name was changed to North Nyanza District.[3] *Nyanza*, a more familiar term, means "lake," obviously referring to Lake Victoria. Today, the fifteen or so different Bantu-speaking groups in this region call themselves Luyia, meaning "those of the same tribe." The Maragoli are among these Luyia groups.[4]

There are hardly any written sources on the area before colonial conquest in 1894, but impressionistic observations by a European traveler to the area in the 1880s describe thriving, self-sufficient communities with plenty of food to eat—at least according to Joseph Thomson, a Scottish geologist and the first European to visit the area.[5] Sponsored by the Royal Geographical Society, Thomson made his debut trip traveling from the coast through Masailand and arriving in western Kenya in December 1883. Thomson's description of Luyialand is not as detailed as we would like (he visited western Kenya largely because the region happened to be on the way to his major destination, Lake Victoria); but it is, for the most part, sufficient to give us a general overview of the area before the arrival of British colonizers.

Thomson tells us of his encounter with the Luyia by first describing their villages: "On the 28th of November, 1883, I entered the village of Kabaras, picturesquely situated on the face of a boulder-clad hill, and surrounded by

smiling fields." The surrounding land, he says, is a "fertile, rolling country watered by a perfect network of rivulets." Farther north toward Nzoia
River, Thomson notes that "the country became more diversified and pleasing, rolling in gentle undulations and dotted over with flowering shrubs."
Careful to make the landscape seem familiar to his readers in Europe, he
remarks on the numerous colossal boulders scattered over much of the area
and compares them to the glacial erratics that dot the fields of Scotland—
although the ones in Scotland were "not so numerous." Approaching Lake
Victoria from the southwestern part of western Kenya, Thomson climbed
the nearby hills, seven thousand feet above sea level, and, looking down
from his promontory upon the broad body of water, saw a "glistening bay of
the Great Lake surrounded by low shores and shut into the south by several
islands.... The view, with arid-looking euphorbia-clad slopes shading gently
down to the muddy beach ... was pleasing."[6]

The inhabitants of this pleasant prospect were apparently "friendly" and
"peaceful," even though he describes their appearance in the most disagree-
able terms: their "heads are of a distinctly lower type, eyes dull and muddy,
jaws somewhat prognathous, mouth unpleasantly large, and lips thick,
projecting and averted—they are in fact true negroes." When the men in
Thomson's caravan entered any of the villages, the local people amicably
shouted, "Yambo" (How do you do?), and they soon proved themselves to be
"peaceable and genial hosts."[7] His impressions of the Luyia people, however,
should be read in the context of his overall trip through East Africa. Before
arriving in western Kenya, Thomson had just passed through Masailand,
a land that, according to the existing European lore, was inhabited by the
"most blood thirsty people in the world."[8] This being the case, it is not surprising that he considered the dull-looking "true negroes" gracious and good-
natured.

Thomson's portrayal of the Luyia may, at first glance, remind one of the
now all-too-familiar notion of the "noble savage," the blissful African sub-
sisting in ignorant heathendom. This impression may not be entirely wrong,
since Thomson, like the other explorers of his time, was prone to exagger-
ation.[9] According to one of his biographers, for instance, Thomson was an
ambitious young man who was always in a hurry and always eager to em-
bark on his next adventure, and so it is very probable that he wrote up most
of his results hastily, adding sensational details that were likely to appeal
to his readers back home in Europe.[10] Yet it would be wrong to dismiss his
observations entirely; other evidence shows that western Kenya was in fact
relatively peaceful in the 1880s, at least when compared with the many East
African communities that had been destroyed by the Arab and Swahili slave

trade.[11] Throughout the slave trade years of the mid- to late nineteenth century, the Luyia remained a stable agricultural people, despite the occasional feud over cattle or land.[12]

Apparently, Thomson could not help but be surprised by "the generally contented and well-to-do air of the inhabitants." Though he duly notes the area's dense population—"almost every foot of the ground was under cultivation"—he still appeared rather obtusely amazed that "the people seem to have some idea of the value of rotation of crops for they allow land to lie fallow occasionally, such parts being used as pasture." Often, Thompson and his caravan passed by "a perfect lane of people, all carrying baskets of food, which they were dying to dispose of for beads. They were honey, milk, eggs, fowls, beans &c., &c."[13] He was impressed—so impressed, in fact, that he deemed his hasty transit through Luyialand "almost like a triumphal progress."[14]

This supposedly innocent land of "honey and milk" was to change in 1894, when the British established a formal administrative center there, in a place called Mumias, the most important trading post on the main route to Uganda.[15] Charles Hobley was appointed to take charge of the center, a position into which he was hurriedly ushered in order to settle a major feud that had arisen between the local people and government officials. This was Hobley's first crack at colonial administration, and he proved marvelously suitable for the job.

Born in northern England in 1867, Hobley was trained as an engineer at Mason Science College in Birmingham. After graduation, however, he soon realized that the "prospects for a young man in England were far from promising," and so he decided to seek better opportunities abroad.[16] In 1890 he left for East Africa to work as a geologist for the Imperial British East African Company (IBEAC), which had the royal mandate to occupy the region that extended from present-day Kenya to Uganda. But on arriving in East Africa, he found that the opportunities for making money were not as promising as he had imagined. The IBEAC was experiencing great financial difficulties and was on the brink of bankruptcy. Indeed, it was precisely because of its financial problems that the company needed a geologist to survey the interior of East Africa for minerals. But no sooner had Hobley begun trekking into the interior than the IBEAC went bankrupt.[17] Eventually, the Colonial Office took over the company's responsibilities, and Hobley found himself a servant of the British Foreign Office, delegated to administer western Kenya from the trading post of Mumias.

The Colonial Office was interested in Mumias largely because it was located strategically near the Ugandan border, a location that ensured Britain's access to Uganda. Aside from this, Mumias, indeed much of western Kenya, was not considered likely to offer much in the way of financial benefit. Unlike the central and eastern parts of the country, western Kenya, at least until the late 1920s, was neither coveted for its mineral resources nor much settled by whites (it was considered too remote and too far from the coast for profitable settler farming). And in October 1894, when Hobley was called to Mumias to settle a feud, the town itself was a relatively quiet village with a handful of coastal traders. With colonial occupation, however, the town grew steadily, and by the end of 1895 it was hosting several coastal traders, a number of porters from all over Kenya, and more than a handful of Sudanese soldiers employed by the government to guard the town.[18] Almost all of the foreigners carried guns.

In fact, the feud that Hobley had been summoned to resolve involved guns. The porters had started selling, in exchange for food, the government rifles they had carried to protect themselves along the road. The Kitosh people (a Luyia group), located to the north of Mumias, were the main buyers of the munitions. But the government officials straightaway smelled trouble, and one, a Mr. Spire, then a presiding officer, feared being surrounded by armed locals and promptly asked the Kitosh to return the rifles. Predictably, they refused. He responded, in September 1895, by sending Sudanese soldiers to secure the weapons, by force if necessary. Although the Sudanese soldiers "fought gallantly," according to Hobley, the Kitosh impaled them with spears, "one by one...eventually annihilat[ing] all twenty five of them."[19]

Hobley, who happened to be in Uganda, was called to settle this dispute and to ask for "reparations" from the Kitosh. But the Kitosh were not forthcoming. Enraged, Hobley sent five thousand "native auxillaries," recruited from local groups, to resolve the issue; when they met with resistance, they simply "shelled and burnt hundreds of Kitosh" as if they were not more than "a nice kettle of fish to fry." "The fact that we had ninety killed and wounded," Hobley reported contentedly, "was a measure of the severity of the contest."[20] In addition, Hobley and his soldiers took some three hundred prisoners, principally women and children, who, according to Hobley, were temporarily detained as "the best means of inducing speedy overtures of peace."[21] They also captured about 1,700 cattle and some sheep and goats. This was the first major encounter between the Luyia and the British in western Kenya. It was hardly a promising precedent.

Violent expeditions like this were in fact common in other parts of Kenya during the early years of colonial conquest. Perhaps some of the best known of these expeditions were those carried out against the Kikuyu and Kamba in eastern and central Kenya.[22] Yet Hobley, in spite of his violent actions, was generally considered a gentler administrator than administrators in other parts of Kenya. Indeed, historians have tended to portray Hobley as one of the few administrators genuinely interested in the "good of the African peoples amongst whom he served"; he was, for example, one of the few white administrators who spoke against white settlement in Kenya.[23] His supposedly real interest in the societies and cultures of Kenyan people can be glimpsed in the pages of his several anthropological books and scholarly articles.[24]

In fact, we are told, this kinder and gentler administrator had hoped not to use violence against the people of western Kenya. Hobley had planned to work through local chiefs to peacefully "lure their influence" and support and to make them submit to British rule through "negotiation, discussion, and fruitful cooperation."[25] He had, in other words, hoped for diplomacy. But, clearly, diplomacy had its limits. Some groups in western Kenya, groups like the Kitosh, for example, felt genuinely threatened by the presence of armed outsiders in their midst and were not always willing to sit back and seek compromise. They felt they had to defend themselves. Other practical reasons also made such diplomatic solutions virtually impossible. Each tribe, as Hobley noted, had "numerous chiefs, and the large number made it difficult to reach a consensus."[26] Consequently, the lofty ideas about "negotiation" were quickly abandoned, and Hobley increasingly turned to violence. Perhaps it was inevitable—even he, the supposedly understanding administrator, believed, "deep inside his heart," that "to have peace [in Africa] you must first teach obedience, and the only tutor who impresses the lesson properly is the sword."[27] Complete submission to British rule is what Hobley, like other colonial administrators, expected from the Africans.

The sword—or, rather, the rifle—gradually became his favored instrument, and the amount of violence in western Kenya increased. The suspicions generated by foreigners, as well as the rise in the number of guns in the area, meant that people felt more vulnerable to the wrath of their neighbors. Ethnic warfare also increased as ethnic groups raided each other for cattle, food, and guns. Claiming that "all real progress was impossible" until the interethnic raiding and fighting had ceased, Hobley ended up dispatching more and more warriors (or "native auxiliaries," as they were euphemistically called, most of whom were from chiefdoms of Hobley's local African allies) to intervene in the feuds.[28]

One such expedition was carried out against the Nyangori, who lived directly to the northeast of the Maragoli region. In 1901, Hobley deployed soldiers to suppress "cattle stealing and tribal feuds" among the Nyangori, and numerous Nyangori men perished as a result of Hobley's intervention.[29]

Reflecting on his punitive tactics, he wrote that it was necessary "to repress at all cost the pernicious system of inter-tribal raiding which has for so many centuries been the curse of this district." He argued that the use of violence was necessary to impress upon the local people who supported him that he was an implacable force. He wanted, that is, for the "tribes to feel in a *vivid* manner the protection we guarantee to afford to the adherents of law and order."[30] He was clearly ready to adopt any method that might help him divide and conquer.

A few months before, in May 1900, Hobley had demonstrated his willingness to use force by attacking the Nandi, an ethnic group that lived in the northwestern part of Maragoli.[31] Apparently, the Nandi had assaulted a trade convoy consisting of "twenty ox-carts, a small escort of police, and two passengers, one a Greek trader, and the other a government clerk of Eurasian origin."[32] Hobley reported that the Nandi had looted all the goods, destroyed the carts, and murdered the two passengers. In response, Hobley deployed a Kitosh-like punitive expedition against the Nandi. They put up a strong resistance, but Hobley and his local warriors were able to subdue them, inflicting "considerable damage" in the process.[33] The Nandi did not relent, however, and continued to ambush foreign traders. Once again Hobley responded violently. "Tribes must be made to understand," wrote the incensed Hobley, "that small parties are allowed to travel about without molestation and that in the event of their being interfered with, the arm of government is far reaching."[34]

The government's far-reaching arm could not be underestimated. By the end of 1904, Hobley, with the help of soldiers recruited from local people, had almost subdued the whole region—though even he could not eliminate all resistance. To do that, he needed something else, something that would extend the government's influence over the locals. He decided that he needed a bureaucracy. So to consolidate his victory, to impress upon the Luyia his unbending authority, he forced them to pay taxes in traditional forms of currency such as glass, cowries, beads, clothes, and labor. He wrote happily about how the payment of taxes was "an outward and visible sign that the particular section had definitely accepted Government control."[35] In theory, colonial occupation of western Kenya, that is, the tactical day-by-day accumulation of power by the British, had been implemented, at least in part, by making the Luyia more accustomed to death and taxes.[36]

The colonial government introduced something else as well. Colonial conquest fostered another kind of violence against the Luyia, something more insidious and devastating than the escalation of intertribal feuds: sudden increases in famine and disease.[37] As a direct consequence of their flight from the British military expeditions, people were forced to bed down in bushy areas inhabited by tsetse flies; there they often contracted sleeping sickness, a wretched disease that causes fatal lesions in the brain.[38] Hobley's response was predictably mordant. Writing about the people's sufferings, he notes that hundreds of "the poor wretches steadily died off" from sleeping sickness; in fact, the disease killed "thousands and thousands."[39] To make matters worse, the Sudanese soldiers and the increasing number of Swahili trade caravans that passed through the area introduced smallpox to the Luyia.[40] The disease spread rapidly, killing hundreds. Last but not least, jigger worms were introduced to the local people by the indentured Indian workers whom the British had imported into Kenya to build the Kenya-Uganda railway. The jiggers burrowed into the workers' feet, causing infection and, eventually, rot. In due course, such infections spread to the local people, who, without the use of their feet, were unable to work their fields and grow crops.[41]

New diseases also ravaged livestock as colonial rule penetrated the region. Colonial officials and the coastal merchants who accompanied them introduced rinderpest into Mumias. Coming originally from the Black Sea and Arabian Peninsula, the deadly foot-and-mouth disease spread in major waves from the Horn of Africa to southern Africa, destroying multitudes of cloven-hoofed animals.[42] Eastern Kenya was hit hard. Describing one such epidemic, Hobley noted that the disease spread so rapidly that it was difficult to dispose of the dead cows: "Their bodies were piled up in the form of a wall, a few yards from the villages which cluster around the mountain, and the air night and day was pervaded by a sickly odour of putrefaction."[43]

Severe food shortages also became common. Since people were constantly on the move, usually running from their new enemies, they did not have time to plant and harvest crops. Moreover, the Luyia who survived the famines and diseases often went to war with each other over what little food and livestock resources remained. Today, western Kenya is dotted with monuments to the wars and diseases of colonial conquest. The name Eldoret, one of the major towns in western Kenya, for example, means "place of killing" in the Nandi language.

⌒∞⌒

Looking back years later, Hobley crowed about his experience in Kenya: "I look back moreover with some pride to the fact that I was one of the early pioneers in that part of the continent, and can without boasting claim to be of the band which helped to win this fair land for Great Britain, furthermore at a small cost and with little loss of life."[44] Many ordinary western Kenyan men and women who lived through those first few years of colonial conquest would undoubtedly have disagreed with Hobley. While the financial cost to the British government may have been small, the loss of life was certainly anything but "little." The wars of colonial conquest and the diseases and famine that accompanied them left many communities in western Kenya crippled by economic hardship and emotional loss.

But as always, suffering is never fairly or equally distributed. Although disease and famine took their toll upon Luyia men, women, and children alike, most damaging was the disruption caused by the number of men killed in the local wars. Left behind were widows and orphans, weak, hungry, and in desperate need of help. By 1902, when the first missionaries arrived in western Kenya, the area was no longer the land of "honey and milk" described, albeit with a bit of embellishment, by Joseph Thomson. It was increasingly a land of families headed by widows, a land of "feeble little lads looking for food," a land of communities in turmoil. It was, we might say, no longer a land so easy to boast about.

CHAPTER TWO

Feeble Little Lads Looking for Food

Willis R. Hotchkiss, Edgar T. Hole, and Arthur B. Chilson were the first missionaries to work in western Kenya. They were descendants of evangelical Quakers who left the eastern United States in the mid- to late nineteenth century and moved westward to seek greener pastures and more religious freedom. These frontier Quakers became evangelical fundamentalists, setting themselves apart from their Hicksite brothers back East, who stressed the need for quietness and waiting upon the Spirit.[1] As they settled in the Midwest, frontier Quakers built self-sufficient communities in which they closely linked spiritual work with physical work; for them, working with one's hands was just as important as reading the Bible or praying. Their evangelical zeal took them to other parts of the world, to the island of Pemba, Palestine, India, Cuba, and Jamaica, where they established Friends Industrial Missions in the latter half of the nineteenth century and claimed to teach the natives "habits of industry," with the ultimate goal of "establishing a self-supporting native Christian church."[2]

Hotchkiss, Hole, and Chilson had a similar agenda for western Kenya. On the morning of April 23, 1902, they boarded a steamship by the name of *St. Paul* in New York and set out for East Africa. The idea of establishing a mission in Africa had actually originated with Hotchkiss, who had lived in Ukambani, eastern Kenya, for four years in the late 1890s as a missionary with a Scottish mission. Hotchkiss claimed that he had been troubled by the "choking atmosphere of moral putrefaction" and by the "physical degradation" of the Africans whom he encountered in Kenya, so when he returned to the United States in 1899, he spoke fervently of "Africa's crying need" to members of his yearly meeting in Cleveland, Ohio, and he urged them to send missionaries to Kenya to train the Africans in the "habits of industry" that would endow them with a much-needed "stability of character."[3]

ARTHUR B. CHILSON.   EDGAR T. HOLE.   WILLIS R. HOTCHKISS.

Arthur B. Chilson, Edgar T. Hole, and Willis R. Hotchkiss (from Friends Collection and Archives, Earlham College)

According to reports in the *American Friend*, the then-leading missionary journal, members of his congregation "understood this need," and within a few months they had collected four thousand dollars in cash and pledges, some of it "given at the cost of much personal sacrifice," for evangelism in Africa.[4] Numerous prayers followed, and after presenting "themselves in humility before the Lord and imploring Divine guidance," members of Hotchkiss's church sent three men to Kenya. Along with Hotchkiss went Edgar Hole, an elder in the church and "a thoroughly trained businessman," and Arthur Chilson, "a minister of the gospel and a skilled mechanic."[5] Allied with a businessman, a mechanic, and a seasoned traveler in Africa and armed with divine guidance, the members of the Quaker church were confident that they could achieve their evangelical goals in Africa. Of course, it was not always easy. As expectations ran up against realities, the pioneering missionaries inevitably encountered cultural conflicts that challenged their preconceptions and hindered their work. Ironically, were it not for the families of widows and for the desperate conditions of fatherless sons who were forced to seek help from the missionary centers, the Quakers' evangelical and industrial work would not have succeeded.[6]

Hotchkiss and his partners arrived in western Kenya from Mombasa on the cool evening of July 6, 1902. It was the rainy season, and the missionaries were actually surprised that the "heat was not at all oppressive."[7] These three missionaries were among the first whites to ride on the newly completed Kenya-Uganda railway. Seated in comfortable new carriages "lighted with kerosene lamps," they rode through "beautiful and varied scenery," through "miles and miles of plains, with just low scrubby vegetation," where they saw "zebras, ostriches, antelope of various kinds feeding in herds"— though they were "a little disappointed not to have seen lions, elephants, or other larger animals" since rumor had it that these animals were in "abundance."[8] As they neared Kisumu, the country "became quite mountainous and they passed through some areas as high as 8320 feet above sea level." After traveling 580 miles, they disembarked from the train at Kisumu, the main terminal in western Kenya. At the time Kisumu was a tiny hamlet on the shores of Lake Victoria and had recently been settled by Indians who had just finished building the railway and were now building little *dukas*, or shops, where they sold basic commodities. The village actually looked as if it was thriving economically.[9]

The missionaries were met at the train station by Hobley, that infamous subcommissioner who had recently subdued the people of western Kenya. Having come to know the area well through his exploits, he offered to show them around and help them settle on a place that would be suitable for an industrial mission. With the help of twenty-eight local porters, they wandered through western Kenya, camping in various places—and like Thomson, the Scottish explorer who had visited the area in the 1880s, the missionaries found the Luyia to be affable. Writing home, they assured their families and friends that they had been "received kindly" by various chiefs who had "begged" them "to settle in their country, and teach their people" (now that the military expeditions had come to an end). For example, when Hotchkiss told one of the local chiefs what their purpose was, the chief apparently responded, "Why don't you build here? I'll show you a good place in the morning." Comparing the friendly reception to his previous experiences in other parts of Kenya, Hotchkiss commented that in eastern Kenya "we could always get a guide to show us the nearest way out of his country, but here the reverse was true."[10]

The region's dense population also struck the missionaries—"a million souls," according to Hobley.[11] Hole noted that the men and women were only covered by "a skin, often un-tanned, and suspended on the left side by a string from the right shoulder. Some of them wore bracelets of wire and beads on their necks, arms, wrists or ankles, and had plumes or horns fastened to the temples of some of the men." The children had "no clothing save a few strings of banana fiber tied around their loins."[12] To Hotchkiss the naked Africans represented a harvest of souls to redeem, a "ready to pick field."[13]

These Africans, this ready-to-pick field, lived in round huts clustered "among the trees" or among "irregularly cultivated land patches." Much of the region's landscape, however, comprised "massive, rolling blue curtained hills" that lacked the timber the missionaries needed for their industrial work, so they soon became desperate to find the destined "place whereunto the Lord hath sent [them]."[14] Already four weeks had passed, but they continued "marching" along the "native paths." On August 10, 1902, they veered toward the eastern part of the province until the company had to discontinue its journey because Hotchkiss was sick with a "stubborn case of fever" and Hole was also "far from well." To get a better view of the area and to determine an appropriate camping ground for his sick partners, the last healthy missionary, Chilson, shinnied up a tree. What he spied from his lookout impressed him: the prospect presented "a tract of land unoccupied by the natives, splendid, heavy timber, with a large stream running through it which has good falls and rapids, splendid drinking water. Hundreds of natives live within reach. The altitude a little high, is 5300 feet."[15]

The supposedly "unoccupied" land was Kaimosi, about twenty miles northwest of Kisumu and ten miles north of Maragoli. The three men were all "unanimous in feeling that this was the place of God's choice," so they went ahead and pitched their tents and established their center here.[16] A few days later, they wrote home conveying the good news; they were happy to confirm to members of their congregation that "all things work together for good to them that love God, to them who are called to his purpose"—so they believed.[17]

The missionaries no doubt wanted to make Kaimosi feel a bit more like home, more like the midwestern landscape they had left back in America — in other words, they tended to see what they hoped to see. For example, they described Kaimosi as a "rolling fertile prairie," when in fact their photographs of Kaimosi reveal a rather hilly and forested landscape.[18] At other times they romanticized the landscape: "Such beautiful views as we have constantly before our eyes," rhapsodized Virginia Blackburn, who, with her physician husband, joined the three men a year later. Virginia was a prolific letter writer who wrote detailed letters to her parents almost daily, sometimes taking rather extravagant rhetorical liberties. "The sunsets here are often gloriously bright," she told her parents in one of her letters, "and so resplendent with gold that it almost seems that the portals of heaven are opened, and a little of the radiance shining down on the world."[19]

Reality, of course, was less welcoming than Virginia's Victorian exuberance would suggest. Sadly, it was not easy to get to this "fertile prairie." The trek from Kisumu to Kaimosi was treacherous, since there were no proper roads and making one's way through the bush was difficult. After making one trip, Emory Rees, a missionary who arrived in Kaimosi two years later, wrote home complaining that "the native paths wind along through bush often higher than one's head. You are shut in by the bushes while an equatorial sun glares at you straight from above. You toil uphill only to find when at the top there is a valley beyond. The nettles sting you, the thistles prick you, the sun scorches you, but every step brings you nearer to Kaimosi."[20]

Initially, in Kaimosi, the three men lived in mud houses with dirt floors, and in due course they fell victim to bouts of malaria and the remorseless attack of foot jiggers.[21] Nevertheless, these "men of God," these men who had received the "Master's call to Africa" and had gladly responded "We will go," were not about to give up.[22] Indeed, the missionaries regarded themselves as intrepid, as men of hardy pioneering stock—descended from ancestors who had migrated to remote areas of Iowa, Ohio, Indiana, and Kansas, built sod houses on the lonely prairie, and eked out a meager, backbreaking existence.[23] In spite of their bravery and perseverance, however, the missionaries were assailed by all kinds of physical afflictions. And yet even as they struggled to cure their ailing bodies, the local people were beseeching them for remedies—*Bwana, nataka dawa* (Master, give me medicine). The ulcers, wounds, malaria, smallpox, and snakebites that pestered the locals cried out for immediate attention, and the three men were overwhelmed by these requests, for they had neither the medicines nor the training necessary to treat the sick. To their good fortune, Elisha Blackburn, a graduate of Hiram College and Cleveland College of Physicians and Surgeons, arrived in Kaimosi the following year in order to "fulfill his call."[24]

Now that the injured and ailing could be directed to the care of Mr. Blackburn, Hole, Chilson, and Hotchkiss could start working to establish their industrial training school, which, they hoped, would teach those who came to the mission station how to saw timber, make bricks, and build square houses (as opposed to the villagers' round huts). The missionaries also hoped that the local people would take up manual work in pursuit of "practical Christianity," in order to "live out in everyday life the gospel of the Lord Jesus Christ." They believed that their endeavors would succeed because "the Negro in Africa, as in America, is attracted by the demonstrative."[25] With typical condescension, they thought Africans capable of imitation but not reason. And Africans were expected to be grateful for the godly example to imitate.

EMORY J. REES.   DEBORAH GORMAN REES.

Emory and Deborah Rees (from Friends Collection and Archives, Earlham College)

The local people were, however, not as malleable as the missionaries had hoped. They were much more interested in the practical advantages of having their diseases healed and their bodies nourished with food than in the gospel or in manual work. In response, the missionaries argued that they needed more help from home to convince the Africans of the value of their work, and especially to assist in translating the Bible into local languages so that the missionaries "could tell the Kavirondo in their own tongue that 'wondrous story of deathless love.'" So they pleaded to members of their congregations in the United States, writing letter after letter soliciting assistance and complaining that "three or five in a million were not enough to stem the tide of heathenism."[26]

One couple, Emory and Deborah Rees, heeded the call for help. Their response was most welcome, for Emory was not only a "gifted teacher" but also fond of "books and study" and was therefore suitable for the translation work. Born in rural Illinois and educated at Urbana High School, the Reeses had been to Africa before; they had taught Zulu children in Durban between 1899 and 1902, and they had also preached among African gold miners in Johannesburg—both offered rare and valuable experience. After a brief furlough in the United States, they returned to Africa at the end of 1904 and made their "difficult" trip to Kaimosi, through the stinging nettles, pricking thistles, and scorching sun, though, luckily, the paths were less impeded by mud since it was the dry month of December.[27]

Treating the sick in Maragoli (from Friends Collection and Archives, Earlham College)

Their stay in Kaimosi was short, for they immediately identified Maragoli, with its dense population, as a particularly attractive area to seek converts. Thus, the Reeses became the first missionaries to live and work actively among the Maragoli. Like the missionaries in Kaimosi, they had to provide food and medicine to the local people to make them strong and healthy before they could begin teaching them the gospel. They had, in other words, to be very practical in their Christianity. In February 1905, for example, the Reeses complained that they had to give smallpox medicine to the many Maragolis who visited their one-room, grass-thatched hut, and they sensationally noted that the disease had become so rampant that "living in Maragoli is much like living next door to the pest house."[28] Unfortunately for the young American evangelists, the Maragoli visited because they needed real food, not the metaphorical "loaves and fishes" promised by the scriptures. When offered spiritual food, they understandably claimed that they did "not understand the good news yet, but when [they] do [they] will accept it."[29] First a good ration of food, and then maybe, on a full stomach, they might accept a ration of faith.

A majority of these visitors to the mission station, whose numbers ranged between twenty and thirty on any given day, were children of local widows.[30] Indeed, these unfortunate, fatherless, and often hungry and weak children were the ones whom the missionaries first targeted for conversion.[31] Most of them had lost their fathers to the colonial warfare of the late nineteenth century or to the major outbreak of smallpox. Their families' condition had been made more desperate as their livestock died of the rinderpest epidemics at the end of the nineteenth century. Having neither fathers nor the cattle normally provided by fathers as bridewealth, young "orphans" (children with only a mother were considered orphans) tended to move to the mission centers before others to do menial work in exchange for food and in order to earn the means to acquire livestock. Mudaki was just such an orphan—"a little fellow of ten or eleven years old, but small for his age. He was bright and vigorous and carried his load without grumbling."[32] Amugune, who arrived at the mission station in October 1904, was "a little, naked, dirty lad of eleven or twelve, interested only in getting 32 cents for a month's work."[33] Ahonya was another "feeble, little lad looking for food," and Vyoya was "a fatherless lad interested in rupees and cattle only."[34] For children such as these, the missionaries offered physical sustenance that was impossible to disregard.

⋘⊙⋙

Yet along with sustenance came the specter of cannibalism. Whites, after all, were believed to be cannibals.[35] And widowed mothers naturally worried that their sons were going to the mission not to eat but to be eaten—not surprisingly, the widows were terrified, and their terror clashed with the young men's interest in the missionaries. As irrational as the tales and rumors of white cannibalism might seem, they had a specific and understandable source: Sometime in February 1905, a government doctor in Kisumu performed a postmortem on an African man who had been killed on the railway.[36] The Maragoli were stunned by the postmortem; they believed that dead bodies contained spirits capable of doing harm if tampered with and that it was very important that corpses be handled carefully and with respect. Cutting up the dead was unthinkable; the dead must be respectfully buried in graves so that their spirits could rest in peace and did not come back to haunt the living. A postmortem was therefore a horrifying violation of one's obligation to the deceased person's remains.

As might be expected, then, news of the incident was received with great horror and anxiety in many Maragoli households and communities. Rees, for example, noted that after the postmortem, each and every Maragoli he encountered gave him a "horrified look and then about all that he could see were flying legs and arms as they scurry off through the bush."[37] Similarly, Hole related that after the incident, "people disappeared behind a rock or bush at the first suspicious movement on [his] part." Distressed, he described how the Maragoli people "passed by him quickly, scarcely turning their heads until they were some distance behind him." Once he discovered the cause of their behavior, however, he gave it the appropriate Christian explanation: "The rumors of cannibalism befitting the devil were obscuring the light that is beginning to shine in this stronghold of Satan."[38] Blaming the devil would become an effective coping mechanism for the missionaries.

The following month brought even worse news for the missionaries as several converts abruptly left the mission center. Rees was disappointed in the lost converts, whom he quickly labeled as "sensual, sin-loving, lost men and women." Because of their flight, he felt the missionaries' efforts had begun to "dwindle and shrivel till they [were] pitifully small," and he discouragingly commented on his failed efforts, saying that "time and again those who seemed to be imbibing the truth and nearing the Kingdom were swept away by powers of darkness." But Rees was not a quitter. In one of his letters home, he told members of his congregation that in spite of these disappointments, he had reminded himself that "the most successful missionary is the one who will patiently, persistently, and systematically sow the seed, keep at it, and hang on the longest without being discouraged." Invoking Psalm 126—"They that sow in *tears* shall reap in *joy*"—he remained confident that the "powers of darkness" would eventually be defeated.[39]

And yet the Reeses could maintain a strong front for only so long. By the end of 1905 it seemed as if events were conspiring to undermine their efforts. For example, in November the Maragoli suddenly barred the missionaries from attending funerals, though they had always been welcomed before. Rees was enraged. He blamed their exclusion on "witchdoctors who were going around telling everyone that whites were cannibals." Complaining in a letter home that the "natives" had continued to look at them with "suspicion," he was forced to conclude that "the past year's progress has been slow and tedious." Unfortunately, to prove the "uncivilized" state of the Maragoli, he sent a picture of naked young men with spears and shields to the *Friends Missionary Advocate* and wrote the following note to accompany the picture: "The natives are sitting in the light and warmth of the Equatorial sun. But they are also in the blackness of utter darkness and of heathendom. You might imagine them looking toward Christendom, and presenting the query, 'Why don't you come to enlighten us?'" But, Rees noted, "this is not the object of their gathering. They have always lived in such darkness and degradation that they know not how to appreciate or desire the light."[40]

The light seemed further and further away as the year ended, since most Maragoli boycotted everything concerning the missionaries. In fact, the two groups remained so antagonistic that a number of Maragoli elders were forced to intervene. When the elders visited Kaimosi to meet with the missionaries, Chilson assured them again that the rumors of white cannibalism were not true. But the elders were not entirely convinced. In the succeeding weeks, things got so bad that Chilson was forced to visit the homes of several of the elders to try to explain to them why the postmortem had been performed. Still, few elders were convinced, and enough suspicion remained that fewer and fewer people visited the mission center during the rest of the year. Commenting on the ruthless desertion in the missionaries' 1905 annual report, Chilson wrote that not much had changed from the previous year and that "visible results in the way of converts have not been many." Nonetheless, he concluded the report optimistically by saying that "the word has been given to hundreds of hearers, and it is our Father's work to give the increase; the work of the Spirit to prepare the hearts and send home the word of life."[41] As usual, Chilson solicited "prayers" from the homeland since "in this tribe of Africa, the darkness is dense, the enlightened ones are few." He reassured members of his congregation in America that he would continue to "work on, and trust."[42]

Evidently, his prayers were answered the following year—though probably in a way more mysterious than he had hoped. In early 1906, drought struck the Maragoli region, and widespread hunger followed as surely as one season follows another. So severe was the hunger that people resorted to the traditional remedy of tying a string around their waist to diminish the hunger pains. I was informed nearly a century later that "the string shrank the stomach." "With a string tied tightly around your stomach," Jane Mirimu told me, perhaps drawing on her own recent experience of food shortages, "your stomach did not make many hunger noises so you forgot about your hunger and just lay there."[43] But the pains when they came were still sharp, sharp enough to force Maragoli men and women to venture once more through the missionaries' doors. The missionaries were elated. They praised the Lord. And they wrote enthusiastically about the "decent" increase in the number of visitors, now from thirty to fifty every week. They could now finally "bring the lost sheep to the Shepherd."[44]

The shepherding moment was short, however. In April 1906, Edgar Hole and a young African man were preparing ground in order to plant potatoes when they came upon a human skull—probably the skull of someone who had been buried long ago and whose remains had been uncovered by a wild animal. Hole picked up the skull. "The African boy," Hole noted, "gave me one look and then ran for his life." He looked as if he "expected some dire calamity to befall him at once." Once a frequent visitor at the mission center, the young man could not be persuaded to return. Hole visited him at his home, "counseled" him, and told him that only "those who trust in spirits and believe the witch doctors" are afraid of touching human skulls. During the counseling session, he asked the young man one supposedly innocent question: "What harm can an old dry bone do to anyone?"[45]

A lot, as it turned out. The missionaries saw almost no sign of Africans at the mission center in the succeeding months. Once again, word had spread that whites were man-eaters. In fact, the news of this incident spread so fast that one of the missionaries noted that the "natives had a sort of wireless telegraphy" and that "any happening for miles around is soon known to every native in the neighborhood."[46] And it soon happened that one of the converts' wives ran away because her relatives frightened her, saying whites would eat her if she continued to visit the mission center—and her husband followed her shortly thereafter. Hole was again frustrated and wrote home grumbling that the Maragoli were "sunken in sin and shame," were "ignorant in morals and religion," and were "poor, child-like, and simple-minded." Again, however, he reminded himself of Psalm 126: "They that sow in tears shall reap in joy." And, as usual, he asked his brethren in the homeland to "join him in prayers."[47]

Despite the prayers, the fear of whites remained so strong that by the end of 1906 only about six converts remained. Among them were the destitute orphan boys Mudaki, Amugune, Ahonya, and Vyoya. They stayed because, as one of their sons told me, they "really wanted to help out their widowed mothers."[48] Yet their mothers did not believe them, did not think the missionary center was a safe place for them, and did not think that their sons were respectful of them. If they had respected their mothers, they would not have tempted the cannibals.

CHAPTER THREE

"What Harm Can an Old Dry Bone Do?"

Inzi ndagwa uguduma gudamanu
Ndorangwa muvandi
Msira, inzi ndagwa uguduma gudamanu
Ndorangwa muvandi
Umwana wange ya gota

I am the bad seed
They winnow me out
Msira [the singer's deceased husband], I am the bad seed
They winnow me out
My son is vanished

So sang the widowed mother of one of the "feeble little lads"—John Mudaki—who had refused to leave the missionary center in spite of the widespread rumors of white cannibalism. Bereaved, marching in slow circles around her husband's grave, Mudaki's mother chanted her lament, hoping that her public expression of grief would make the male members of her community keep her son away from the missionary center. If her son did not return, she feared she would never see him again, would be left to live in loneliness and isolation and poverty, and would become to others the "bad seed" that must be thrown away.

In the mid-1990s, I had several conversations with John Kefa, Mudaki's son. Kefa, a primary school teacher, had recently been forced to retire. Only fifty-two years old, Kefa looked healthy and energetic, but he was unsure how he was going to spend the remaining years of his life. Still, he remained in good spirits, grinning and cracking jokes—actually half-jokes—about how the Kenyan government was increasing mortality rates by forcing people to retire in their early fifties. Now with far too much time on his hands, he was happy to receive me when I knocked at his door to inquire about his stubborn father—at least he could momentarily put his "brain to some use" by talking with me about Kenyan history and about his family.

It was not hard to get him started. Kefa vividly remembered the stories he had heard from his father about the reaction of his widowed grandmother to the rumors of white cannibalism. We spoke one morning in October 1994, while we sat in the living room of his square mud house with its corrugated iron roof.[1] The more he remembered, the more animated he became: "My father went to the missionary center because he really wanted to learn how to read. He could also get some food there. In those days there was a lot of hunger, you know. But my grandmother feared whites because whites did strange things." As he continued, he studied me to see if I believed him. "They were strange, and she was afraid that they would kill my father and eat him up. So when my father went to the center, that gave my grandmother *ke-henda mwoyo* [worries of the heart]." In due course Kefa let me know that his grandmother had worried that his father, as the firstborn son, would not take care of her as expected. He looked up and appealed to me directly: "If he died, who would protect her? Who would provide for her? You tell me."

I hesitated but was finally able to ask the obvious question: "Didn't your father think that he was helping your grandmother by asking the missionaries to give him food for your uncles and aunts?"

"You are right, you are indeed correct that way. But the stories of whites as cannibals were too real, too scary. My grandmother was scared and cried all the time while singing lamentations," Kefa replied, and then gallantly began singing one of his mother's laments for me. He ended with a shrug of his shoulders—"Eh! My father's behavior brought my grandmother *kehenda mwoyo*. See, she sung this song loudly so that she could get help from people. People would say, 'Poor Msira's widow, she has so much *kehenda mwoyo*.' Then they would talk to my grandmother and help her out with my father's troubles."

Kefa first heard the details of his father's conversion to Christianity from his grandmother, who had died when Kefa was nine years old. His father had also told him of his conversion, but he gave a slightly different version of the story. For example, his father acknowledged the prevalence of rumors of white cannibalism, but as Kefa indicated, he was careful to deny complicity in spreading them; he told his son that as "a civilized, forward-looking man," he did not believe these rumors—unlike most people in the village. In his mind, the willingness to listen to the teachings of the missionaries had freed him from the tales of white cannibalism so that he could pursue "things that would bring him progress." According to Kefa, his father was proud of the fact that he was one of the pioneering Christians in Maragoli, and Kefa too was pleased to have had a Christian father.

The essential outline of Kefa's story was echoed by that of Maria Doresi. Petite and highly energetic, Doresi was born in the late 1920s, about twenty years after the rumors peaked. "It was generally thought," she told me, "that whites ate people in the old days. But in my days, in the days when I was growing up, they had stopped eating them."

"Did people really believe that whites ate people?" I asked.

"Yes," Doresi responded enthusiastically. "They believed that whites ate blacks. I am telling you the truth. I want to tell you the truth because I know you want the truth." When she was growing up, she said, "parents were very harsh, and if you went to the mission, they would whip you so hard. So hard that you bled."[2]

Another informant, Berita Visero, offered more graphic details of the post-mortem incident that had started the rumors of white cannibalism. Visero, also in her seventies, was generally quiet and shy, but her face came alive when I asked her about the postmortem scandal in Kisumu.

"Yes, I used to hear these stories from my grandmother," she remembered. "My grandmother used to say that whites would get a sharp knife and cut the stomach of a dead man. They would then dig into the body (like you dig into the stomach of a chicken) and sometimes remove the kidney or the intestines, sometimes the heart. Can you imagine removing someone's heart?" Whites, she told me, "scared people because they were acting like hyenas." "You tell me," she said, and then patted my wrist: "only hyenas could do things like that."[3]

I asked Visero about Edgar Hole's discovery of the skull. For the sake of argument, I took Hole's position and told her that I did not see anything wrong with touching a dead person's skull—after all, during my high school days in western Kenya, we had often held and examined such skulls in our biology classes, and no harm had come. But she responded with her certainty unchecked: "You are young," she insisted. "In those early days—and even now—you do not touch the remains of the dead just like that. Maybe if you are in school. You see, you have to be scared. You have to wonder whether the spirits of the dead person will come to haunt you."

She looked at me intently to see what I thought, then went on to instruct me on the protocol for dealing with dead bodies. "You see," she said, "dead men were supposed to be buried and not cut up. So what the doctor did was such a bad thing. People were scared. They were scared of whites because whites did strange things."

I continued to press, asking if she was aware that African doctors performed postmortems in several major hospitals in Kenya.

"Yes, I know that," she replied, and to exhibit her knowledge of the subject she offered up the names of people she had known whose bodies had been surrendered to postmortem. "Their bodies were cut up," Visero told me, "because the people died suddenly and people suspected that they had probably been poisoned." In these cases she felt that the postmortems had been justified because they helped rule out the possibility of poisoning. "But," she said, "in the old days that was not necessary; in the old days people were primitive, so they had every right to be scared of whites."

For people in western Kenya, apparently, slicing open the stomach of a dead man conjured up the image of an animal, a goat or sheep, being slaughtered for food or, worse, the image of a hyena feasting on a carcass. And Hole had, unforgivably, handled the skull of the dead person the way one would indifferently handle the bone of a chicken or a goat. So given the context, the inferences of the Maragoli about cannibalism were not as outlandish as they probably seemed to white missionaries—but even so, the misunderstanding had real and, indeed, powerful consequences for members of the Maragoli community.

The rumors of cannibalism were not the only reason Maragoli men and women feared the white missionaries. According to one implausible story, whites had the capacity to transform Africans into *amajini*, or "mermaids." After all, "whites were really clever people," Erika Semo explained to me one December day, when I asked her to tell me what she had heard about the whites while growing up in the 1930s and 1940s. Semo, a tall, stout woman with an imperious gaze, recalled that whites were thought to have had "all kinds of technology, and people were afraid that they would use the technology to transform or kill them." "So," she speculated, "people were thinking of the technology when they ran away from whites. In those days, people would say things like 'If whites could walk on four feet [referring to cars], they could also transform you.'" She chuckled and then for emphasis opened wide her yellow-brown eyes, discolored by years of quinine treatments for malaria.[4]

But Semo was hardly finished. Still eager to share the details, she shifted in her chair so she could face me more directly and quietly sighed: "Eh! Eh! My father brought my widowed grandmother *kehenda mwoyo*. Much of it. I tell you." And she did tell me, recounting in detail how her grandmother had sung several lamentations to demonstrate her sadness and to solicit sympathy from members of her community. Little by little, with mounting enthusiasm, she began to recite one of the lamentations herself:

Omwana wage goi
Umuyayi wange goi
Nangorendi goi
Yangotera ku va missien goi
Nagwi irijini

My child
My son
He has vanished
He has vanished with the missionaries
He will become a mermaid

As she sang, her weary voice grew louder; she lifted herself from her chair and began, slowly, to dance in circles, as her grandmother would have danced around the grave of her grandfather. After a few minutes she stopped abruptly, stared at me, and whispered with utter conviction, "My grandmother hoped that the men in the village would talk to my father and ask him not to go to the mission."

It was not an easy episode to forget, and so a few months later I spoke with Mark Luvusi, an ex–World War II veteran, about Semo's stories of whites using technology—particularly about their supposed ability to transform people into mermaids. Of course, I wanted some kind of explanation, and in more general terms, I hoped to find out what white technology had meant for people of his father's generation.

"Oh! I think people thought that whites had a brain that could do many things, a brain that did not just heal diseases, but one that could also turn you into *amajini*."[5]

"But mermaids are usually found only in the ocean," I interjected. "How could the mermaids live here in Maragoli where there is no water?"

"But that is the point," he answered and went on to tell me that he had grown up hearing stories of how "in the old days" whites or Arabs had captured people and transported them to the coast to sell them to "people of other lands." It was when they were at sea that they were turned into mermaids.

"But mermaids are usually white and not African," I remarked.

"Yes, you are correct. But," Luvusi added, "people believed that whites had the technology to transform you so that you looked like them. People used to say that whites looked like ghosts. So they transformed you so that you looked like a ghost. And that is what scared most people." Always it was technology that enthralled them. "You know," he continued, "all the nice things whites have now, things like bicycles, refrigerators, cameras, and cars, were very strange things to many Africans in the early days. Now people want these things, but in those days people used to run away when they saw these things."

Luvusi's comments may describe the predictable unease felt regarding the unknown, but they are also interesting because the Maragoli had not suffered from the Arab slave trade. Nevertheless, they had evidently heard—and warily construed—the rumors of whites and Arabs' capturing and selling people on the coast. It is most likely that these stories reached western Kenya from Bunyoro and Buganda, in present-day Uganda, the nearest place from which people had been traded to the Arabs as slaves. It is also possible that Luvusi was recalling historical knowledge he had acquired from school—such stories were part of local history, so to speak. Regardless of his sources, it is clear that stories of the slave trade portrayed whites and Arabs as people who took Africans to the coast so that they could convert them to mermaids. For what purpose it was never said. Still, these stories, along with the violence that accompanied the colonial conquest of western Kenya, naturally made the Maragoli suspicious of the motives of the white newcomers. It is no wonder that many of them fled at first sight, scurrying into the nearest bush whenever they glimpsed a white person—or the ghost of one. It is also no wonder that mothers, especially widowed mothers, feared for the lives of their unprotected sons.

For widows the situation had become positively intolerable—they feared they were either about to die from hunger or to have their sons eaten or turned into mermaids. To find some way out of the impasse, widows were eventually forced to confront and negotiate the controlling structures of patriarchy—structures from which, as widows, they were of course excluded. They had no choice. Fearing for their sons' lives, widows were routinely forced to enlist the male members of their communities, usually fathers or brothers-in-law, to help prevent their sons from going to the deadly mission stations.

Marita Beywa found herself in just such a situation when her son, Shem Vyoya, another "feeble little lad," began living at the mission center. I spoke with Berita Kasaya, Vyoya's daughter, about her father's decision to convert to Christianity and move to the mission. She told me that her grandfather had died, leaving her grandmother with seven children. Her father, as the eldest son, had no option but to work on the missionary farm in exchange for food to feed his younger bothers and sisters. Without this work, the hunger her father's siblings suffered would have been intolerable: "They felt a lot of hunger. . . . I am telling you, in those days there was so much hunger. And the only way to survive was to tie a string around your stomach and then lie down. That way you did not feel the hunger that much."[6] Despite the fact that Vyoya brought food to his family, his mother did not approve of his trips to the mission center: "My grandmother was desperate and needed the food, but she also feared for her son's life because of the stories of white cannibalism. It was a really torn situation, I tell you."

Afraid for her son's life, Kasaya's grandmother was in time forced to ask her brother-in-law to speak with Vyoya and discourage him from associating with the missionaries. If Vyoya refused to heed, the brother-in-law was granted permission to beat him until he acquiesced. When I asked Kasaya why her grandmother herself could not stop Vyoya from going to the mission center, she looked up with sorrow: "I think my grandmother was defeated. She was really defeated because she had repeatedly asked my father not to go to the mission, but my father would not listen. So she asked my great-uncle because she thought that my father would listen to him."

"Why did your father obey your great-uncle and not his own mother?" I asked.

"Because he was a man. A real man. And if a man provided such a beating, the child got scared."

I asked her about the actual beating.

"It was a real hard beating. With a raw stick full of water. Hayeah! It was a really hard beating," she replied.

When I asked whether the child could really get hurt from such a beating, Kasaya paused. Tears welled in her eyes as she began to recollect her own experience. Widowed in her early fifties, she had been forced to resort to the same methods as her grandmother. After her husband died, one of her sons became a drug addict, and Kasaya, too, found it necessary to ask her brother-in-law to beat her son so that he would stop taking drugs. Choking back tears, Kasaya went on, "It was a very sad situation because you were frustrated with your son. You were defeated. You wanted to show him a lesson, to make him a better person, but then when he showed up with bruises you felt so sad. You felt so sad because he was your child. But then," she told me, "you were defeated. You were defeated because this was your son and you loved him." Her son eventually died from an overdose.

As awful as I felt for stirring up these memories, I still wanted to know if she regretted having asked her brother-in-law to beat her son. Kasaya

Mary Lusiola with author, 1995 (photo by author)

gave me a quick glance and then looked down, ashamed. "Yes," she quietly admitted.

Kasaya's father, as I later found out from one of her neighbors, had withdrawn from the church briefly in response to her great-uncle's pressure, but he returned to it later and eventually became one of the mission's most prominent converts. This, apparently, was little consolation to his mother.

Her story is not unique. James Ahonya, yet another one of the first "feeble little lads" to visit the mission station, also caused a great deal of trouble for his mother. Ahonya had become an enthusiastic Christian convert, but his mother was not at all pleased with his conversion. I spoke with Mary Lusiola, Ahonya's niece, and she recalled that her grandmother had been forced to ask her great-grandfather to beat Ahonya after he began showing up at the mission center.[7] Our conversation was revealing.

"Why couldn't Ahonya's mother discipline her own son?"

"Ahonya wouldn't have listened the same way, because kids fear men more than women. Don't you know that men have more power? They are respected more. They are respected more because they are men. Don't you see?"

"Why do the men have more power than women?"

"Because they are men."

"But why do men have more power? Really?" I persisted.

"Because they are men. Don't you know this?"

I paused for a moment while Mary stared at me blankly in a manner that suggested I was some kind of alien not to know what was basic knowledge to her and to everyone else in the world—everyone in her world, that is. So I put my question to rest and instead asked her to describe for me how severe the beatings had been.

"I do not know exactly. Some people used a big stick. Yes, a stick when you beat a child, because a stick gave a good beating," she replied.

"If your grandfather had so much power because he is a man, why couldn't he just talk to Ahonya and tell him not to go?"

"I am sure he talked first. But you know, the children used to sneak into the mission for food, thinking that their parents wouldn't know. That was when they needed to be beaten and taught a lesson."

Of course, this did not explain why the children would not have been—more than anyone else—frightened of whites because of tales of white cannibalism.

"They were frightened," she explained, "but sometimes the children sneaked in because they saw that whites had food, and kids, you know, cannot hide hunger the way we adults can. So that is when they went to the missionaries."

"Couldn't Ahonya's mother have asked her father-in-law to provide food instead of a beating?" I asked.

"What you are saying makes sense, but sometimes there was drought, locusts, and there was hunger everywhere and everybody got hungry, but adults were good at hiding hunger."

Ahonya did not forgo his visits to the mission, despite the severe beatings he received from his grandfather. But his refusal to give in did not necessarily mean that his grandfather's power as a "man" had been diminished. According to Lusiola, Ahonya's grandfather was still considered a "real" man because he had heeded the call for help from a widow: "As a man, he tried all he could to prevent Ahonya from moving to the mission center, and Ahonya's mother recognized this." This gesture, this attempt to help, clearly mattered to Ahonya's mother—even though it had been unsuccessful.

Like Lusiola, most of the women I spoke with attested to the power men had over them.[8] "Men have power, you know"—this was the reigning mantra. Interestingly, most of these women seemed not to resent—at least openly—the power the men had over them; instead, they insisted that men were supposed to use their power to help them. Almost unanimously they maintained that it was men's duty to help women in need, especially widows. "A real man," they told me over and over again, "is a man who helps out and takes good care of women."

In order to receive help, however, widows like the mothers of Mudaki, Vyoya, and Ahonya had to appear vulnerable, largely by demonstrating their *kehenda mwoyo*, "worries of the heart." Only if their grief was sufficiently on display could they expect to receive any sympathetic support from the men in their community. In fact, the open and public display of their grief was one of the means by which they shifted some of their burdens onto men. Once the local men had witnessed a widow's demonstration of *kehenda mwoyo*, they usually felt called upon to protect their masculinity; that is, to make themselves feel like men, they had to answer a widow's petition of grief. And evidently the pressure was sometimes felt so keenly that Maragoli men would even agree to use violence against a widow's son to bring him into line.

That said, we should also note that some of the men no doubt helped widows for reasons other than simply to protect their masculinity. Their motives were often mixed. For example, Kasaya was quick to note that her father's uncle had feared for her father's safety just as much as his mother did—he, too, had heard the rumors of white cannibalism and believed them: "I think my great-uncle thought that my father would be killed by missionaries, so he tried to save him." She insisted that there was more to this kind of male action than the purely selfish motive of wanting to protect their masculinity. "He saved him," she told me, "like you would save anyone in danger, whether a relative or not. See, people are people with blood in their bodies, and you should try to help out anybody who is in danger." She punctuated the comment with a decisive nod.

Be this as it may, it is still important to note the difficult position widows found themselves in when forced to ask men to physically discipline their sons. As Kasaya explained to me, she, like other widows, terribly regretted the physical violence perpetrated against her son. It is, after all, one thing to describe such cruelty as a kindness and another to be forced to solicit it and witness its results. But the widows' worries were genuine: their sons, whom they expected to take up the duties of their deceased husbands, might be harmed—possibly eaten—by whites. As the rumors of white cannibalism circulated to every homestead, to every nook and cranny in western Kenya, there seemed to be no choice left them. If their sons would not return home, they had to oblige the men to intervene—physically if necessary. It would take another decade for the widows to begin to feel comfortable around the missionaries and to understand that most of the missionaries had good intentions—at least compared with whites like Mr. Hobley, the callous administrator who had helped to precipitate the warfare, disease, and famine that had been responsible for killing so many of their husbands.

CHAPTER FOUR

Lessons in Practical Christianity

Despite the misunderstandings in the initial encounters between the Maragoli and the missionaries, years went by, the rains came, people cultivated fields and harvested crops, widows struggled on, and the missionaries ate no one. In fact, young men like Mudaki and Semo, who had disobeyed their widowed mothers by frequenting the missionary centers, were thriving. They ate well at the centers, and the missionaries provided them with the medicines they needed. Under the close tutelage of their benefactors, the young men spent their days working in the fields or in the household, learning to read and write and listening to the missionaries discuss the Bible. The converts were expected to forgo their so-called superstitions and instead take up Western habits of hygiene—washing with soap, wearing clothes, and keeping their homes clean and tidy. They were also expected to value, even covet, material goods and—as true capitalist Protestants—work hard to get them. Missionaries' letters, reports, and diaries often complained that the converts, whom they condescendingly labeled "boys," were indolent and apathetic and needed to learn the "dignity of labor" to deter the temptation to steal.[1] Supposedly, the Maragoli only needed to transform their laziness to industry and to earn their keep, and then they would become less "prone to take what is not theirs."[2] So the missionaries encouraged their new converts to "use their hands to make bricks and to build with them a comfortable home that is suitably furnished or grow crops from which they can realize means to buy clothing and other necessities."[3] Hard work would turn the Maragoli into self-sufficient, conscientious, and, above all, honest men and women—"becoming a Christian does not mean merely learning to read and write and becoming a school teacher or a preacher, but it does mean to be a steady, industrious man or woman, living out in everyday life the gospel of the Lord Jesus Christ."[4] These were, in short, the tenets of "practical Christianity" and, as one missionary put it, among "the many many things the poor ignorant Maragoli" needed to learn.[5]

The missionaries' plan was for the converts to master the ethical and economic—as well as the religious—codes of practical Christianity and then move away from the missionary centers to outlying areas and establish their own Christian villages. There, ideally, they could spread the teachings to their new neighbors. These Christian villages, called *iliini* (line), were so named because the houses in them were laid out in two straight lines on either side of the road and because their residents were presumed to live in a morally straight and narrow manner. But learning a new way of life is never simple, and unsurprisingly, a number of misunderstandings arose between the new converts and the missionaries.

⋅∞⋅

The Quaker missionaries had a long list of "heathen practices" that they wanted their new followers to abandon so that they could take up practical Christianity. For example, the missionaries were often shocked that the Maragoli did not seem concerned about organizing things in straight lines, so the missionaries began teaching their followers to develop a "straight eye" and to ensure that they used it when building houses and planting crops.[6] Everything had to be lined up, squared up, and partitioned. Righteousness was apparently right-angled. This was one of the starting points of practical Christianity: what the converts needed was a square house with windows, doors, and partitions instead of "an ordinary, beehive grass hut with one low opening for a door and with children, chickens, cows, and numerous goats" squeezing through.[7] After all, a square house, a house with clear straight lines, made it possible for one to fit in a square bed, a table, and a chair—the prerequisites of civilization. A square house also allowed for the partitions that would make it possible for the Maragoli to live in accordance with Protestant notions of privacy and morality. What could be more backward and immoral than to have husband, wife, and children sleeping in the same room, let alone chickens, cows, and goats? As a metaphor for life, "straight" signified order and civilization: right angles meant right living.

The house also needed to be clean and tidy and have a smooth floor, preferably made of concrete—though dirt would do so long as it was hard packed and thus less likely to attract jiggers. God forbid, no cow dung. In any case, the floor was not to be slept on. In the new house, in the clean, partitioned, square abode, a true Christian, a Christian whose everyday life reflected his or her beliefs, would sleep virtuously on a bed with a mattress and covers, not on a papyrus or banana mat. So, for example, in one of her letters to her parents in America, Virginia Blackburn bemoaned the fact that she had to teach her "'boy' over and over, line upon line, precept upon precept how to get the covers straight when making a bed." She regretted that her "boy" had no "straight eye" and thus liked to "cata-corner" or use shortcuts. She, nonetheless, reassured her parents that she was teaching the Maragoli to understand that "becoming a Christian does not simply mean a changed soul, it also means a changed life."[8]

The bodies that occupied the house also had to be clean and tidy. And properly clothed. Roxie Reeve was happy, for example, when one of her students asked her "heathen" grandmother to find some money "to go buy a dress instead of wearing that old skin." She was equally pleased when the same student repeatedly implored her "heathen" grandfather to "take a bath."[9] Adelaide Hole was delighted when "the natives dressed cleanly and neatly for the Sabbath."[10] And Deborah Rees reported that she gave the converts "lessons in the clothing of their bodies, proper family relations, management of their homes, and dealings with other natives."[11] She believed that such lessons would help cleanse the "gross darkness and awful sin in which their fathers and forefathers have languished until mental, moral, and spiritual powers have been stunted, warped, and deadened."[12] Clearly, the relationship between a clean, clothed body and Christian salvation could not be driven home too carefully.

The Christian body also needed to be free of tattoos and other ritual markings. Tattooing the body, especially the face, with wide symmetrical circles was considered sophisticated adornment among many ethnic groups in Kenya. But to the missionaries, to people like Edna Chilson, for example, tattoos were "so awful, so cruel" as to deform one's soul. After witnessing a tattooing ritual, Chilson described the scene: "The blood was running from the gashes, streaming down the body and standing in pools on the ground. The girl in her agony would raise her hands, hardly able to suppress the cries of pain only to be laughed at by those looking on." For Chilson, this ritual was so "ghastly" that she felt compelled to pray that Christ's "light might speedily dispel this dense darkness with its awful superstitions and customs."[13]

The missionaries prayed equally hard that the Maragoli would abandon their heathen burial rituals. Virginia Blackburn once witnessed such a ritual. Walking through one of the villages, she encountered a large party of men, women, and children performing "a sort of half dance, half march, up and down, every few seconds giving vent to a mournful wail, but keeping time and keeping step with one another." "It was a sight," she wrote, "to see these naked black bodies swaying back and forth, some smeared with red clay,

A circumcision dance (from Friends Collection and Archives, Earlham College)

some half covered with white clay." After a few minutes the party was invited to the house of the deceased. Outside, only a few yards away, a couple of men were just beginning to dig the grave "with sharpened sticks to loosen the earth and using their hands for shovels." Blackburn, whose letters and diaries were often detailed and eloquent—at least in comparison to those of the other missionaries—provided further detail: "They made the grave about four feet deep," and when the grave was ready, "the two men went inside the house and in a few minutes came forth bearing the body of the woman on a cowhide. They placed it in the grave on the left side with knees drawn up closely to the body. After a little delay, a woman came from the hut, cut away all the little strings and ornaments from the body, and took off the piece of goat skin from about the waist. Then the men filled up the grave." "This is Funeral Kavirondo style," Blackburn observed with an obvious note of condescension.[14]

Although the burial ritual was "blacker than anything" she had ever seen, she was nonetheless happy to have attended, because it made her aware of local practices and, more important, she could use it in the future as a negative example. Knowledge was power. If she could convince the Maragoli to abandon these heathenish practices, she would be able to help them "learn the relationship between the physical body and salvation" so they could conform to Christianity.[15]

Other missionaries also found the burial rituals especially vexatious. Even Edgar Hole, who usually wrote curt and precise letters, indulged in

Clay decorations for a mourning ritual (from Friends Collection and Archives, Earlham College)

meticulous descriptions of the ritual. "The funeral," he wrote, "consisted of noise, dancing, wild wailing and some genuine grief, coarse jesting and song which told of the dead man's doings and cause of his death, the brandishing of spears, the flourish of the club, a whirling, howling, and sweating mass of naked savages." Hole concluded rather discouragingly that "black though heathenism be in the daily life of the people with nothing to think of but sensual desires, it is blacker still in the presence of death."[16]

Another major concern of the missionaries was the Maragoli habit of making sacrifices to ancestors in the event of illness. Like many other Africans, the Maragoli believed that unhappy ancestors were the cause of sickness, and in order to regain their health the sick had to appease them by offering up a chicken or a goat.[17] This had several consequences. For instance, converts who became sick often felt duty bound to go home and offer a sacrifice, usually because their relatives had made urgent appeals. Though the sick were more likely to get well by taking the missionaries' medicines, such appeals were hard to resist. As we might expect, however, the missionaries dismissed as sinners those who gave in to the temptation to make sacrifices. On the other hand, they almost canonized those who managed to resist. For instance, Ahonya and Amugune were singled out for unrivaled praise when they refused to offer sacrifices when their children fell sick; and when the children eventually died, they "absolutely refused to permit the usual dancing and wailing so common at heathen funerals." To the missionaries this represented clear evidence of their success. Ahonya and Amugune were indeed the "true children of God" and were now counted on by the Quakers to help lead their friends and relatives to "practical Christianity."[18]

⸱⸙⸱

Despite the fact that some of the converts were able to adhere to the tenets of practical Christianity, the missionaries did not always appreciate Maragoli interpretations of the teachings. In 1908, for example, Emory Rees told a curious story about Vyoya, the convert we met in the previous chapter (his uncle had severely beaten him for visiting the missionary center). Rees reported that Vyoya ran away from the mission center every time he made a small mistake, when he burned or spilled food or broke a cup or glass, for instance. However, he shyly but consistently returned to the center after a few days had passed. When Rees asked him why he had disappeared, he answered, "I was afraid that you would burn me in the stove because the Gospel says that those who sin will burn in the fire."[19] Rees was plainly shocked to hear Vyoya's literal interpretation of the gospel; he had assumed that converts like Vyoya, who had spent a significant amount of time at the mission center and could read the Bible well, would have a better grasp of the teachings.[20] But of course, reading and comprehending are two different things.

For another example of the misunderstanding, we can to turn to a letter by Roxie Reeve, an unmarried female missionary.[21] In 1918, she wrote home to say that during a meeting with the wives of the Christian converts, one of the women stood up and urged others to pay attention to Reeve's message because she looked "well," referring to Reeve's "double chin and big and strong" body.[22] The woman also called attention to Reeve's "big hands," which she hoped would dish out "large amounts of food." Obviously, Christianity was considered as a means to an end, but not always the one the missionaries had in mind.

In May 1919, when the number of students attending Sunday school lessons at the Maragoli center suddenly decreased, Roxie Stalker, another unmarried female missionary, became concerned. During one of the meetings she asked a student why the other students had not shown up for classes. "It is because you don't give them scraps," the student replied. She had not realized that her alms had served as bait. Determined to explain the true state of affairs, Stalker gave the students a lesson on selfishness, virtuously informing them that when a group of white people were given anything, they tried to divide it equally and, if there was any choice, to give others the best piece. However, one of the students quickly spoke up and asked, "Oh, don't you and Miss Reeve always get yourselves more and better clothes than you do us?"[23] We have no record of her response. Nevertheless, we can imagine that the new converts' immediate concerns with food and clothing easily superseded their interest in, or their proper understanding of, biblical teaching. It is hardly surprising that immediate needs often trumped spiritual insight.

Similar misunderstandings occurred concerning an issue related to "selfishness": the idea of property ownership. The Maragoli apparently didn't get it. In 1918, for example, Mira Bond, one of the missionaries in Kaimosi, wrote home complaining that "one of the hardest things" for the Maragoli to learn was the difference between "thine and mine." The Maragoli had "a code of their own," she grumbled, "and the things we call stealing they merely call taking." She recounted an incident in which a young man had been "very hungry and sick Saturday night, so he went down to the [missionaries'] garden and got a bunch of bananas." According to Bond, the man "did not consider it stealing and as he needed them he took them." She responded by calling on the services of Hole, asking him to speak to the man and "get him to see that taking other people's things without asking was stealing." On another occasion, Mrs. Bond wrote, another convert had taken some meat off the porch of one of the missionaries, and when he was accused of stealing, he said, "I did not steal it, I just took it."[24] Clearly, "taking" and "stealing" were slippery concepts for the Maragoli—if something was needed and available, where was the harm in using it?

At other times, the converts put the teachings of the Bible to surprisingly unintended uses. For example, a woman told Roxie Stalker the following story during a "probationer's class" (a class in which those who felt they had sinned or wronged others came forward to confess): "One day," began the female probationer, "a neighbor's cow got my dress and began chewing it. A second time the same cow came and chewed my dress, but I did not get angry with my neighbors or have any trouble with them. However, I asked my husband to help me settle with our neighbors and see if we could get them to keep their cow at home." Her story then took an interesting turn when her husband applied scripture for his own purposes. "My husband," the woman continued, "said that he would not help and gave as his reason the case of Eve leading Adam into trouble and said that he did not want to be led into trouble by his wife."[25] She admitted that she had gotten angry with her husband, and for that she felt sorry. This was what she felt the need to confess.

The missionaries and their converts obviously lacked a shared knowledge of metaphor and allusion and so were constantly misinterpreting one another. Without the cultural context of Western Christianity, the locals inevitably interpreted the Gospels according to their own lights. To Vyoya, for example, the metaphorical "fires" due the sinner were literal fires—his literal understanding of concepts like "sin" and the "fires of hell" was a perfectly reasonable interpretation for someone who had not learned to read figuratively or typologically. On the other hand, Reeve and Stalker's students appeared to be learning other lessons all too well and doing precisely what practical Christianity seemed to expect of them: desiring material wealth and improving their physical condition. The students had taken this to heart; in fact, Stalker and Reeve had come to consider the students much too acquisitive. Stalker, in particular, self-righteously denounced the students for their covetousness by quoting an admonitory verse from the New Testament: "It is easier for a camel to go through the eye of a needle than for a rich man to enter the kingdom of God." But coming from the missionaries, who had so much more, this no doubt puzzled the new converts.

Unfortunately, such misunderstandings became fairly common, even when the converts tried to meet the missionaries halfway. In one of her discussions with Stalker, a female convert told the following story: "When a woman gives birth to a child and if she sees that it has all its fingers and toes, eyes, mouth, nose, ears, and is perfect physically, then she is pleased. But if she sees that it is deformed, even only one part, she will throw it away. Or again if the white man has a motorcycle and it is all good except for one little piece of iron, then it is spoiled for running." So, the woman concluded, "if a person tries to be a Christian, although he goes to church, leaves off all his heathen customs and tries to please God, yet he is guilty of breaking one of God's commandments, if for example he does not pay his tithes and offerings, then he cannot enter the kingdom of heaven."[26] Stalker was dismayed at the woman's analogy—or, rather, she did not realize that an analogy was being made and actually believed that the woman was advocating disposing of children with deformities. She felt compelled to write a letter to the *African Report* to assure its readers that no such actions had taken place. In fact, the missionaries had stopped the Maragoli from throwing away children with deformities.[27]

Evidently the missionaries could be literal minded as well. Stalker not only missed the point but failed to see that the convert was offering a parable of her own, in imitation of those told by the missionaries. In reality, the woman was disapproving of the missionaries' emphasis on backsliding, and she was subtly appealing for more forgiveness—mothers do not throw away a baby with a single deformity, and white men do not throw away motorcycles because a part breaks, and therefore the missionaries should not throw away a new convert just because he or she may have slipped for a moment into some heathenish practice.

But more often than not the missionaries tended to be forgiving so that they might keep those they had converted within the missionary fold. When, for example, Mudaki got sick and gave in to his mother's pressure to make sacrificial offerings to his ancestors, Elisha Blackburn was "sad to see him go, but prayed that he may come to his senses" and return to the mission center. Sure enough, Mudaki "came back to his senses" and to the center. He was put on probation for two months, during which time he had to maintain the requirements of practical Christianity. He performed well: "he prayed, bathed, worked hard in the garden, and obeyed all the rules" and eventually was released from probation.[28] Similarly, James Lumadede was put on probation after his wife had compelled him to offer sacrifices to the ancestors because two of their children had died in infancy.[29] So, too, was Peter Obusi, who had stolen out of the mission station to go back to his village to attend "heathen circumcision ceremonies." Obusi returned to the station and begged for forgiveness so that the "shackles" could be "removed from his heart," and he asked that the heavy iron bracelet he wore during the ceremony be removed from his wrist and converted into "a useful knife."[30]

If forgiveness was required, so was prayer. The missionaries constantly counted on prayer, on God's kindly intervention, to give them the patience they needed to work with the Maragoli and get them to adhere more strictly to the teachings of practical Christianity. Roxie Reeve prayed when a girl of about eleven years old ran to the mission center because her father wanted to marry her to an old man; when the girl's father and two uncles soon followed and insisted that she return home, Reeve prayed some more—with tears "very near the surface" of her eyes—as she watched the girl walk away with the men. Sure enough, the girl returned to the center after a week. "God was," according to Reeve, "working, but so different from anything" she had expected.[31]

Stalker also believed that God had answered her in October 1918, after she had spent hours praying that the converts learn the important relationship between salvation and practical everyday life. For example, one day while Stalker was putting her clothes away a woman came in and asked to be given something, so Stalker gave her a piece of an old gingham skirt. The woman thanked her profusely; she "bowed, shook hands with me, pranced around, started to the door then came back and repeated the performance." Stalker was "pleased" with the woman's gratitude and with the ways in

which she "expressed it," all the more so because the woman had learned
that she could not simply "take" what belonged to others; she had learned
to ask for permission.[32]

Apart from asking God for guidance, missionaries found other ways to
get the Maragoli to listen to them: in fact, they sometimes expediently contrived to make the lessons of the Bible serve their own agendas or their own
convenience. Stalker, for example, was not averse to using scripture to evade
a conflict. She reported that one day five of her female coverts had run from
the mission "pouting and mad about something." She set out to hunt for the
girls and "found them about a quarter a mile away up on top of one of the hills
talking with some other girls." She managed to persuade them to return to
the missionary station. One of the girls told Stalker that they had run away
because Stalker was, apparently, their "enemy." Instead of scolding them,
as she would normally have done, or clarifying her relationship to them,
she instead "read them a Bible story and had a prayer with them." Then she
asked the girls to tell her what the Bible says about how they should treat
their enemies. "We should forgive them," one of the girls said. Stalker nodded her head in approval and then added, "We should love them and pray
for them."[33] Evidently, the Bible could also be used to extricate the missionaries from whatever social predicament they encountered. It was often
easier to quote scripture than to unravel the Maragoli understanding of the
situation.

∽

Regardless of the tactics used by the missionaries to win over and keep converts—whether prayer, rewards, or the shrewd manipulation of the Bible's
message—the missionaries had, by around 1919, begun to feel that many
of the men at the mission center had achieved "satisfactory results." The
missionaries' success was, in fact, quite remarkable: by December 1919,
Rees noted, there were about two hundred converts at the Maragoli station.
He wrote proudly of how the men and women were "deepening in their
Christian lives and are evidencing a much keener desire for salvation of
others."[34] Some of the new Christians were quite anxious to move to the surrounding areas to start small schools and churches.

Mudaki, Amugune, and Vyoya were among these enthusiastic converts.
Amugune, for example, was so eager to prove himself that he "voluntarily
severed his connections with the white man's purse in order that he might
prove that he is not a Christian for the white man's money." Rees was
sorry to lose Amugune's help but was "glad to see his independence and

New Quaker converts, 1919 (from Friends Collection and Archives, Earlham College)

courage."[35] Similarly, Vyoya was so "honest and hardworking" that he willingly handed to the mission center part of his monthly wages as a "voluntary offering to be used in the work of the Lord."[36] Although these "future workers of the church" were, according to the missionaries, a little "imperfect" in the way they preached the gospel, they were still capable of "bringing the knowledge of Christ to lost men in the outlying areas."[37] They were, that is, ready to move to *iliini*, to Christian villages with houses, churches, and schools all lined up in two straight rows. By the early 1920s converts like Amugune and Vyoya had started up at least ten of these villages, each with about thirty families.[38] The Christians in these villages constituted, according to one of the missionaries, "the germ of the missionary spirit."[39] Indeed, the new Christians would take a great deal of pleasure in spreading the "germ" to many communities in Maragoli, infecting the more susceptible of its members.

CHAPTER FIVE

Living "in Line"

On a clear sunny morning in January 1995, Shem Olovoga told me a poignant story about his family's eviction from their house by Christians who sought to establish a village ("a line") on his father's land.[1] Olovoga was a neighbor of my mother's and still lived in the same mud hut (or at least a version of the same hut) that he had occupied when I was growing up. Tall and slim, Olovoga was in very good health for someone in his midseventies, unlike most of the people his age in the village. He was still able to till his land, to plant, weed, and harvest his crops. His wife, Inyanza, had died several years earlier.

But as I recall, even while Inyanza was still alive, Olovoga did the farmwork all by himself; Inyanza was a drunkard and disappeared for months at a time, sometimes years, before suddenly showing up again at her husband's homestead. Rumor had it that she lived with different men, fellow drunks, in a place called Idakho, near the town of Kakamega. Her homecoming was sometimes theatrical—she often turned up costumed in layer upon layer of ripped dresses and old *lesos*.[2] And one dared not ask her where she had been, because she would shout humiliating insults at her inquisitor. Of course, as children we looked forward to the spectacle of Inyanza's return; it was a rare performance. But she received little sympathy from her husband. Olovoga would not let her enter his hut. So Inyanza usually set herself up in Olovoga's banana grove, where she built herself a shed from maize straw and subsisted on the generosity of the villagers. I remember vividly how my sister and I and the other kids in the neighborhood would sneak behind the shed and watch Inyanza as she modeled for herself the vibrant, tattered dresses. If she happened to spot us (as she often did when we laughed at her grinning self-admiration), she would run after us, calling us names, cursing our mothers, our dead fathers, and even our ancestors for bringing rascals like us into this world. We seldom had other occasions for such hilarity.

Olovoga, on the other hand, was known in the village as a good story-teller and was one of the people we village children approached whenever we wanted to hear something about the war or about *wabeberu*, the colonizers. He particularly enjoyed telling us stories of his conscription during World War II and of his regiment stationed at a place called Voi, near Mombasa. Proud of the fact that he had been a "soldier," he was nevertheless disappointed that he had not gone all the way to the coast, where the main military center was located.

Olovoga began his story that January morning in 1995 as he would for schoolchildren in the village: "A long time ago in the days of the missionaries, my mother was cooking the afternoon porridge in our hut when she heard people talking loudly outside. One of them, the chief of the village, called out her name, 'Respah, Respah.' 'Who is it?' my mother yelled from the hut. 'Where is Visero [Olovoga's father]?' the man asked.

"My mother," continued Olovoga, "ran out to see who was calling. Standing before her were two male Christian converts and the chief of our area. My mother thought that the men had come to collect tax, so she wanted to run away and hide because my father was not around and she did not have the rupees. In those days people used rupees, not shillings." He paused and looked at me inquisitively to ensure that I had taken note of the differences in currencies.

"'We are looking for Visero,' the chief said. My mother told him that my father had gone to visit his relatives in another village. The chief replied that they needed to talk to my father because the Christians were going to take over our land. My mother wondered what that meant. She had heard of the evictions in other places, but none had happened in our village. My mother and father had lived on the land for a long time and had even buried my grandparents on the land. It was my father's land for many years." Olovoga paused again, gazed at me intently, and said softly, "You know, in those days people didn't really own land the way we do now; when you lived on land for a long time, it simply became yours, because clans owned the land in those days.

"So," he continued, "the chief told my mother that she should tell my father that they should either become Christians or leave the land so that the Christians could start a line there. Because my father liked to drink and smoke tobacco [Olovoga himself was a chain smoker] they refused to convert. The chief came back again and again, but my father was not around so he told my mother to give him the message.

"'Tell him,' the chief pleaded, 'he should either stop drinking and smoking and become a Christian or move by tomorrow.'

"As you can imagine," Olovoga told me, "my mother was surprised because she didn't know what was going on. Somehow, she didn't think the chief was serious. The next day my parents left in the morning to go find out where they could go live. When they returned, they found all their belongings in the yard and their hut torn down. The chief and his Christian people had evicted them. My mother cried, wondering where to go. The chief gave them some rupees and told them to go find a place to stay. They went and lived as *avamenya* [refugees] with people of other clans. And this is how my people became *masikini tu*, paupers, just paupers." Olovoga stared at me, signaling that the story was over.

Apparently, scenes like this were common throughout the late 1910s and early 1920s as Christians sought to establish their villages.[3] The evictions obviously bred ill will: the evicted felt their rights utterly violated, and those they went to live with felt infringed upon and, worse still, infringed upon by distant clan members to whom they felt they owed little. "The evicted families felt like beggars, just beggars," Olovoga recalled.

Another man, James Keverenge, whose family was evicted in a manner similar to that of Olovoga's parents, told me how the money offered as compensation could never replace people's emotional attachment to their lineage land. "People never forgot the ways in which the Christians treated them; they carried the grudge with them everywhere." Keverenge protested, "How can you forget something like that, that kind of outright evil treatment?" Somberly he recollected how the Christians had simply thrown away the belongings of the people who refused to convert and then, in hardly any time, had erected a new house for a Christian family. "The Christian families worked together cooperatively and built the houses within a few days," Keverenge remembered. "The men put up the poles, thatched the roof, while the women were plastering the walls with mud, and the house was finished in a week. What could anyone do? What could anyone do, especially since the Christians were backed up by the chief?"[4]

There were no easy answers. The relatives they went to live with, for example, were not entirely happy to receive them. Olovoga related to me how the distant clan members they went to live with treated them badly: "They would wait until our maize was ripe and then just take some without asking. See, the hosts felt that because they had given us land to build a house and grow crops they could simply claim the crops as well. So, you see, that kind of situation was not a good one for many people like us."

The parents of the young Christian men, especially the widowed mothers, also felt wronged by their self-righteous and often imperious sons. One of the widows' hopes had been that after spending several years at the missionary stations, their sons would at least have the decency to return to their homestead and be there for them when they needed help with daily chores. This rarely happened. Just as important to the widows was the fact that the young men had deserted their lineage land; they had, in other words, ignored the significance of the land as the burial places of their fathers. The graves were sacred, and honoring the land where one's husband or father had been buried was a solemn family responsibility. To abandon the burial ground was to abandon the whole family.

Maria Demesi, a grandchild of such a widow, commented on her grandmother's wounded feelings when her son (Maria's father) had moved to one of the Christian villages: "My grandmother was left alone, just alone like that, just like that." Demesi described the loneliness caused by the departure in the customary way: it increased her grandmother's "worries of the heart." It was, she said, "really a bad thing for the mothers when their sons moved to the villages; that gave many widows *kehenda mwoyo*."[5] Another grandchild, Matayo Jumba, spoke even more poignantly about his grandmother's hurt feelings. "See," he said, "it was a great insult when a son that you had nursed on your breast and had struggled to raise—all alone—moved away and deserted you just like that."[6]

Widows "wept" for their sons, others "clicked their tongues" and "cursed" them, while others simply "shook their heads" in disbelief as they watched their sons construct their new houses, step by step, indifferent to the sorrow caused. First, holes were dug in four straight lines to fit poles for the walls; poles were inserted—in four straight lines; the roof was carefully thatched; and finally the walls were plastered with mud and the floors with cow dung. The converts then moved their belongings—their pots, hoes, safety pins, milk jugs, and millet—into their new square house. The move was momentous, of course, and the careful proportions, the painstaking precision, and especially the symmetry seemed alien and eerie to the nonconverted. Straight lines were not found in nature. It was all alarming.

In the eyes of the locals, the physical appearance of the Christian villages was dramatic. Not only did each Christian village have a church and an elementary school—this in itself was an extraordinary change—but the converts also laid out their houses, walkways, and gardens in nice, neat straight lines, in complete contrast to the nonbelievers' huts scattered haphazardly over the ridges and valleys.[7] Moreover, the square houses in the village were

A typical square hut in a Christian village (from Friends Collection and Archives, Earlham College)

often decorated in square and rectangular patterns with white clay from the riverbed. Some of the houses even had neat rectangular flower gardens in their—square—front yards.[8]

Most of the new houses had one or two windows (usually in the living room) and were partitioned into four sections: a tiny cooking area, a small room for cows and goats, a living room, and a bedroom for the parents and infants. In some rare cases, the walls were covered with posters of Christ's crucifixion or of the apostle Paul that the owners had acquired from the missionaries. Wooden stools or benches were likely to be the only pieces of furniture in the living room. A kerosene lantern made from a tin can provided light in the living room; the kitchen was lit only by the fire from the hearth. The older children usually slept in the living room on banana mats, surrounded by chickens nonchalantly strolling and clucking about the room. The children's parents, on the other hand, slept in the bedroom on mattresses of animal skins slung between tree poles and covered themselves with cotton blankets purchased from the local Indian merchant.[9] In these new orderly homes, the converts practiced their Christianity and tried to "live out the gospel of the Lord Jesus in their everyday lives."[10]

The villages also had dormitory-type huts, constructed for adolescent and teenage girls and boys. Each village had six or eight of these dormitory huts, and all the girls and boys in the village were expected to sleep in them—separated by gender, lest they be tempted to engage in premarital sex. The girls and boys who resided in these huts were expected to grow up to be

Grinding millet (from Friends Collection and Archives, Earlham College)

strong Christian men and women, good husbands and wives, and nurturing parents.[11]

The girls received lessons from their elders in specifically Christian ways of doing housework and farmwork and providing child care. The lessons kept them busy. A typical day for the girls began around six in the morning. Barely able to keep their heads up, they walked the few yards to their parents' houses to collect pots with which to fetch water from the river; on their way home, with pots nimbly balanced on their heads (another important skill for the ideal Christian woman), they would search for leaves to sweep the floors of their parents' house; afterward, the girls would clean themselves with soap—as, of course, befitted future Christian mothers. They then left for school. As soon as they arrived, they were required to gather at assembly and recite the Lord's Prayer—it was crucial that the girls ask the Lord to "lead them into green pastures" and "away from temptation" before commencing the day. Then they spent about two hours learning rudimentary reading and writing skills in the local vernacular before heading back home around noon.[12]

Very little leisure was granted them at home. The girls' afternoons were almost fully occupied: searching for firewood in the bush, collecting vegetables, and grinding maize with the millstone, all chores designed to help their mothers prepare for the evening meal of millet mash (*ugali*) and vegetables. Often the girls carried out these chores in groups, usually with the girls they lived with in the "dormitory."[13]

After supper, they returned to their sleeping hut, telling stories to one another until they fell asleep, stories of origins and of *amanani* (ogres)—and, of course, stories about of the value of work. "In the beginning people did not have to work," began one of the folktales, "but a woman became annoyed with her dog for eating food without doing any work and tied a hoe to its tail and sent it to dig. The dog went off singing, 'The woman is stupid, she has tied a hoe to my tail, but I don't dig.'" According to the story, whoever heard the dog singing or saw it digging would soon die, and so God, afraid that all people would die, "ordered people to take their hoes and do the digging themselves with their own hands."[14] This was the beginning of work—the so-called curse of the dog among the Maragoli and other Luyia groups.[15] The folktale underscores the necessity of work for the benefit of all in the community.[16] And it at least partly explains how the girls came to understand why women like themselves and their mothers were saddled with most of the physical work—it is women, after all, who in the story are responsible for bringing hard labor into this world.

Women endured the curse of the dog by working long hours in the fields and the household. The most intense labor periods occurred during the cultivation months of February through June and September through November. The women who grew up in the villages remembered their mothers' waking up at six during these busy months, splashing their face with water, grabbing their hoe, that cursed tool, and heading straight to the garden. In February they prepared the ground by themselves, sometimes as much as three acres, in order to plant the crops of cassava, beans, pumpkins, potatoes, sorghum, millet, and, increasingly, maize (all planted together in a mixed-up fashion). They weeded the crops in March and May, then harvested beans in June and the maize, sorghum, and millet in July and August. They repeated the same procedure during the short September through December growing season. The postharvest period did not necessarily bring relief for the women: they had to dry the grain by spreading it on papyrus mats and then laying it on the roof of the house, where it was exposed to the strongest sunlight; once it had dried, they searched for long, thin sticks for flaying the sorghum and millet to separate the grain from the chaff. This was not an easy task; the millet chaff, for example, was highly allergenic and, like poison ivy, could cause burning and itching upon contact with the skin.[17]

As the grain dried, the women could sometimes take time off to visit with each other and talk about their recent harvest, their children's behavior, and their in-laws' nagging, or they might also gossip about their neighbors, comment on each other's outfit, hairstyle, and so on.[18] But too soon the women were forced to return home to cook the evening meal for their husbands. Normally, the women took turns preparing the meal for all the husbands in the village: primarily a thick paste called *ugali* made by grinding corn or millet between two stones into a smoothly textured flour and then mixing it with hot water and stirring vigorously—this was normally served with beans or pumpkin leaves boiled in water and seasoned with salt or bean sauce. The women always presented the meal to the men, respectfully with both hands, and humbly bowed before they departed to the kitchen, where they sat with their daughters on a cow dung floor and ate. They were, after all, expected to "fear" and "respect" their husbands and act with humility toward them. Such dutiful catering to men's needs, as studies of Christian women in other parts of Africa have shown, signified true Christian femininity.[19]

The curse of the dog, however, continued to haunt the women in other ways. It was inexorable, inescapable. In addition to all the work in the fields and in the household, it was the duty of an older woman with children to be a good mother. This meant continuously monitoring a daughter's ethical behavior and teaching her the necessary deference to and reverence for her father and brothers, as well as older men and women. All the mothers considered each and every girl in the village their own daughter, and so they keenly watched their behavior to ensure that the girls did not behave in unbecoming ways—particularly, acting in any way that might be sexually tantalizing. If such wayward behavior was ever spotted, they immediately reported it to the girl's parents, who disciplined her by giving her buttocks a good lashing.[20] Occasionally, the young girls received severe beatings (not unlike those that older men gave to the widows' disobedient sons).

The boys usually slept in small round huts known as *idisi*. Before they fell asleep, they also told each other stories about work, mostly about herding cattle. Their stories often celebrated ingenious acts in which they outwitted wild animals or tricked giants in the bush. One much-told tale concerned a "lost boy" who escaped from a giant's captivity. While herding cattle the young boy had encountered a giant, who immediately tried to kill him. "Please do not harm me," the boy pleaded with the giant, "and I will go and be a herder of your cattle since you are the chief of the giants." The giant agreed and took the boy home with him. After taking care of the giant's cattle for two years, the boy began to think about ways he might escape and go back home. One day he said to himself, "Oh, I see much trouble here ahead of me herding these cattle, so I think it would be a good thing just to run away and take all the cattle home with me." So when the giants were busy drinking beer and enjoying themselves, the boy started walking back home, taking with him the giants' cattle. An old woman saw the boy and tried to warn the giants by singing, "The herder that you brought here is taking away your sheep and cattle," but the giants were too busy having a good time to pay attention to her.

The boy kept walking toward his home, and when he reached a large lake, he sang to it: "Water divide and stand up on the side that my father came from [the right], and you, water, stand up on the side that my mother came from [the left]." The water did as he requested, and he and the cattle crossed over to the other side, and then he sang again for the water to resume its place.

Soon the giants realized that the boy was missing, and they followed him and tried to recapture him. When the boy saw them coming, he stood at the edge of the lake and sang to it, asking it to open, and the lake did. But as the giants were crossing, the boy asked the lake to close back over the giants—and as they were drowning, the boy raced home. As he neared home, his sister heard his voice and told her mother, "I hear the voice of my brother who was lost." Her mother struck her with a stick because she thought she was deceiving her, but soon the boy arrived in the homestead with all the cattle. All the neighbors went to meet him singing and dancing with joy. They even killed a bull for a feast to celebrate the boy's homecoming.[21]

As they dozed off, the boys, I am sure, marveled at the herder's magnificent feat and possibly connected it with the story of Moses parting the Red Sea, which they most likely had heard from the missionaries. Then, like the girls, they woke at around six in the morning and, like the "lost boy," took the cattle, sheep, and goats into the woods to graze. As soon as they returned home, they washed up and left for school, where, along with the girls, they recited the Lord's Prayer and then learned reading and writing until around noon. Their afternoons were occupied with taking care of the animals, making tools, repairing houses, and, occasionally, hunting for meat.

In the evenings the young men often sat with their fathers in the front yard and waited for the women to serve them food. While waiting they sometimes listened to their fathers expound on the tenets of Christian masculinity, which to them generally meant protecting women—that is, ensuring that the women had enough land to plow and did not face physical danger from their neighbors or wild animals. Men were also expected to negotiate bridewealth for their daughters, a responsibility that demonstrated their patriarchal authority. Other responsibilities included clearing new land for cultivation, milking cows, and cutting down large trees for firewood or for building houses. Men, of course, were also expected to take care of bereaved widows, assist them with their new needs, and thereby mitigate their "worries of the heart." In this regard, Christian masculinity cohered nicely with Maragoli masculinity.

Generally, the converts observed the Sabbath dutifully. They avoided manual labor like herding or tilling the land and, like Christians everywhere, attended church in their Sunday best to pray for nonbelievers to accept Christ. They sang hymns—such as "Shall We Gather by the River?" and "Showers of Blessings"—that Deborah Rees had translated into Luragoli. Like the children at school, they also recited the Lord's Prayer. And the more faithful ones brought offerings, compelled by "the simplest translation of Malachi 3:10": "Bring ye all the tithes into the storehouse, that there may be meat in my house, and prove me now herewith, saith the Lord of hosts, if I will not open you the windows of heaven, and pour you out a blessing that there shall not be room enough to receive it."[22] So when they dug up yams or potatoes, they put them in piles, nine for themselves and one for God. The women collected their offerings in baskets, which they placed on their heads, and walked, erect as ibis, the few miles to church to present the church headman with the offerings.[23]

Even as the converts prayed for the nonbelievers, they made a conscious effort to distinguish themselves from them. They saw themselves as "civilized," in contrast to the "primitive" nonbelievers, and it was not uncommon for the Christians to show off their wealth, proudly parading about with their blankets and hoes or their bright cotton clothes.[24] Perhaps it was inevitable that practical Christianity turned some of its converts toward vanity.

Though they may have tried to distinguish themselves from the nonconverts by acting superior, some of the converts failed to strictly adhere to the tenets of practical Christianity. Some of them, for example, continued to offer sacrifices to the ancestors or participate in circumcision and burial rituals. They did so stealthily, of course, hoping that the other Christians would not find out. Rachel Chahonyo, who was acknowledged to be a strong Christian, agreed to offer sacrifices after three of her children died in infancy. In one of my conversations with Belisi Mutiva, Chahonyo's daughter, she admitted that her mother had offered sacrifices because she was desperate to have healthy children: "I was the first child to survive after the sacrifices, and my mother had four more children after me, all who lived to be old men and women." I asked her whether her mother really believed that offering sacrifices prevented her children from dying.

"She had to believe that," she said. "People in the Christian villages did what they had to do to survive."

"Was your mother then considered a sinner?"

"Not really, I don't think so," she replied self-assuredly. "Other people, even good Christians, offered sacrifices too. People gossiped about it, but nothing happened to my mother."

More important, the Christians retained the practice of widow inheritance, whereby a brother or a relative of the deceased man inherited his wife, who then became a member of her new husband's household and was able to remain a member of the village community—and thereby, at least according to the missionaries, increased the number of polygamous households. For the missionaries, widow inheritance was uncouth behavior. Yet as Esteri Vugutsa, who grew up in one of the Christian villages, told me, "If your husband died, especially if you were young and had young children, you had to get someone to take care of you."[25] The process was usually straightforward. After burial there were two important ceremonies: *olovego* and *lisara*. *Olovego*, a hair-shaving ceremony, was performed immediately after burial. Everybody who was related to the deceased, or who had come into contact with the deceased right before he died, was expected to get his or her hair shaved off. The purpose of this ceremony was largely to purify the living, as it was believed that the hair was susceptible to catching the disease that had killed the departed.[26] The *lisara*, or remembrance ceremony, took place anytime from two weeks to three years after burial. This was a significant ceremony for remembering the dead, but it was also when those who owed cash or other debts to the deceased were expected to pay them back to the family. This was also the time when the elders proposed that someone, usually a brother of the deceased man or a member of his lineage, inherit the widow. The widow was never forced to accept the man, and she was usually given an opportunity to state her wishes long before the choice was made. Although the inheriting man usually had a wife or wives of his own, the widow was not seen as entering a polygamous marriage. She also had the right to choose a man from another clan; however, if she did, the man was expected to pay back the bridewealth. Widow inheritance was generally practiced only with women of childbearing years; an older widow usually remained alone on her deceased husband's land or moved in with her older son.[27]

Other traditions that some of the Maragoli found hard to set aside in spite of the teachings of practical Christianity were rituals surrounding warfare. In a revealing incident, Emory Rees related how he visited one of the communal villages and found a lone tree standing in the center of one of the homesteads. When he asked about the strange-looking tree, the owner of the household denied that there was anything unusual about it. But after repeated pestering, he relented and explained to Rees that sacrifices were made under the tree in time of war. He told Rees that warriors used to gather under the tree to sacrifice a chicken and have a blessing pronounced upon them. After these ceremonies the young men went off to battle, certain of personal safety and of victory. The custom had declined with the coming of the British, the owner of the homestead claimed, but the sacred tree was still feared and revered by his people—in spite of the fact that they were Christians.[28]

Some of the Christians, however, managed to keep the tenets of practical Christianity more exactingly. Amugune, whom we have already met, was one of them. Almost all of my informants held him up as the ideal representative of Quaker life. Amugune defied Maragoli culture in many ways. For example, he went to Kaimosi hospital and had a white missionary doctor perform his circumcision (the Maragoli custom required that circumcision be performed at the river by a traditional circumciser).[29] Moreover, he allowed his wife to eat chicken and eggs, foods prohibited for women by local customs. He even refused to receive bridewealth for his daughter (although my informants said that in his old age he changed his mind and decided to ask for the marriage price—and actually got it).

Sadly, misfortune struck Amugune when, in a period of about seven years, he lost three children in infancy. And yet he still refused to offer sacrifices. Maragoli converts and nonconverts alike believed that his misfortunes were the consequence of his radical beliefs. For instance, his mother believed that Amugune's children died because his ancestors were angry with him for breaking the taboos. She became convinced that the only way any of Amugune's children were going to survive was for him to offer sacrifices to the ancestors. Amugune refused to be swayed.[30] Others attributed the death of Amugune's children to the fact that he had been circumcised at the hospital and not at the river, where his blood was expected to blend with the soil and strengthen his sperm; the conditions of his circumcision, the Maragoli believed, rendered his sperm too weak to produce healthy babies.[31] Others claimed that Amugune's children died because he had allowed his wife to eat chickens and eggs—the story goes that these foods left his wife's womb too weak to sustain healthy babies.

Like Amugune, Ahonya insisted on keeping the tenets of practical Christianity at all costs, and he too refused to appease his ancestors with sacrifices—even though he had lost his wife in childbirth and two of his children in infancy. Even worse to the disbelieving was the fact that he had buried his children in coffins, another new and unfathomable custom. More misfortune followed when Ahonya married again and lost his new wife in childbirth; this too was ascribed to his refusal to offer sacrifices.[32] I spoke with Ahonya's cousin, John Majani, who told me that Ahonya's mother had asked several village elders to persuade him to offer sacrifices, but he refused. "Since Ahonya was now an adult," Majani told me, "his mother could not ask the elders to force him to change his mind by beating him up as she had done when he was younger." All she could do was to ask them to give him advice. The elders could also disparage him by slandering his masculinity, by emasculating him, that is, for causing his mother "worries of the heart" when he should have been helping her with her grief as befits a "real man." And they tried this. But Ahonya remained adamant; he believed that he was no longer bound by the rules of the community of nonbelievers.[33]

⟡

All things considered, most people who lived "in line" were in a very real sense "practical" in the way they understood and practiced the new religion—though the kind of "practical Christianity" they engaged in was somewhat different from that envisioned by the missionaries and their Maragoli spokesmen. The converts were cautious and shrewd. They usually took up practices they felt useful from their old culture and the new culture of the missionaries and blended them in a circumspect way that allowed them to meet their spiritual and everyday needs. This pragmatism sometimes meant that the converts could not observe the more abstract codes of practical Christianity—like relying on prayer for guidance. Offering sacrifices seemed more practical, more judicious. Indeed, they were remarkably astute. For many converts, living "in line" was soon deemed necessary preparation for greater acceptance into the wider colonial community; that is, the Christian villages became a way of reconciling the new spiritual faith of the Maragoli with their temporal needs of food, shelter, and education for their children.[34] By the mid-1920s, the men who had moved to the Christian villages were, in most cases, flourishing economically. In fact, their economic and social status had become so eminent that their widowed mothers began to reconsider their objections to their sons' conversion and migration to the villages—and they came to regret the violent beatings that they had asked their in-laws to inflict on them. Their sons' new lives seemed to be, at least for the time being, not so bad after all.

CHAPTER SIX

The Impact of Gold Mining

In December 1939, Willis Hotchkiss, a former Quaker missionary in western Kenya, reminded readers of the *Friends Missionary Advocate* of the hidden riches in the Bible by telling a story about the discovery of gold in western Kenya. "One day," wrote Hotchkiss, a white farmer "hard hit in the wake of the depression following World War I" showed up in western Kenya in the late 1920s and set about exploring the streams and riverbeds around Maragoli and the neighboring areas. As he "patiently sifted the sand and gravel the natives thought he was mad." But "he found little reddish yellow particles amid the wet sand and gravel." He had found gold, and his discovery quickly drew others into a quest to pursue the "gleaming streaks down into the bowels of the earth." Always the didact, Hotchkiss urged his Bible students to emulate the patience and tenacity of the farmer who had discovered gold; they should read the Bible carefully and diligently and not "picnic on its surface, never dreaming of the exhaustless riches waiting to be appropriated by faith," and he counseled them to avoid a life "impoverished in spirit, oppressed by doubts, prey to fear, strangers to comfort, perplexed, burdened, defeated." The riches of the Bible, he assured them, would turn "their gloom into gladness, their mourning into singing, their perplexity into certainty, their sinful defeat into glorious victory."[1]

Hotchkiss's biblical metaphors capture nicely the earthly expectations of the white gold prospectors when in the early 1930s they discovered gold in Kakamega, ten miles from Maragoli. They excitedly dreamed that Kakamega "would develop into another Johannesburg."[2] Starting in 1931, white settlers syndicated companies, and individual prospectors from places as far away as London and Johannesburg confidently descended on Kakamega to begin alluvial and reef mining.[3] By 1933 roughly three hundred Europeans were engaged in gold mining in an area of approximately 420 square miles.

The newcomers built "substantial houses" with extra land set up for "gardens, open garages, carpenter's shops, and machine houses."[4] Some of the estates were almost the size of native settlements, and everyone predicted that a full-scale mining town was on its way.

As the prospectors gloried in the new discoveries, the Friends missionaries worried about how the mining would affect the Africans. In their reports home, Fred and Alta Hoyt, then missionaries in Kaimosi, wrote that they feared that the new "secular civilization," the "hotels, banks, and other buildings" the mining companies were constructing, would distract the Africans from the "services of church and school"—up to that point the only "unusual attractions" available to the Africans. They worried that Kakamega would turn into a boomtown to which "all kinds of Europeans" would come, and they concluded, nervously, that it would be "a bad thing for the Africans."[5]

Their concerns were well founded, since the discovery of gold arguably helped set into motion events that would end up disrupting the relatively idyllic Christian villages and that would indeed test the commitment of many Friends to school and church. The new discovery exacerbated the already-brewing tensions over land and over the meanings of material goods, and it complicated relations between convert and nonconvert and between family and community.

∽

While the rest of the country suffered the economic slump and the decline in prices for agricultural products brought about by the Great Depression, the discovery of gold in western Kenya provided a much-needed economic stimulus for the local people. The peasants in western Kenya had already suffered their share of misfortune at the beginning of that decade, as locusts and drought had destroyed their crops for three consecutive years.[6] Flying swarms of locusts had infested the area, gnawing through maize and millet stalks with frenzied persistence, once at the beginning of the long growing season in February and again, shamelessly, during the shorter growing season in September and October. Local people organized major locust-beating campaigns to combat the invasions. Men and women, young and old, grabbed sticks, pots and pans, brooms, blankets, or whatever makeshift weapon they could get their hands on and ran to the fields to beat the pests away, shouting curses, ululating, and singing chants that commanded the pests to fly off and drown in Lake Victoria, in far away Embo, or Luoland.[7] Others lit fires near the fields, hoping that the smoke would drive the locusts away. These

Locust plague, 1931 (Friends Collection and Archives, Earlham College)

sinister, plaguelike scenes are described extensively in missionary and colonial records. The locust beatings sounded much like the desperate beatings that I took part in as a child in the 1970s, in which the fires, the violent slapping at the crops, and the thumping and tramping of feet through the fields often ended up causing more damage than the locusts themselves.[8] In those bleak years of the early depression there was not much to harvest; in spite of the peasants' efforts, the locusts destroyed nearly 60 percent of the crop between 1930 and 1932 and caused severe hunger in much of Maragoli.[9]

The locust invasions instigated an exodus of people to the mines to secure jobs and earn money to buy food. In 1933, for example, at least seven thousand African men from the local areas worked in the mines and related industries. These workers contributed to a 20 percent increase in the number of men who depended on wages in the district. A large number of the workers were from Maragoli; in fact, according to the district commissioner (DC), the Maragoli were "the most favored tribe for underground work." Desperate for cash to buy food for their rapidly growing population, the Maragoli were willing to sign on, usually for the month-long contracts preferred by the mining companies.[10]

Wages in the mines were higher than those on the nearby sugar, tea, and sisal estates.[11] In 1935 the average wage for surface and underground workers was nine shillings, and at least 3 percent of these workers earned between two and five times as much. Other mine employees—namely, clerks, carpenters, drivers, domestic servants, and hospital assistants—were paid twelve shillings per month, and in these jobs at least 13 percent earned wages two to five times higher.[12] In contrast, agricultural laborers on sisal estates earned as little as five shillings per month.[13] By 1934, some miners were apparently becoming so dependent on wages that the local labor officer claimed that a "special mining class was springing up fast."[14]

Gold mining was clearly transforming Kakamega and its environs. Günter Wagner, an anthropologist trained at Columbia University and the Universities of Freiburg and Hamburg, Germany, recorded some of these changes in his book *The Bantu of North Kavirondo*.[15] Sponsored by the International African Institute, a London-based organization concerned primarily with the impact of modern conditions on the Africans, Wagner did intensive ethnographic research in Maragoli between 1934 and 1938. He wrote a detailed ethnography of the Maragoli in the 1930s, covering such popular topics as religion, rites of passage, kinship structures, trade, and diet. In describing the changes wrought on Kakamega by the mining industry, Wagner noted how this once "quiet district station with a few Indian *dukas* and a native market" was now "bustling with life." He noted that the economic life of "a far greater number" of people had been affected by the "market which the mining companies and individual European claim holders offered for foodstuffs, timber for building and mining purposes, mats, &c."[16]

Maragoli experienced some of these changes firsthand. As it was strategically located between Kisumu, one of the busiest centers in the colony, and Kakamega, more traffic passed through Maragoli than through any other region in western Kenya—indeed, an all-weather road that connected the two towns went through Mbale, Maragoli's major market.[17] Mbale was not simply a local market; it was a regional market that attracted buyers and sellers from as far away as Nandi and Luoland. In the mid-1930s, Wagner spent a great deal of time in Mbale, recording the numerous local and imported items sold in the market and observing the "bargaining and haggling" that went on there. He described Mbale as "a large open field flanked by a main motor road." On the field was "a large storage shed for maize, a butcher's shop, a small brick building with cement floor and a corrugated iron roof, a hut for scraping hides and skins, and a large and airy shed for shade drying of hides," all laid out in straight lines and interspersed with a number of "square huts or stalls serving as stores, 'tea rooms,' and tailors' shops."[18] In

the market the Maragoli and their neighbors bought and sold locally produced goods like maize, beans, fish, grinding stones, baskets, quail cages,
and cattle. On the other hand, in the stores, or *dukas*, "enterprising Maragoli
who had learnt trade from their Indian tutors" sold imported items such as
"cigarettes (only *King Stork*, an East African brand), Sunlight toilet soap,
paraffin (sold in bottles), matches, tea, sugar, Amerikani (calico), khaki drill,
thread and needles, safety pins, writing pads, envelopes, ink, pens, lavender
powder, and combs."[19]

In addition to Mbale there were sixty-four other markets in the district,
a number of which were easily accessible to the local Maragoli. The district also boasted two hundred African *dukas* in 1937, and a number of
these stores were located in Maragoli. For example, of the sixty-two traders
Wagner surveyed in Maragoli, thirteen specialized in imported goods: "two
bought coffee and tea at Kisumu and sold it from their houses, three others
sold sugar and soap from their houses and at the main market, two traded
in new and second hand clothes which they bought every other month from
Nakuru or Nairobi, and six were owners or part owners of roadside dukas."
All the traders cultivated their own gardens, and about half of them had
other occupations as well. Of the six store owners Wagner interviewed, two
were also trading in cattle, one was buying up and selling maize, and another
was a preacher or interpreter for the Friends African Mission. "One of the
tea and coffee traders was also a partner in a water-mill company and made
bricks, and one of the sugar traders sold groundnuts as well." According to
Wagner, these petty traders were likely to make a profit because "all the articles were in a steady demand on the part of a broad section of the African
population." Wagner noted that the turnover of goods was "fairly rapid and
the trade does not carry any considerable risks such as are involved in keeping large stock."[20] The increasing demand for consumer goods was clearly
encouraging a spirited new entrepreneurship.

In other major markets in the area, Indian merchants owned larger stores
and sold luxury items like sewing machines, bicycles, plows, hoes, shoes,
hats, and belts, goods whose consumption rose dramatically in the 1930s.
Basing his knowledge on a recently finished economic survey of the area
in 1937, the DC reported that the sale of these "luxuries" had "curiously
enough increased." Sewing machines were particularly popular, and reports
of their increasing numbers abound in the records. "One of the noticeable
features in the reserves," noted the DC proudly in his 1937 annual report,
"is that the verandahs of all Asiatics have sewing machines that cost 300
shillings each."[21] Similarly, Wagner observed that there were seventeen tailors working on the verandas of African *dukas* in Mbale, each one of them

Bicycles, hats, and shoes as symbols of wealth and increasing materialism (Friends Collection and Archives, Earlham College)

"equipped with a sewing machine and such accessories as the tailor's scissors, tape measures, &c." Anxious to protect their trade, the tailors had in fact organized themselves into a "tailors' union" that determined the prices for the various kinds of garments they made and also enforced certain "standards of cleanliness." "The busiest of these tailors," Wagner noted, "used 144 yards of Amerikani cotton a month."[22]

Indeed, tailors became quite popular in the 1930s. The figure of the tailor, always an African man, attired in a khaki shirt and shorts and seated behind a Singer sewing machine, appears over and over again in the colonial and ethnographic literature of the time. In a photograph taken by one of the Friends missionaries, for example, we see numerous yards of cloth hanging on a line on the veranda of an Indian *duka*, while a tailor sits on a stool behind the cloth, pedaling the sewing machine. On a bench in front of him, young girls and boys sit waiting for him to finish sewing their garments. Meanwhile, a young Indian man stands at the edge of the *duka*, looking out into the distance, catching some fresh air. According to the DC, tailors were in such high demand in the 1930s that, in 1937, nearly 60 percent of the goods imported was cloth for making garments.[23]

Goods circulated more widely in the 1930s than before. Wagner noted, for instance, that "the introduction of money and the creation of transport facilities" had led to a "considerable increase in local traffic in goods as well as a steadily growing trade with the outer world."[24] Gold mining had certainly contributed to this change. However, gold mining in western Kenya did not have a major economic impact colony-wide since gold constituted only a small part of the total domestic exports—so small, in fact, was its contribution that even at its peak in the late 1930s gold provided only 10.7 percent of the exports from the colony, trailing behind many agricultural exports, such as maize and coffee.[25] Even in the years of depressed agricultural prices in the early 1930s, the value of the gold bullion was never more than a small part of the total value of domestic exports. In general, then, many prospectors made a minute profit, and the government drew very little direct revenue from the industry.[26] Nonetheless, the social impact of gold mining on Maragoli remained undeniable.

Joshua Chavulimu, a nonconvert who had worked in the mines, detailed some of these changes for me. Chavulimu was in his midseventies and nearly blind when I spoke with him in 1994 and 1995; he wore outdated glasses that looked as if they had been fitted sometime in the 1950s. Although he could barely see, he could hear fairly well. I visited Chavulimu often and usually found him sitting and smoking a pipe in front of his mud hut, with its rusted, reddish-black corrugated-iron roof, while his wife, Belisi, sick and tired of taking care of him, constantly yelled at him for being who he could not help being: a frail blind man who could not help her with chores around the homestead. Chavulimu was glad to see me (or simply hear my voice), for my presence, he claimed, prevented Belisi from yelling at him—as he put it, "Belisi respects you and wants to impress you."[27] Belisi was indeed very friendly toward me and often gave me a big hug and offered me food and drink. Chavulimu and I talked about all kinds of things, but he was particularly very excited to talk about his work in the mines. He had had various jobs there: from mining to cleaning offices to cooking to working as a messenger at the hospital. He was proud of his former work and had left the mines with regret (when they closed in the 1950s), forced to return to Maragoli, where he barely had enough land to grow food to feed his family.

Despite the fact that the mines had been closed nearly fifty years earlier, Chavulimu's recollection was vivid. And he did something special for me: he reenacted the payday scene for me. "Imagine," Chavulimu began, "a European clerk, dressed in a khaki shirt and shorts, seated under a tree on a chair with a desk in front of him. A group of workers, wearing eager and anxious expressions, are seated in front of him." Chavulimu is one of them.

The clerk calls his name, "Joshua Chavulimu." "Me, saa [Yes, sir]," Chavulimu replies and marches toward the clerk as though he were marching at an army camp. He bows his head before the clerk. The clerk counts several coins while Chavulimu nervously looks on. He hands Chavulimu the money. Chavulimu receives it with both hands, bows his head again before the sir, says, "Asante, Bwana [Thank you, Master]," and walks away. The clerk calls the next worker on his list, and the scene is repeated until everyone gets paid.[28]

It was fascinating for me to watch Chavulimu come alive and demonstrate the movements of the various participants, imitating their voices and body movements with a vitality that I had never seen in him before. Many of the men receiving the wages were Maragoli, half of them belonging to the so-called heathen, or nonconvert, groups.[29]

"Some of the men had never touched money before," Chavulimu told me. "So when they got paid, they went out and spent it; they bought all kinds of nice, sweet things." These workers were not at all like the frugal wage earners we read about in places like South Africa, who tended to save their money to buy cattle with which to marry more wives.[30] Very few of these Maragoli mine workers spent their money on such long-term investments—largely because they worked a mere ten miles from their homes and could easily go home to their families, who demanded that they provide them with some of the new goods that were being sold in the markets and *dukas*.[31] In fact, it was impossible for the workers to escape their families' demands, for even if they decided not to return home at the end of the month, their families would track them down in Kakamega and demand that they provide for them. "If you didn't go home after payday, you would come from the mines and find your wife waiting for you at the mine gate so that you could give her some money before you ate it all," recalled Petero Kilivia, another nonconvert who worked in the mines.[32]

According to Kilivia, the workers usually left for Maragoli the day after they got paid in order to rest for a couple of days before resuming work. They often bought sugar and tea—the "nice sweet things"—for their families. Other workers indulged a bit more, however, and bought head scarves, pots, lanterns, and cups for their wives and mothers; they even bought Vaseline, which, according to Wagner, their wives took pleasure in smearing "liberally" on their faces, legs, and hands.[33]

Indeed, the nonconverts' displays of the new goods gradually became more elaborate and ostentatious. Kilivia told me how the nonconverts who had never drunk tea before did so for the first time in the 1930s: "Your wife would prepare tea and bring it to you in the yard and you drank it in an enamel cup openly. You know," he noted, "not many people had cups like that in those days, so when you drank tea in a cup people thought you were doing well.

"New goods were becoming available in this land of ours for the first time," Kilivia explained. "The Indians brought them and sold them in Lunyerere market, and if you had money you bought them, whether you were a Christian or not." As might be expected, the nonconverts cheerfully flaunted their new material goods just as they had seen the Christians do.

The Quaker converts responded quickly and sanctimoniously: they mocked the nonconverts for what they saw as their inability to appropriately use the goods of civilization. In particular, my informants commented on the use of Vaseline by the nonconverts: "You know, the non-Christians smeared the Vaseline and it looked like cow grease, and when it combined with dust, their legs looked like they had been smeared with clay," said Respah Musimbi (his parents had been Quaker converts, and he remembered their disgust).

I asked Musimbi whether the nonconverts were the only ones who liked Vaseline. "Yes," she replied. "See, the non-Christians were heathens and liked greasy, shiny things; they wanted their legs and arms to shine, but see, that shining was heathenish; it is what people did before Christianity came and civilized us."[34] To Musimbi, the nonconverts were "dirty."

Chavulimu also told me that the Christians mocked the non-Christians for living in round houses: "Some people would say, 'How can you eat on plates and drink in cups when you live in dirty round houses with *kesonga*?'"[35] Shaking his head in disapproval, he continued, "You see, the Christians were very proud people. Eh! Very proud. They never thought that anybody else could be like them."[36]

The mockery of nonconverts did not end with their supposedly inappropriate use of the goods of civilization. It extended to the other realms of their lives, to moral and spiritual matters, for example. As the economic changes occurred, new sects like the Pentecostal and the Salvation Army began to appear in Maragoli, as in other parts of Kenya.[37] Independent African churches like Waroho, Dini ya Israel, and Divine also began to grow rapidly.[38] These sects were quite different from the Friends; they tended to be highly evangelical, and their gatherings were often "characterised by the most extravagant forms of hysteria and emotionalism."[39] The leaders of these churches claimed that they "could raise the dead, heal the sick, cause the dumb to speak, the blind to see." At their meetings the members often dropped "down in swoons in dozens," confessed their sins, and "prayed and prayed hysterically." Their services lasted hours, often from "9 A.M. till 6 P.M. and then went on through the night till dawn."[40] Adorned in long white robes or dresses marked by large crosses, the members of these churches marched down the road in procession, singing, drumming, and clapping deafeningly. Unlike the Friends' strict and narrow understanding of the Bible, the new sects interpreted the Bible liberally, so that those who were polygamous, drank beer, or smoked tobacco were still welcomed. The nonconverts who had been marginalized by the Friends naturally found a comfortable place in these new churches.

The Quaker converts soon came to resent the new religions—not only because they were encroaching on their territory but also because they saw their practices as uncouth. "See," said Musa Miremu, recalling the Quaker attitudes toward the new sects, "many Friends saw the drumming and marching of the new churches as sinful. So they didn't think that the new religions were serious. The Friends believed that one has to approach God with respect, not dancing like a madman like the Israeli or Waroho." They also criticized their white robes and crosses. "The crosses were too elaborate for the Quakers," Miremu added. "They liked to keep things simple. And the swooning and the Holy Spirit stuff was seen as heathen. You see, those are things that civilized people who had become Christians from the beginning had left behind."[41]

The criticisms of the new sects were, in many ways, a symptom of deep internal problems that had begun to beset the Friends church both locally and abroad.[42] Among the missionaries in America a big rift was emerging between the younger "Modernists," who ironically wished to return to the old Quaker tradition of waiting for the Spirit to reveal itself to an individual, and the older "Fundamentalists," who were more evangelical—evangelical, that is, in the modest Quaker fashion. This rift made it hard for the Friends to attract missionaries to western Kenya, and as a consequence, many centers went without a missionary for years.[43] Because of this neglect, some African Friends began to defect to the new religions, where some actually felt more at home than they had with the Friends. Why not practice the new, less demanding, more exciting religion in which you could have it both ways—where you could find salvation and practice polygamy or drink alcohol or smoke without being ostracized?

The Quaker missionaries wrote with understandable disappointment and regret about these desertions. "The real Christians have been strengthened while the pretenders have dropped out," reported Fred and Alta Hoyt about the state of affairs in Kaimosi. Many of the converts, they noted, "have been careless in their Christian activities, and have done nothing to help get the gospel to those who have not yet been reached," and they bemoaned the "new and very subtle forms of superstitions that were creeping in some areas where they were least expected.... One form which is common among the men," the missionaries wrote, "is called *kokola buvira* [witchcraft]." According to this belief, illness was caused by other people. The situation had become so bad, one missionary wrote, that some of the local Christian leaders had decided to take part in a ritual that involved chewing up some herbs and spitting out the mixture on the affected area to heal the disease.[44]

The desertions also affected the financial resources of the church. "There had been a great falling in giving which is not all due to financial depression but also to cooling off in interest," Alta and Fred Hoyt wrote to the Quakers in America. "This has resulted in there not being enough money in the church treasury to pay teachers, so many have had to teach for little or nothing."[45] In 1933, Jefferson Ford, a missionary in Broderick Falls, north of Kaimosi, reported that he had expelled forty-nine backsliders who had "fallen into gross sin." Moreover, of the 159 people Wagner surveyed in 1936, 30 percent described themselves as backsliders, 60 percent as Christians, and the remaining 10 percent as pagans.

Colonial officials also took an interest in the defections. In a way, officials were pleased that the Quaker monopoly of the area was quickly coming to an end. Relationships between the missionaries and the colonial officials had soured because the missionaries had opposed gold prospecting in western Kenya. Writing in his annual report, the DC gloated, "The Friends have alleged that the Pentecostal Mission in Nyangori has 'poached on preserves.'... It seems," he elaborated, "that the normal casual pilgrimage of the local man in search of a belief that both comforts and cheers—like Grant's Morella Cherry Brandy—is from the Friends to the Pentecostal or Salvation Army." And finding them far less authoritarian, the converts tended to adhere to the "breakaway sect."[46] In other words, the new sects appeared to offer much more freedom. Like cheap brandy, they were certainly cheerful and comforting—especially on the pocket.

⸱∽∞∾⸱

The Friends' tendency to mock and sneer at others came back to haunt them. Unfortunately, they could not contain their bitterness, and it spread like wildfire through their insular Christian villages. My informants told me over and over again that "jealousy finished *iliini*." They observed that the Christians became more and more covetous as material goods increased in circulation in the 1930s. They competed with their neighbors in the acquisition of goods—a destructive desire to keep up with the Joneses (or shall we say the Amugunes or the Vyoyas or the Avugwis) began to emerge. It was not uncommon for the Christians in the *iliini* to peek at and sniff about in each other's kitchens to find out whether the household was cooking with oil or the traditional bean sauce, whether they were drinking tea with sugar or without, or whether they were cooking in a metal or a clay pot.[47] Such pettiness would begin to erode the once strong and cohesive Christian communities.

Indeed, class divisions in the villages intensified as some converts took advantage of the increased consumerism to expand their economic ventures. These converts, men like Yohana Amugune and Mariko Avugwi, set up butcher shops, as well as shops that sold grain in the major markets. Many of them became actively involved in trade politics in western Kenya and established organizations such as the North Kavirondo Chamber of Commerce, whose proposed goals were to "represent the common interests of farmers, craftsmen, and traders before the district commissioner, to keep its members informed of the prices, to explore new means of fostering internal and external trade."[48] Established in 1933, the chamber of commerce blossomed rapidly, so that by 1937 it had about three hundred members. The chamber of commerce's other major concerns were to "curtail competition from Indian traders in the reserve, eliminate license fees payable by African traders, ensure that the Maragoli had access to private loans from LNC [Local Native Council], and ensure that the Maragoli got permission to grow coffee." The members fought hard for their rights to be recognized. Some of the men became so prosperous—at least by village standards—that they were able to afford luxuries such as "leather shoes, lounge suits, raincoats, hats, topees, suitcases, wrist watches, alarm clocks, &c."[49]

Commenting on the class divisions, Wagner noted that some people still lived in "low, circular mud huts with their peaked straw roofs"—huts that still looked "exactly as Joseph Thomson, the first European who visited the district in the year 1883 had described them"; but, he continued, every now and then one saw "a red brick house with a straw or corrugated-iron roof, the home of an African teacher, trader, or Chief."[50] The discovery of gold had contributed to this change.

In fact, gold mining never generated the kind of certainty, confidence, or contentment that Hotchkiss had promised to those who mined the Bible in his letter to the readers of the *Friends Missionary Advocate*. Mining the Bible for spiritual truth was not the same thing as mining the land for gold.

In fact, gold mining had given rise to a secular civilization that helped destroy the Christian villages by tempting people away from the church and village schools. But this so-called secular civilization, with its materialism and commercialization, was only the beginning of the end. Worse times lay ahead.

CHAPTER SEVEN

Land Conflicts in the 1930s

A long with the other changes, the discovery of gold in western Kenya gave rise to severe anxieties about the loss of land: peasants feared that the colonial government would appropriate their land, as it had done in eastern and central Kenya.[1] To be sure, land had always been a sensitive topic in Maragoli due to the region's high population density; as we have seen, European travelers to the area at the turn of the century often commented on its overcrowding and attributed the high population to Maragoli's good climate, which provided ideal growing conditions for a variety of crops. Moreover, the population had grown steadily during the first three decades of colonial rule, so that by 1932 it had nearly doubled to about 590 people per square mile, making Maragoli one of the most densely populated regions in Africa.[2]

Reasons for the population increase abound in scholarly accounts, but the general conclusion is that sustained high fertility and decreasing mortality rates combined to increase numbers at about 4 percent each year.[3] The Maragoli themselves, however, offer different explanations for the rise in population. They attribute it to a rise in *fecundity*.[4] According to Maragoli elders, the capacity to procreate was closely linked with warm blood (*amasahi mahiu*), while impotence was believed to be a result of cold blood (*amasahi mazilu*). The elders alleged that fecundity increased in the decades immediately following colonial conquest as people began to eat new foods—sugar, bread, oil, and avocado—that possessed aphrodisiac powers that "burnt the body and the blood" and thus eliminated ritual periods of sexual abstinence that the Maragoli had previously observed to facilitate child spacing.[5] My informants also commented on how the new foods made women fat, which they believe turned their wombs into fertile places to nourish healthy babies:

"The new foods made women nice and fat and fertile, and they gave birth to many children," one of my informants assured me.[6]

Of course, more babies meant more mouths to feed and more money spent on the supposed necessities introduced by the colonials. The cultivation of cash crops like maize, then, became more and more important; cash crops provided the means by which Africans could enter the economy. And, in turn, land became an even more coveted resource. To make matters worse, the demand for land was aggravated by the Great Depression of the 1930s as the prices paid for maize declined, requiring the peasants to cultivate more land in order to grow more crops so they could earn an income adequate to feed their larger families. Inevitably, land became a major source of tension, and people fought for its possession more intensely than ever.

Litigation over land, however, was not necessarily a new thing for the Maragoli. Land conflicts had become fairly common even before the 1930s, and officials had been forced to make a detailed study of the native land tenure system in the district in order to make recommendations as to what "rules should be enacted to govern the occupation rights of tribes, clans, families, or individuals."[7]

⟨∞⟩

The threat that the new mining ventures posed to land rights cannot be underestimated. In fact, in the rush to mine the gold, a whole range of new and insidious violations of African land rights were introduced, many of which were utterly demeaning in their refusal to acknowledge the Africans' rights. Because of the controversies surrounding land seizure by white settlers in the Rift Valley and in eastern and central Kenya in the 1910s and 1920s, government officials had been forced—largely by the agitation of the Africans—to recognize African rights to land in the designated African areas, the so-called reserves.[8] In 1930, officials actually passed the Native Land Trust Ordinance, which stipulated that no European could occupy land that was currently owned by Kenyans: "the reserves," it said, "were for the use and benefit of the native tribes of the Colony for ever." The ordinance further stated that if for some reason officials needed to use some of the land in the reserve for public (not commercial) purposes, "an area equal in extent and, if possible, in value should be added [to the owner's land]." Moreover, the ordinance maintained that "no lease could be granted nor exclusion made before the Central Land Board had obtained the views of the Local Native Council (LNC) in the area concerned."[9] The LNC was a body sanctioned by officials to oversee the concerns of Africans in each district and consisted almost entirely of African men; members of the LNCs became some of the most vocal people in many Kenyan districts.[10]

Kakamega happened to be such a reserve area. Yet in the case of Kakamega, officials defied the stipulations of the ordinance, and they even refused to compensate the affected Africans with land of equal value as specified in the ordinance. Instead, they chose to pay them back with cash, which, of course, was of limited benefit to the dispossessed since there was no longer any land to buy with it. Officials objected to using "equal" land as a form of compensation because they believed that the mining period would only be brief and, so they claimed, it would not be "practical" to use land to pay the peasants evicted by mining companies. The officials further defied the ordinance by refusing to confer with the LNC as mandated. Such a consultation, one official alleged self-servingly, would merely be "a farce" since it would add to the aggravation of the Africans. "On every single occasion," he noted, "if we went to the natives concerned or the Local Native Council, they would say 'we don't want to do it'; and we should then have to say: 'it doesn't matter whether you want to do it or not; it has got to be done.'"[11] At least he was honest.

Inevitably, then, the officials went ahead with their plan without checking with the Africans. On November 12, 1931, the colonial secretary introduced to the Legislative Council meeting in Nairobi a new law authorizing the temporary exchange of land for cash in the areas where gold deposits existed. The secretary argued that the settlers needed to undertake mining to recover some of the losses they incurred in agriculture due to the depression. The all-white Legislative Council did not need much convincing. They voted unanimously to institute the new law, and by the end of 1931 European miners were free to appropriate land as they wished.

The news was bound to be poorly received by the peasants in and around Kakamega. To begin with, the cash compensation that the miners offered in exchange for land was often not enough to cover the losses incurred by the peasants. For example, Rosterman, the leading mining company, leased 155 acres for twenty-one years at five pounds per acre and paid the affected peasants a lump sum of ten pounds per acre.[12] Given the acute land shortages in the area, ten pounds was certainly not enough money to sustain a family for a year, let alone twenty-one years. Moreover, in cases where the Africans refused or hesitated to agree to the leases, the miners simply occupied the land with force. Often, one missionary noted, "a native would get up some morning and find a European driving stakes and digging trenches across his gardens."[13] The violations were absolutely ruthless, and the victims could do little or nothing.

The officials' failure to honor the 1930 ordinance particularly infuriated members of the LNC and of the North Kavirondo Central Association (NKCA), an association whose members were largely adherents of the Friends missions and worked to meet the needs of Africans.[14] Their grievances were highlighted over and over again by the DC in his annual reports, partly to make his bosses in Nairobi (who had been instrumental in passing the new law) aware of the crisis that mining was causing in the district and partly to show that Africans were perpetually stubborn and ungrateful: "It is idle to pretend," reported the DC in 1932, "that [gold mining] is regarded by the natives with nothing but the gravest suspicion and distrust.... Any advantages which they obtain, such as market for their produce and opportunities of obtaining wages," the DC noted, "all pale into insignificance beside the ever-present fear of losing their land, and in addition the inconvenience and disturbance to which they are frequently subjected to by mining operations. It must be repeated that the idea that occupies the native mind to the exclusion of all else is the fear of losing land." The native, wrote the DC with no sense of irony whatsoever, takes refuge behind the Native Land Trust Ordinance and asks "why land reserved for him 'for ever' should be in the constant and increasing occupation of Europeans."[15]

This was clearly the question that vexed the Africans the most. Instead of answering the question, however, the DC tried to disparage the LNC and NKCA members by dismissing them as "semi-illiterate" men "obsessed with the enormous belief of their own value," men who, to him, did "not appear to have the ability and intelligence displayed by the Kikuyu Central Association."[16] The DC's slander was relentless: for example, responding to a memo drafted by members of the NKCA about the injustices committed by mining companies, which "dug ditches and trenches on land belonging to peasants," the DC dismissively replied that "it has been explained time and time again that the gold, if present, must be worked, and that inevitably removal of individual natives must take place to allow for mining leases."[17]

Unable to prevent the merciless land seizures, members of the NKCA and the LNC at least tried to be present when peasants were being compensated with cash, so that they could help ensure that the miners actually paid for the land. Yet the cash compensations, as I have noted, did not even begin to ease the peasants' sense of loss. As Hugh Fearn, an economist who carried out research on land consolidation in Kenya in the 1950s and 1960s discovered: the compensation paid, whether for loss of land or for disturbance, never acted as a corrective for the feelings of insecurity that the mining invasion created in Kakamega.[18] "The memories of the disturbance and the fear of insecurity engendered by the advent of mining," wrote Fearn, "would hamper future discussions of land tenure reform in western Kenya."[19]

The anxiety over land spread to Maragoli, where, in fact, a few scattered gold deposits had been found. Maragoli was technically off-limits to the miners because officials feared that mining in this densely populated area would create great havoc.[20] Nonetheless, the Maragoli, like everyone else in the area around Kakamega, worried that Europeans would seize their land, and they felt forced to tighten their grip upon it.

The tension was felt most intensely in the Christian villages, where there occurred at least four distinct scenarios. As we may recall, the Christians had practically evicted the nonconverts in order to establish their Christian villages in the early 1920s. The Christians had in fact seized the nonconverts' land in much the same manner in which the white settlers had taken over African land decades before: with force and without scruples. And the nonconverts continued to hold grudges against these intruders—again much as the Africans now felt toward the white miners. As pressure over land increased, the nonconverts began to fear that they might never recover their land in the Christian villages, and they began to demand that the Christians vacate their land. Furthermore, the kind hosts who had taken in the nonconverts several years earlier were now pushing them out, because they, like everyone else, were beginning to feel the pressure to protect their land. This was the first scenario in the Maragoli community's reallocation of lands.

The second scenario involved conflict among the Christians themselves. Some of the people who had agreed to convert to Christianity in order to retain their land began to demand that later converts, who had long since joined them and shared the property, either pay them rent or else leave. These older converts, whose conversion had—in their minds—given them a kind of indemnity, viewed the newer Christians as outsiders, even as squatters. Usually, a dispute over payment of rent and other compensation led to evictions of more recent converts who refused to move voluntarily or who could not afford to pay the rent.

The third scenario involved the land that the Christian squatters had left behind when they moved to the Christian villages. Their relatives who had stayed on the land began to claim it as their own. They argued that the land had reverted to them when the Christian converts had abandoned it by moving to the Christian villages. A few of these relatives had even begun to sell some of the land—which leads us to the last scenario. In the 1930s the value of land had more than quintupled, so that a field that cost 10–20 shillings in 1925 went for about 100–150 shillings in 1937.[21] Eager to capitalize on the increased prices, people tried to sell whatever land they could profitably dispose of—even contested land. Once the land was sold and the sale agreement signed, it was often difficult for the original owners to recover the land. For better or worse, land conflicts such as these forced people to turn to the courts to help them sort out the problems. And a little later, when we turn to the situation of widows, we will see the extent to which tensions over land disrupted communities. As usual, the developments put widows in particularly awkward positions; they were forced, for the first time, to appear in court and defend their rights over land. It was not easy for the widows, because the colonial courts of the 1930s were difficult to navigate.[22]

◦◦◦

Land litigation in Maragoli has a complicated history. Before colonial occupation in 1894, a council of village elders presided over any land conflicts that could not be solved within the family.[23] Such conflicts were, however, rare because land was relatively plentiful. In these communities, male members of each lineage communally owned the land on which they, their children, and their wives lived.[24] Each man was allowed only use-rights to the land. Each, however, maintained a personal claim to land he had cleared (the Maragoli practiced shifting cultivation, whereby first clearance meant temporary ownership). These claims had also extended to the man's widow (or widows). Thus widows, with their children, cultivated land that had belonged to their deceased husband's lineage, and they continued to use the land until the soil was depleted of nutrients, at which time they shifted to another piece of land owned by their lineage, just as they and their husband had done while they were still alive.[25] If members of a particular household let their land lie fallow, it reverted to the jurisdiction of the lineage elders, who, in essence, were the overseers of all lineage land. The elders ensured that only household members were able to farm their lineage land, and the elders protected it against members of other lineages who might cross the boundaries over to land that was not theirs.[26] As local land administrators, then, the elders were expected to represent individual Maragoli men and women in matters concerning land disputes, since land belonged to the whole lineage and not only to individuals.

Violations of land boundaries carried heavy penalties. Normally, each witness in a land dispute (all the witnesses were male) carried his spear and shield and made his statement to the assembled elders by brandishing his spear and thrusting it into the ground at the conclusion of his statement.

When the boundary was decided, representatives of each side stuck a spear into a nearby tree and took a vow to respect the boundary. It was believed that anyone violating such a vow would die. If a death occurred that was popularly ascribed to such a violation, the tree would be cut down and destroyed to prevent any further deaths.[27] Because violations of this ritual were considered deadly, people naturally tended to respect other people's land rights.

This ritual continued to be useful during colonial rule; however, its impact began to diminish as chiefs, usually young men who had collaborated with the colonizers, replaced the traditional elders. The new chiefs possessed little or no traditional authority and were often seen as illegitimate in the eyes of their subjects—making it harder for people to perform their roles in overseeing the ritual seriously. Nevertheless, because the chiefs now presided over land disputes, they quickly became influential, and the elders, who had traditionally exercised judicial power, were little by little "driven into an attitude of apathy, of sulky acquiescence or even of hostility."[28] Eventually, they became so angry that colonial officials were forced, in 1910, to restore their judicial authority.[29] Nevertheless, the authority of the elders had been so badly damaged that it could not be recuperated easily. And understandably, the chiefs—even though they retained their executive powers—resented the fact that they had to relinquish their judicial powers to the elders. The predictable result was that the chiefs did not always enforce the elders' verdicts with sufficient resolve.[30]

In the end, this quibbling tended to diminish the stature of local courts. People simply did not take the court verdicts seriously. Meanwhile, the colonial officials retreated—in fact, they refused to intervene at all, claiming rather lamely that it was against their principles "to interfere with indigenous institutions."[31] The officials' lack of supervision, however, resulted in "corruption and inefficiency," as the chiefs and elders began to look for personal gain at the expense of the whole community.[32] By the 1930s corruption and bribery had become so rampant in the tribunals that colonial officials were forced to intervene. They were particularly concerned that the chiefs and elders were swindling court revenues that they had collected in the form of fines—the issue of fair court verdicts was not necessarily a priority.

Throughout the early 1930s, then, officials instituted several changes designed to prevent court workers from stealing cash from the courts. For instance, they "reduced the number of tribunals and of elders sitting on each tribunal; they introduced a panel system consisting largely of elders nominated by chiefs; they paid court workers a fixed salary; they built modern court houses and ensured the separation of the executive and the judiciary."[33] New officials were put into place, including permanent presidents and vice presidents, mainly young educated men appointed by the DC in consultation with the chiefs of the locations concerned. Chiefs were permanently banned from presiding over cases in the tribunals.

The changes enhanced the profiles of African courts and made it especially hard for court workers to steal the court revenues. After visiting one of the courts in western Kenya in the late 1930s, for example, Arthur Phillips, who was appointed by the colonial government to study all the native tribunals in the colony, noted that the conduct of proceedings in the courts had, "at any rate as far as external appearances are concerned, reached a stage at which it is within measurable distance of the normal standard expected of British courts." He described the courtroom as "well built, spacious, and of suitable design." Adjacent to the courtroom, Phillips reported, were lockups for prisoners and the clerk's office with a built-in safe; he also noted that the members of the tribunal sat "on a raised dais" and that the low sidewalls of the courthouse were flanked by "covered verandas," which provided additional accommodation for members of the public who wished to listen to the proceedings.[34] The rest of the furniture in the courtroom included chairs, tables, and two witness stands, which in civil cases were occupied by the plaintiff and defendant.

Impressed by the ways in which the elders conducted the proceedings in the new courts, Phillips noted that one distinctive feature was that the elders "took the floor" and administered the oath to witnesses. Standing beside each of the witness boxes in turn, the elder conducted cross-examinations in a manner—Phillips imagined—"of an attorney in a Hollywood court scene." The rest of the elders sat back and listened self-importantly to the proceedings. Afterward, the different parties and members of the public were required to withdraw while the elders deliberated their verdict. Finally, one of the elders rose and announced the tribunal's decision, at which time all the other elders would clap their hands to signify their concurrence. Meanwhile, a clerk sat at a table on the dais and took notes.[35]

This appearance of professionalism could be deceiving, however. Phillips noted that corruption and nepotism remained a serious problem. Deeply entrenched clan rivalries were often played out in the new courts, pitting neighbor against neighbor, clansman against clansman—and the courts often continued to be partial, since theoretically they remained under the influence of chiefs. Chiefs appointed the presiding elders, and they tended to appoint people from their own clans, whether they were qualified or not. Commenting on the corrupt nature of this process, the DC described the degree of ill feeling engendered as "remarkable."[36] "The Chiefs' influence," wrote the DC, "was naturally resented by other clans whose claims to any consideration

were ignored." An "immediate uproar," the DC noted, was the natural response of many people.[37] Unfortunately, the local courts often became un-
principled venues of nepotism, making it difficult for many people to trust
leaders to treat them fairly.

Nevertheless, more and more people were forced to turn to the new
courts to help them solve their land problems. Among them were widows
who were compelled to appear in the courts and defend their rights to land.
Katarina Libese was one of the widows. In March 1995, I had long conversations about her experience with her daughter, Janet Iravoga. Iravoga was born
around 1925. She told me that her mother had lived in one of the Quaker
villages, and after her husband died, she had hoped that she could continue
to use his land, located just outside the Quaker village, to grow food for her
seven children.[38] Despite the fact that she had cultivated the land for the
previous decade, her brother-in-law decided to sell it. When she discovered
the land was no longer hers, Libese asked him to rescind the sale. He refused,
and Libese then sued him before the elders of the newly established colonial court in Mbale. According to Iravoga, her mother appeared in court—
"with her body trembling"—where she told the African court elders that she
needed the land to plant maize to sell and support her family. She got the
relief she wanted: the court elders ordered Libese's brother-in-law to withdraw the sale and let Libese use a portion of the land.

And yet Iravoga told me that it was not easy for her mother. In spite of
her mother's grievances, in spite of her anger at her brother-in-law, she was
expected to "speak silently" and not "look men in the eye." She had to be
"submissive and behave with fear and respect towards men for them to
listen to her." Anger, Iravoga told me, "boiled in my mother's heart and not
on her face," and she was able to speak in public "without looking the men
in the face, in the eye." The elders would not have supported her had she
behaved otherwise—and "because the elders were true men, real true men,
they understood my mother's pain."[39]

Marita Shemegi, whose mother was widowed in 1933, also noted the importance of proper female behavior in the new colonial courts. I spoke with
Shemegi about the difficulties facing widows who appeared before the court
elders in the 1930s. "Women had to be women in those courts; they had to be
submissive if they ever hoped to get help from the elders," she recalled. "See,
but it was good to speak like that and to be obedient as long as this behavior
got you what you wanted. See, in those days people were fighting over land,
and as a widow it was important that you secured land to grow food and feed
your children."[40]

Jonesi Jumba also related her widowed grandmother's experience before the court to defend her rights to land. Jumba told me that when her grandfather died, the owners of the land on which they lived in the Quaker village forced her grandmother to pay rent. Because she could not pay what they demanded, they threatened to evict her. So she turned to the court and related her inability to pay to the elders, who then requested that she be allowed to pay a reduced amount. Jumba told me that the court elders had helped her grandmother because they were "real men who wanted to make sure that widows were helped." "But," she qualified, "my grandmother spoke silently and did not look the men in the eye. So the elders felt that my grandmother really respected them, and they helped her."[41]

According to the court records in the Kakamega Provincial Record Center, several other widows found themselves in similar situations. I came across the case file of a widow by the name of Erika Kisiru who had sued Matayo Odanga, her brother-in-law, after he had appropriated her deceased husband's land. According to Kisiru, Odanga had promised "to take care" of her after her husband had died and left her with five young children. But as it turned out, Odanga was more interested in her deceased husband's land than in making her his "wife." While in court, Odanga admitted that the land in question belonged to Kisiru's deceased husband; however, he argued that he had used the land for seven years to plant maize and hoped to use it for only two more years. The elders ruled in favor of Kisiru, arguing that "according to customary law, a widow cannot be evicted from the land of her husband. She obtains a life interest in the shamba or shambas she was cultivating at the death of her husband. In this case Kisiru has a right to the land, not only because she is a widow but because she has a son to whom the land should revert at her death."[42] The file did not give any details of Kisiru's behavior in the court, but most likely she, too, acted like a "good woman" and "spoke silently without looking the men in the eye."

⚬

The mothers of Shemegi and Iravoga, Jumba's grandmother, and other widows were obviously happy to secure their land so that they could support their children. But the land was also important to them because it contained their husband's grave: the grave not only kept their husband's memory alive but was also crucial to warding off "worries of the heart." At the gravesites widows composed and performed their lamentations, singing them loudly while walking around the grave, in order to remind members of their communities that they were widows and needed help with their socioeconomic problems. Lamentations like the one below revealed the loneliness felt by the widows and obliged members of their communities to come to their aid:

> Murinange ndemeye, ye ye
> Nyumba yarinyumbira
> Murinange ndemeye, ye ye
> Murina wange, yatsia kuvaya hai? ye ye
> Ndemeye, ye, ye
>
> My friend, I am alone
> The house is too big for me alone
> My friend, I am alone
> My friend, where have you gone to visit?
> I am alone, I am alone[43]

The courts did not hear these lamentations. Nor were all widows lucky in getting their views heard in the courts; many still had to give up land despite their behavior as "good women" and despite their staging of such symbolic rituals. For example, Ronika Vusha, a widow, was evicted from a Quaker village, and when she tried to return to her husband's land, she discovered that her brother-in-law had sold it to one of the chiefs. She sued her brother-in-law, but she was unable to get the land back. In her case file, the clerk wrote, "case dismissed, Lubanga [the chief] has shown evidence that he paid for the land."[44]

Torkas Isigi found herself in a similar situation. I interviewed Isigi's son, Petero Kisala, who told me that his mother and father had moved to one of the Quaker villages in the mid-1920s. When his grandfather died, sometime in the early 1930s, he was buried back on his lineage land. A few years later, overwhelmed by the congestion in the Christian village, his grandmother decided to go back to her husband's lineage land and claim the area surrounding her husband's grave. But Shem Mutiva, his great-uncle, would not let her. Isigi sued. Even though Isigi "spoke silently" and gave a detailed history of the land and whom it had belonged to (by listing all her husband's ancestors), the elders did not rule in her favor. Mutiva, as it turned out, had sold the land to Mariko Beywa, a prominent man in the village and a relative of the chief. While in court, Beywa produced the sale agreement letter, and the elders nodded in approval as they scrutinized it. "What could my mother do?" Kisala asked as he looked at me pleadingly.[45]

Berita Kaziva, another widow who lived in one of the Christian villages, also lost her case when the court ruled in favor of a prominent villager. Her brother-in-law, who had inherited her as a widow, sold land that had belonged to her husband to a prominent member of the village. When I spoke to her son, Mariko Mukiri, he recalled that his mother suffered a great deal because she did not have land on which to plant crops and feed him and his six siblings. "Eh! My mother really suffered from *kehenda mwoyo.*"[46] Luckily, a neighbor sympathized with them and gave them a piece of land. Such swindling of land, and the evictions that accompanied it, appears frequently in the court records, and most widows were not as fortunate as Berita Kaziva.

Though widows were perhaps the most vulnerable, court records indicate that others, mostly poor people, were also victims. Mariko Muteve, for example, was forced to give up rights to his land because his brother had sold it to another man. Originally, Muteve's family had been kicked off their land by Christians when they commandeered it to establish a village. His brother Petero Muse had become a convert and stayed behind. When the Christian villages started to disintegrate, Muteve's brother sold off his brother's acreage. When sued, the buyer, Meshak Kisivura, produced the signed agreement, and the court officials ruled in the buyer's favor.

In his testament to the officials, Muteve brought up his poverty, noting that he had three wives and twelve children whom he needed to take care of. "Mimi masikini tu [I am simply a pauper]," he told the elders. But the officials refused to take this into consideration. In the case file the clerk simply wrote, "The elders have investigated this case thoroughly and have found that the land belonged to Petero Muse." That was the extent of the explanation. No details were given as to how Muse acquired the land, and no mention was made of the obvious fact that the two men were blood brothers and therefore were expected—according to tradition—to share the land. Muteve's claims were most certainly dismissed because he did not have nearly as much political influence as his brother, who happened to be a member of the North Kavirondo LNC. Muteve thereafter languished as an *ummenya* (refugee) in the hills of Maragoli, living on a mere acre of land, on which his twelve children and three wives coexisted uncomfortably in crowded mud huts and tilled soil that was so depleted of nutrients that the only crops he could grow were cassava and sweet potatoes.[47]

Ultimately, the evictions and the ensuing shuffle of people and land marked the physical end of the *iliini*, the once-idyllic Christian villages. Moreover, the rearrangement of people, much like the process that had created the Christian villages in the 1920s, resulted, ironically, in people from different lineages living together. Now it was not religion that was giving shape to the village communities but money and political clout. These had become the major influences. By the late 1930s, it was not uncommon to find a Quaker living next to a polygamous member of the Salvation Army or Pentecostal church. Nor was it uncommon to find a well-to-do man, most likely an adherent of the Quaker church, living next to a poor man who senselessly drank *changaa*, the potent local brew, and cursed loudly late at night as he passed the proper and peaceful household of his Quaker neighbor. The center of these changing communities was clearly becoming something other than the village school and church. Members of these communities were forced to figure out how best to live in their changed environments with their changed (and changing) neighbors—and it often meant dealing with a newfangled legal bureaucracy that they could not understand or trust.

PART TWO

Family Life

CHAPTER EIGHT

Educating "Progressive" Sons

On Sunday morning, February 15, 1927, H. O. Weller, the superintendent of local education, was eating breakfast when he received news that a group of Maragoli elders were waiting outside and wanted to have a word with him. The superintendent finished eating and then received the thirteen men, "a deputation of Africans of good position," led by Mnubi, a local chief. One of the men summarized their needs thus: "The population of the two Maragolis is very large. . . . In the two Maragolis there are 43,000 people, of whom 20,000 are *children* [his emphasis], and schools are urgently required."[1] When Weller asked them what kind of schools they wanted, they replied, "Half mission and half government . . . a school like Maseno."[2] After the delegation of Africans had finished, the superintendent genially responded by discussing the funding and location for the school, to which, he reported, the "deputation made no difficulty at all."[3]

On May 7, 1927, the same delegation turned up again at Weller's house with—for them—the vast sum of two thousand shillings, which, according to Weller, they had "collected on their own initiative" largely from the adherents of the Friends Mission to fund the school. They asked Weller to "take it into safe custody for them." He took the money and then wrote to inform the DC of the meeting, telling him that he had been "much impressed with the earnestness of the deputation, their ability to put their case, their statistical knowledge of the population in the area, and the evidence of prosperity and religious enthusiasm [he] observed." He emphasized that he did not want to be "associated with the refusal of the demand or even with the delay in complying with it" and suggested that the government "reply sympathetically to the request and that open action on the report might be taken to start the school."[4]

The DC was not pleased with Weller's suggestions; in truth, he was as-tonished by what he saw as the superintendent's hasty enthusiasm and cited a number of major procedural mishaps in Weller's correspondence. The DC basically wanted Weller to consult with him before he took money from the Africans.[5] Weller remained persistent, however, and he went on to make a strong case for the school and even arranged for an elementary day school to be established in Mbale by the end of 1927. Its aims were "to provide a school where boys may advance in their studies beyond the usual grade (standard II) of a village school, to at least IV standard; to train boys for at least two of the following vocations: agriculture, carpentry, shoe-making, tailoring." The plan was that after finishing their study the pupils would proceed to the more advanced Native Industrial Training School in Kabete, near Nairobi, or they would be "ready to go out at once and earn their own livings in the reserve."[6] The school was certainly an improvement over the missionary village schools, which focused on simple literacy—even though it was not as highly thought of as the Maseno Boys School, an elite primary school whose graduates became highly sought-after clerks.

Education continued to preoccupy Maragoli leaders in the 1930s and 1940s. As land shortages became acute, as conflicts arose over schooling, and as the desire to earn more money to buy newly available consumer goods in-creased, the leaders looked to education as the only way for their sons to ad-vance in the colonial world, a world that was rapidly enveloping them. Dur-ing the 1930s, members of the North Kavirondo LNC passionately discussed ways to improve education in their district. The Christian village schools had simply whetted their appetite. Now they wanted more. They wanted a more selective education that would endow them with proficiency in read-ing, writing, and speaking English and give them instruction in subjects like history, geography, and science. They hoped that a liberal arts education would enable their sons to take advantage of positions of authority that were slowly beginning to emerge in the colonial economy. Even more, they hoped that their sons would attain well-paying white-collar jobs like those held by Europeans, especially since life in the villages—and the missions—had be-come less secure and dependable.

The Africans' demand for improved education was not isolated to west-ern Kenya. In the 1930s in central Kenya, for example, and indeed throughout much of Africa, African leaders urgently sought higher education for their sons.[7] In fact, the missionary elite among the Kikuyu people in central Kenya had been at the forefront of this movement in Kenya and had begun to push for higher liberal arts education in the early 1920s to help compensate for the severe land shortages they faced because of the white settler occupation.[8]

The colonial government had started to consider these demands when in 1924 the Phelps-Stokes Commission visited Kenya. The commission was a white American organization that focused on the "education of the Negro in the American south" but also claimed to be interested in "pan-African education." Jesse Jones, a white American and self-proclaimed "expert" on Negro education, headed the commission, whose objective was to carry out an extensive survey of African education so as to determine how it could be "best oriented towards improving rural life."[9] In Kenya, as in other parts of Africa, Jones argued vehemently for his theory of "educational adaptations," which he had passionately advocated for blacks in the American South.[10] His argument was primarily that Africans should acquire the tools necessary to elevate their underdeveloped status, just as the American blacks had taken up the "plow, the anvil, the hammer, the broom, the frying pan and the needle" when they began their work "as freemen on the plantations and in the towns of the South." Jones believed that training Africans in the "simples of health and home life" would help develop Africans "along their own lines," just as, he claimed, blacks in the South had done.[11]

The commission's recommendations, arriving in timely fashion in the midst of the education controversy, gave an international seal of approval to many of the ideas the colonial officials had been toying with in Kenya. They confirmed the officials' notion that practical education was the way to go, that their "civilizing mission" must be carried out, and that returning to and improving life in the village should be the eventual goal of educated Africans. These ideas crystallized swiftly, and a Jeanes School, modeled on black schools in the American South that focused on teaching simple rural industries, was established in Kabete, near Nairobi, in 1925.[12]

The colonial officials greatly appreciated the commission's recommendations and circulated several memos praising and rehashing them. For example, H. S. Scott, who had worked in India and was the director of education in Kenya, commended the commission and opined that an academic education had corrupted the upper classes of India, having too often "turned out 'baboos' and failed B.A.s," and should not be applied to the rest of the colonies.[13] Similarly, J. W. C. Dougall, an official in the Department of Education in Nairobi who prided himself on having done "extensive research in native education" and wrote several guidebooks for village teachers, was happy when the commission confirmed his idea that "rural science was the appropriate program for the underdeveloped situation of Africa."[14] The Reverend J. W. Arthur of the Church Missionary Society in Kikuyu, after sojourning in South Africa for only three weeks and acquiring—so he claimed—an "in-depth" knowledge of African education, applauded the commission by declaring, "There is no doubt that the native degenerates when brought in contact with Western Civilization. He acquires wrong notions and picks up bad habits. He loses respect for his own religion and customs and it is our duty to give him an education that will fit him for life under the conditions imposed upon him." "I am convinced," he wrote, "that a mere literary education for natives is a grave mistake," for it would "bring very serious danger to the Empire as witnessed in recent events in Egypt and India."[15] "If we are to profit by [the] education errors of those countries," Arthur insisted, "we must concentrate on vocational training."[16]

Colonial officers in western Kenya similarly lauded the commission's observations. The PC of Nyanza confidently went ahead and made proposals in line with the commission's recommendations, even though he admitted in his memo to the chief native commissioner in Nairobi that he was "not sufficiently an educationalist to know exactly the best way" for government to "take a larger share in the education of the natives in the reserve." Nevertheless, he confidently concluded, "Education should train boys in such a way that they may go back and improve life in the reserves by practicing better habits of cleanliness and industry." The PC insisted that successful schooling would "turn out boys who are really efficient for the demands of modern civilization and able to carry out technical work on farms, estates, etc." "On the one hand," he suggested rather heavy-handedly, "we do not want to turn out numbers of boys with literary training only who will never do any honest toil in their lives again but spend their time wandering about in beautifully creased trousers and stetson hats and on the other hand we do not want to produce semi-illiterate *fundis* [carpenters] who cannot build a small house or make a door frame without supervision." He emphasized that he needed to "produce a native who is completely educated for whatever path of life he may wish to follow," and, more important, "to educate the black man to be what we think he ought to be."[17]

African leaders in North Kavirondo, however, would have none of this. They refused to let colonial officials act unilaterally, and they insisted quite forcefully on taking a major role in determining and shaping the future of their children. In general, the missionary-educated black men of the 1930s and 1940s were not as docile and compliant as their predecessors had been. They not only had strong ideas on black education but also had quickly learned that they could effectively debate with the Europeans and challenge their ideas. More often than not, they had attended the meetings of the North Kavirondo Taxpayers Welfare Association and had seen the defiant manner in which its members responded to colonial officials.[18] Or they may have been present at a rally held in Kisumu in the mid-1920s by Dr. James Aggrey, an African American protégé of Jesse Jones, at which he urged Africans to demand that missionaries teach them English so that they could "communicate with the rest of the world."[19] Even more important, they may have heard of the first major African protests in 1922, organized by an indignant African clerk and telephone operator in Nairobi by the name of Harry Thuku, in which Africans demanded better education and protested land losses, tax increases, and forced labor.[20] Regardless of the source of their inspiration, it is important to note that the black men with missionary educations were becoming fiercely independent and would not let colonial officers decide, single-handedly, the trajectory of their lives or, for that matter, those of their children.

Throughout the 1930s, members of the North Kavirondo LNC debated their sons' education with uninhibited enthusiasm. Missionary bashing became a favorite theme—so much so that the DC, who was required to be present at all the LNC meetings, was forced to come to the missionaries' defense by reminding the men that the missionaries had "taught them what little they know."[21] Nevertheless, the men continued to viciously denounce the missionary village schools and derided them for "teaching simple vernacular only." Some of the members spoke even more daringly, asserting that they wished to set up an alternative school that would "set a standard for mission schools to emulate."[22]

The DC, who was not entirely happy about having to attend every LNC meeting, regretted the time he "wasted" listening to the men debate: "The doubtful gift of oratory, which seems to have been granted to the Africans in such excessive measure, reveals itself at every meeting." Annoyed and discouraged, the DC ended up complaining in one of his annual reports, "The discussion of the most unimportant question is enough to bring ardent orators to their feet, ready to argue on the point (or off it) with a wealth of irrelevant detail, which usually flows on interminably until checked by the chair."[23] Given all the excitement over African education, this observation may not have been off the mark. The men, I am sure, enjoyed being able to express their opinions and, in doing so, may have taken certain oratorical liberties. But that is not the point.

Rather, the point is that Africans who had naively accepted their rudimentary education from the missionaries were, for the first time, beginning to question the validity of such an education. They were questioning its larger purpose in and for the colony—that is, they wondered whether this very basic education would allow their sons to secure high-paying jobs that would help them escape the ache and indignity of manual labor. So, for example, like African leaders in other parts of Kenya, the earnest delegation of

Maragoli men who had visited the superintendent of local education, Weller, on that Sunday morning in February 15, 1927, wanted schools that would teach their sons English and other liberal arts subjects so that they could compete successfully for jobs on a national level. And they worked hard to set up such schools.[24]

The LNC finally opened up one such a school in 1932: the Kakamega Government School ("Government" in the name importantly distinguishes it from what the leaders saw as the less sophisticated missionary schools). Since the government had given Africans permission to tax themselves in order to promote local development, they had used a large chunk of the collected money to set up the school—an extraordinary 200,000 shillings, the highest amount ever allocated for a school by any LNC in the colony.[25] English and other liberal arts subjects were included in the curriculum, as well as a few technical subjects like carpentry and tailoring. Apparently, we are told, the members of the LNC did not mind this technical aspect of the education as long as they felt that the school was their own and they had full control over it.[26]

Improvements in African education, driven largely by African initiatives, occurred in other parts of western Kenya as well. In 1938, for example, the government turned Maseno Boys School, the prestigious primary school, into a secondary school. Similarly, the Catholic school in Yala was transformed into a secondary school in 1939. The boys in these two secondary schools studied for a Cambridge Overseas School Certificate, a very coveted document that opened up economic opportunities for many. In addition, Kaimosi Boys School became a full-fledged primary school in 1939. It was to these advanced schools that parents hoped to send their sons.

⌒◈⌒

Some of these parents were widows, of course. With their husbands gone, they in particular hoped that their sons would be educated in these schools and assume the financial duties of their deceased husbands. According to Petero Azigare, whose father died in 1935, "My mother wanted me to receive pure teaching—not just to learn the Bible and agriculture. She wanted me to advance, so she sent me to Kakamega Government School."[27] The same distaste for manual work was expressed by James Visero, who had also been educated at Kakamega: "My mother did not want me to do manual work at school; manual work was something you did at home." "At school," he told me, "you were supposed to look smart and respectable and learn to speak English like an Englishman."[28] But of course the big question remained: how were parents, especially widows, going to afford their sons' advanced education?

Unlike the village schools, which children could attend at no cost, the new advanced schools charged school fees—and the fees were much higher than any expense parents had ever incurred before. In the 1930s and 1940s, for example, fees were between thirty and forty shillings per term.[29] This was not a small amount considering that an average salary for the highest-paid professions, such as clerical or teaching, ranged between forty and sixty shillings per month.[30] But the learning conditions were also better than those of the village schools; the buildings, unlike the grass-thatched mud huts of the village schools, were made of brick and corrugated iron, and inside, students sat on benches and used inkpens to write—not the sticks in the dust that the less fortunate generations before them had used. The new schools, in short, required much more capital to maintain, and the costs were naturally passed on to the students and their families. Without doubt, they fell particularly hard upon widows, since they had no husbands to work for wages.

To help out disadvantaged people such as widows, the North Kavirondo LNC initiated a bursary scheme for "orphaned" boys who were bright but whose mothers could not afford the cost of their schooling.[31] But these bursaries were often misappropriated, and in many cases widows were once again forced to rely on the coercive discourse of the "worries of the heart" in order to have access to needed funds. Kezia Avugwi, the mother of Peter Avugwi, was one such widow. In 1936, after passing his intermediate school exams, Avugwi applied for one of the bursaries in order to attend the Kakamega Government School, but he was rejected.[32] He tried again the following year, but no luck. One day in May 1938, both he and his mother put on clean clothes and walked about seven miles to discuss the matter with G. E. Webb, the inspector of schools.

I spoke with Avugwi, a slim seventy-something with long spiky legs that looked as if they had been sharpened by suffering. He spoke casually in a low voice, and between pauses he managed to tell me that his mother had informed the inspector of the LNC's negligence concerning her needs. She had even showed him her son's report card, which plainly verified his good marks. As Avugwi recalled, "My mother told Bwana Webb that her husband had died and left her with six young children who needed food and education. She also told him about how the *teminari* [LNC] people had refused to help her—even though I had earned excellent grades." She was ultimately telling him, Avugwi believed, "about her worries of the heart, about her problems. And the inspector listened."[33] He sent mother and son home and asked them to check back in a month's time.

True to his word, Webb began to investigate Avugwi's case and discovered that during that year "the boy who had been offered a bursary by the LNC had not even passed his elementary examination and that the father was a particularly rich member of the LNC."[34] (Such blatant nepotism was not uncommon, as the inspector discovered; there had been several such incidents.) Some action needed to be taken. So in 1938, Webb, after much opposition from members of the LNC, passed a law that required the government to take over from the LNC the responsibility of assigning bursaries.[35] The following year, he ensured that Avugwi was one of the bursary recipients, and Avugwi proceeded to attend Kakamega Government School. He remembered this particular moment vividly. Patting my wrist to alert me to the gravity of what he was about to say and to ensure that he had my absolute attention, Avugwi looked at me directly and said, "Bwana Webb was a true *msungu* [white man]. A real, true *msungu*. He did a good job of taking care of poor widows."[36]

Avugwi was not the only one who praised local white missionaries and colonial officials. In 1939, for example, Yohana Ndanyi, the son of Ronika Ajema, a widow, passed his intermediate school exams but had no money for advanced schooling. I spoke with Ndanyi in the mid-1990s, and he, like Avugwi, told me about a difficult journey to higher education. "My mother and I left home very early in the morning before the cocks began to crow and walked to Kaimosi," began Ndanyi. "We went straightaway to the headmaster's office. Mr. Kellum greeted us very nicely. My mother told him that I had passed my exams but lacked school fees; she gave him my report card. And the headmaster looked at it for a long time without saying anything." Ndanyi paused for emphasis, then proceeded: "The headmaster looked at me and said, 'You look like a strong young man. If I asked you to cut grass for the school during the school holidays, would you do it?' I looked at him and said, 'Yes,' and that is how I was able to attend Kaimosi Boys." Even now, he was eager to point out Mr. Kellum's generosity: "Bwana Kellum was a true European; . . . he helped many other Africans, just as a true European should."[37] As in Avugwi's case, European paternalism was greatly appreciated by Ndanyi and his mother. But Ndanyi also spoke poignantly about his mother's own efforts to ensure that he got an advanced education: "My mother sold either a chicken or a goat [a substantial sacrifice] in order to earn money to buy my school uniform or books."

While some widows like Ajema and Kezia were lucky to get help from Europeans, other widows struggled on single-handedly to earn the money they needed to send their sons to school. Those who had large enough plots of land could work harder to grow extra maize to sell—and they were usually able to mobilize the labor of their whole family. Older male children milked cows, assisted in calf birthing, cut firewood, and helped with weeding, harvesting, and preparing the ground for planting; the younger children helped by chasing birds that threatened ripening grains and by taking care of their even younger sisters and brothers.[38] The older girls searched for firewood, fetched water from the river, and ground grain. By organizing the labor of all the family members, widows could at least hope that their sons might obtain lucrative jobs after graduation and help out with the financial needs of the entire family.

Interestingly, the widows who did not have many children to help with farmwork were often the first to experiment with new crops and labor-saving devices. These widows enthusiastically adopted new tools, crops, and farming techniques, and some even spent a little more money to buy hybrid seeds that had higher yields; others invested in sharper hoes so they could weed faster. Some of the widows devoted the time they saved to cash-generating activities, like trading in maize.[39]

But selling grain was, unfortunately, not always profitable. In the 1930s, the low prices of the Great Depression forced widows to work even harder to market their maize. They, like other peasants, were forced to carry their maize to the distant town of Kisumu to get better prices for their grain from Indian merchants there. In the early 1930s a sack of maize sold for three shillings in Maragoli, whereas an Indian merchant in Kisumu would pay up to four shillings for the same sack.[40] A difference of a single shilling was worth the trip to Kisumu, even though the ten- to fifteen-mile journey was not an easy one, as indicated by the lamentations composed by widows as they journeyed west to that lonely port city of western Kenya:

Andere eh, Andere eh, Andere eh
Rero nangone mkambi,
Mkambi yu Odiaga

Andere eh [her deceased husband's name]
I will be sleeping in a camp
In the camp of Odiaga

Odiaga was a prison camp in Kisumu near the market where the maize was bought and sold, and since the distance to and from Kisumu was more than a day's walk, the women were forced to sleep there. Not surprisingly, they saw their trip to Kisumu as a trip to the prison.[41]

I spoke with a son of one such widow, and he provided details of the sacrifices his mother had made to send him to Kakamega Government School. Shem Kavaya, a heavyset but frail man in his seventies, had been an eldest child and therefore obligated to take care of his five siblings: "Our mother would be gone for several days to sell grain in Kisumu, and when Mama returned she was too tired to do anything; her ankles were swollen from walking to Kisumu, and her eyes were swollen too because she had not slept well for two days." I asked Kavaya why his mother had felt it necessary to make such an effort. "You know, she was a widow and had to struggle to survive; she also wanted me to go to school so that I could help her and my siblings. So that is why she had to go to Kisumu to get more money for the maize."[42]

⋄

Whether widows relied on colonial officials or missionaries or whether they struggled alone to educate their sons, they did so because they wanted their sons to secure lucrative jobs and eventually help them meet their financial needs. According to the widow Elisi Musimbi, "You sent your son to the new school because you wanted him to make enough money, to be seen as someone with *maendeleo* [civilization] and speak English like an Englishman." Only then, Musimbi noted, "would you be assured that he would get a job as a clerk and help you out; only then could he become a real man."[43] But how realistic were these expectations? How realistic were their aspirations, given colonial officials' dismissive attitude toward the highly educated African, toward a man who did not want to return to the rural areas and do manual work as he was supposed to do?

⚜

CHAPTER NINE

The Burden of "Progressive" Sons

Peter Avugwi finally finished his schooling at Kakamega Government School and in 1945 secured a job as a division II clerk at Kenya Railways and Harbors in Mombasa. His starting salary was sixty shillings a month, which he used to buy food and other household amenities; he did not need money for rent since the railway company provided him with a two-roomed house, a living arrangement seen by many rural folk—and no doubt by railway company officials—as adequate.[1] After all, Avugwi had a whole house to himself, while in the rural areas up to seven people could be expected to share a space of similar size. He did not need to support his wife and children on a daily basis because they lived in Maragoli, where they were able to subsist on produce from the family farm.

In reality, however, the living conditions of a "migrant" worker in the city were different from the rosy picture envisioned by rural people. Prices for basic commodities like salt, sugar, and milk increased in the 1940s and 1950s, making it difficult for migrants—even relatively well-to-do ones like Avugwi—to make ends meet, let alone have money to spare for their families in the rural areas.[2] Not surprisingly, then, Avugwi could afford to return to Maragoli (about five hundred miles from Mombasa) only once a year, even though as a railway employee he was entitled to an occasional free ride. Before heading home he also needed to save enough money to buy clothes and luxury items for his mother, six siblings, wife, and four children. As "a real, working man," Avugwi pointed out, he could not go back home to his family empty-handed: "It was very important for me to return home 'in style,' as a man who had made it in the city, because this is what everybody in the village, including my widowed mother, expected me to be. To them I was a civilized man and needed to act like one."[3] Avugwi cheerfully remembered his family's celebrations upon his return from Mombasa, giving special prominence on the setting of the festivities in his elegant—and, above all, square—mud house with four windows and a corrugated iron roof. He also reveled in his neighbors' awe at the butter, bread, soap, cooking oil, and padlocks that he brought from the city—"all, all our neighbors stopped by to see me, and my wife would cook tea for them and serve it to them with bread and Blue Band [margarine]; people really appreciated it because such foods were rare."[4]

Avugwi retired from the railway in 1980 and used his retirement bonus to set up a small *duka* in Mbale market, where he sold general supplies such as sugar, medicine, tea, and milk. Most of our conversations took place here in the concentrated clutter of the *duka*. Although he spoke about his youthful days in Mombasa with excited nostalgia, he never romanticized his experiences; he was always careful to point out the darker, more problematic side of his success. "See," he told me, "because I was a successful man, everybody in the village expected money from me, and my mother insisted on it. To my mother my giving away money like that was a sign that she had raised a successful son. So I gave away shillings here and there, and a shilling was a lot of money in those days." Avugwi looked at me with his wide eyes and paused to make sure that I understood the significance, the weight, of a shilling and of his act of giving it. "A shilling was a lot of money in those days, I tell you," he repeated.

The euphoric gatherings at his homecoming lasted for only a week, yet in the course of that intense week of feasting and celebration the food was quickly consumed and the supply of shillings was hurriedly depleted. Once the party was over, Avugwi was in a difficult situation: he had either to return to Mombasa or stay in the village and succumb to a sense of inadequacy because he could not provide any more for his family, neighbors, and relatives. Avugwi chose the former. He returned to Mombasa reluctantly: "I went back to Mombasa because I had no money left." It was easier to be poor in Mombasa than in the village. "See, in the village I was 'a man of means,' 'of progress,' 'of the city,'" he explained with a loud laugh; he was considered "almost a European" and a "provider" in the village; he could not just sit around the village without money in his pocket. After all, members of his family and village could not—or would not—believe that it was possible that he could run out of money.[5]

I asked Avugwi's mother, now in her eighties, to remember what she could about her son's days on the coast. She sighed deeply and said, "I am glad that Avugwi has now retired and can stay around to take care of me." When he worked in Mombasa, she saw him rarely—"he visited only for a week"; she grumbled that her son's short visits had disappointed her because her son was "a very important man and I wanted him to stay around so that his presence could be felt in the village."[6]

Avugwi's predicament was hardly unique. In April 1995, I tracked down Yohana Ndanyi, whose mother, as we have seen, pleaded with Kellum to let him into Kaimosi Boys School. After graduating, Ndanyi had become a clerk, as his widowed mother, Ronika Ajema, had hoped; he worked for the Power and Lighting Company in Nairobi until 1983, when he retired and moved back to Maragoli. I frequently visited Ndanyi in his tiny, dilapidated brick house whose once-shining corrugated iron roof was now dark brown and full of holes that allowed a steady stream of rain into the house. Since my visits occurred during the rainy season of March and April, I often sat with him and his many grandchildren surrounded by enamel basins that rapidly filled with rainwater.

Since his retirement, Ndanyi had become a farmer of sorts. On his four acres of land he grew string beans and maize and also kept several head of cattle. In the early 1990s, string beans had become one of the leading new export crops in Kenya.[7] Private companies contracted peasant farmers to grow the beans, gave them the seed to plant, and advised them on when to pick the ripened crop; the farmers then took their produce to nearby collecting centers, where it was weighed and priced accordingly. The beans were flown to France and Britain overnight, where they were sold to some of the finest supermarkets and restaurants in London and Paris. But it is hard to satisfy the palates of exclusive consumers in Harrods' Food Hall or those who wine and dine near the Louvre in Paris, and more often than not, the farmers' harvests were rejected for one reason or another—color, texture, size, and so on. The requirements became so stringent that many farmers eventually gave up the crop altogether, and by 1999 not a single peasant grew string beans. They had all returned to growing maize. "At least we can eat maize," one of the peasants told me. "The beans, we could not eat them, and our efforts went to waste."[8]

While the novelty of string beans lasted, though, Ndanyi was one of the few people who managed to make some profit, because he had the money to hire workers who could pick and deliver the crop promptly enough to ensure freshness. He paid his workers with money he earned from migrant workers who rented two-room mud houses that he had built in Kakamega with his pension funds. Ndanyi was in many ways a slumlord, for he never kept up the houses, and by 1998 they had deteriorated into uninhabitable shacks. Yet at the end of every month he got into a *matatu*, one of the notoriously overcrowded minibuses that transport people all over Kenya, and went to Kakamega to collect rent from the tenants.[9]

On one unusually dry April morning, I visited Ndanyi while his grand-children were in school and not running around to interrupt our conversation. We had one of the most detailed and, I think, frank conversations that I had ever had during my stay in Maragoli. I arrived at his house around nine in the morning. Ndanyi was drinking *chai*, sweet tea that is prepared by stirring tea and milk and sugar together in the same pot and boiling it. Erika Mwanika, his second wife, an Akamba woman he had married while in Mombasa, offered me some of the *chai* in an enamel cup. As I sipped the sweet brew, I asked Ndanyi about his job in Nairobi.

"It has been over ten years since I retired, and I am doing well. I am trying to do farming. Too much hunger around here. It is not like in the old days," he replied.[10]

Ndanyi went on to tell me about his life after he graduated from Kaimosi Boys. After leaving, he had obtained a job as a clerk in Nairobi, and by the early 1960s had built himself a brick house and also bought land and built a house for his mother. He was particularly proud of his house. Initially, he did not have enough money to complete the floor, so it was plastered with cow dung until 1971, when he replaced it with a cement floor. In that same year he also made another, even more prestigious upgrade: he replaced the house's wooden shutters with glass windows—giving it, I should say, a nice touch of practical Christianity. The Reeses would certainly have been pleased with the conditions of his life—at least until the roof began to fall apart.

In a soft, reflective voice, Ndanyi told me that many people had looked up to him because he was a clerk in Nairobi. "I often came home at Christmas, during celebration time, and bought all my family members gifts and also gave neighbors and relatives something small [money]." I asked Ndanyi how he managed to afford to buy the gifts for everyone on his salary of seventy shillings per month. "I started saving in September," he said. "Christmas was a good holiday because many people returned to the village and we could catch up with news of other people." But Christmas was also a time when the demands on "progressive" sons like Ndanyi become outright taxing, since successful people like him were expected to display their material wealth and compete with other families to determine which was the best dressed or the most bounteous in offerings of food. The Christmas holiday could indeed become a time of intense rivalry—and "keeping up with the Ndanyis" the villagers' newest mania.

Ndanyi's mother even towed him along to church to show him off. Because he had become so "civilized," he was often asked to judge the choir groups that sang at the Christmas ceremonies and determine which group sang best. I tried to imagine the scene: a young, plump Ndanyi in spectacles

Girls' choir during Christmas celebration, 1960 (Friends Collection and Archives, Earlham College)

(pictures of him hung all over the wall in his living room), wearing a cheap gray suit, sitting in the pew wiping beads of sweat from his face in the December heat and jotting down points for each choir group. After two hours of competition, Ndanyi would rise from his seat and, with assumed authority, announce the winners, calling out the third-place group, then the second, and finally the winners. The three top choirs would each receive a present, usually Bibles or hymnbooks, before everyone slowly dispersed to eat rice and chicken, a special Christmas treat.

According to Ndanyi, his mother considered him a "clever man of means, an important civil servant," and was therefore very proud. However, like Avugwi's, Ndanyi's visits to the village were often cut short. "The money was gone *kabisa* [completely] in about a week's time, and I had to go back to Nairobi to make more to keep up my status," Ndanyi reminisced, rubbing his palms together to indicate his empty pockets. Predictably, his mother, Ajema, complained about the brevity of his stays. One day, I asked her to tell me about Ndanyi's visits. "I wanted Ndanyi to visit me longer than he did," she answered, "so that he could take care of me. It was very important that his presence was felt here. After all, his father had been an important man in the village. But when he came and left quickly like that, you felt alone."[11]

While the festiveness of Christmas might have helped diminish the problematic aspects of the demands for money, the obligations of funerals did not. Every now and then Ndanyi was forced to return home to attend a funeral, especially those of important persons. This is what his mother—and the village—expected of an educated, successful son. "My mother felt that since my father had been an important person in the village, one of the first people to convert to Christianity, I had to maintain my father's status since I was the firstborn," Ndanyi said.[12] At the funerals, it was important that Ndanyi show up dressed in a suit and tie. He was also expected to make the largest contribution for the funeral expenses, and since the amounts of the contributions were read out loud, he dared not embarrass his mother with a tightfisted gift. The demands on the "progressive" man seemed endless indeed.

Apparently, there were plenty of ways to let others down. Ndanyi, for example, disappointed his mother by making a polygamous marriage. To a Christian like his mother, polygamy was unbecoming behavior, especially for a "proper" man like Ndanyi. Perhaps she would have been a little more forgiving had his new wife, Mwanika, been a Maragoli. But Mwanika was an Akamba from Machakos, in eastern Kenya, and thus in his mother's eyes was a total "foreigner"—a foreigner from a tribe that she believed produced "witches" who could enchant "your son so that your son refused to come home." Akamba women—for that matter, all women from eastern and coastal Kenya—were believed to greedily "get attached to your son, just like a tick on your body that sucks away your blood."[13] Such stereotypes were common among the Maragoli; when growing up I repeatedly heard people utter these stereotypes of other tribes with unrepentant zeal, as though the Maragoli people had no faults of their own.

I came to know Mwanika well during my years of fieldwork, and I liked her very much. She was a cheerful, strong, and generous woman whom I had seen help her mother-in-law out around the homestead—despite the unfortunate start with which their relations had begun. Mwanika fetched water from the river for Ajema, cleaned her house for her, and plastered her floor with fresh cow dung every two weeks. So as much as I did not want to interfere in this rather-delicate family feud, I felt a strong obligation to defend Mwanika. I told Ajema that I thought that her daughter-in-law was a good person and went on to list what I saw as Mwanika's strong points. I even risked sounding pedantic by reminding her that there are good and bad people in every community and that I found her stereotyping of the Akamba women troubling. Ajema was adamant. She insisted that Mwanika's good behavior was a result of the "influence the Maragoli people had on her." "See," she tapped my wrist and informed me, "she is now a Maragoli, she speaks our language, so she is a good person. But she was not like that when she first married Ndanyi."[14] I remained silent. I asked no more questions about the foreign women from eastern Kenya.

Of course, Ajema was not the only widow with high expectations for her progressive son. Elisi Vyoya, another widow, had also expected a great deal from her son, Mariko Mutiva, who worked as a clerk at Kenya High School in Nairobi, a school that catered largely to European and Asian students. Mutiva visited Maragoli once a year for one week only, usually during Christmas. He did not make nearly as much money as Avugwi or Ndanyi. But like Avugwi, he bought clothes and food for his mother and his seven siblings, as well as his own wife and children; he also paid fees for the advanced schooling of his two brothers. Mutiva told me that his mother often complained about his short stays, but as he put it, "I could not stay longer without the money to maintain my image as a progressive man."[15] Indeed, many of the men I spoke with mentioned their mothers' unreasonably high expectations of them. "My mother thought I was a 'big' man and asked for money, but I did not always have the money to give her," remembered James Kazira, another widow's son.[16]

Still, widows whose sons worked far away from home in Nairobi or Mombasa had fewer opportunities to be frustrated with their sons than widows with educated homebound sons, whose improper behavior might be a source of daily disappointment for their mothers. The sons who remained in Maragoli often became teachers and were thereby among the most respected members of the community—more so than even the clerks from the city. They were, after all, allegedly gifted people who had taken up the task of introducing children to the knowledge they needed to succeed in the European economy.[17] But this respect came at a demanding price: they were expected to serve as sterling examples to younger children, to become superlative models of progressive behavior.

James Muliru's case is an eloquent illustration of the pressures placed on sons who stayed in the village and worked locally. After receiving his diploma from Kaimosi Intermediate School, Muliru had become a teacher at one of the elementary schools in 1955. In general, Muliru was a dedicated teacher, and many of his students advanced to intermediate schools in the area. Muliru, like Mutiva, Ndanyi, and Avugwi, had built square mud houses with corrugated iron roofs—one for himself and another for his mother. She was, of course, delighted by this. In addition, he managed to save enough money (it took him seven years) to buy a bicycle, a possession even more prestigious than a house. As far as material goods were concerned, Muliru was right where he should be.

But Muliru was far from ideal in other ways. He was polygamous—and he had not just two but three wives. Worse still, he slept with several young women in the village and produced several out-of-wedlock children. Muliru also had a great liking for *changaa,* a potent and dangerous local millet brew.[18] Perhaps this habit would not have been so bad had Muliru drunk at home and not exposed his drunken state to the rest of the village. But often, unable to walk home in his drunken stupor, Muliru would fall asleep on the road or in the bush. As his younger brother recalled: "Our mother was sad because Muliru did bad things in the open. Some people began to laugh at my mother, saying things like she thought she was educating a *msungu* [white man]. But they would say, 'Look at his behavior, a *msungu* doesn't do this.'"[19]

Such embarrassment was not confined to Muliru's mother. Katarina Libese, one of the widows we met in chapter 7, who had fiercely fought to claim her land rights, also suffered considerable shame as a result of her son's behavior. As we have seen, Libese had endured a great deal in the fight with her brother-in-law for rights to use her land, grow crops, and sell them—all to make enough money to send her son, Matayo Keya, to school. Yet of all the men and their families I talked with, Keya seemed to reflect least the attributes of "progress" envisioned by widows with educated sons. Though a teacher at a primary school, like Muliru, Keya never built himself a square house; instead, like many other people in the village, he continued to live in a round, grass-thatched house with cow dung floors. Furthermore, Keya spent most of his money on *changaa.* In fact, he drank so hopelessly and so frequently that he was often unable to walk home and ended up sleeping outdoors by the roadside. He never had any money left to buy clothes, so he always walked around in the same torn shirt and pair of trousers, and those unlucky enough to sit in the same room with him were inevitably treated to the potent and intoxicating aroma of stale alcohol and sweat.[20] To make matters worse, he even sold the clothing his humiliated mother had bought him to buy *changaa.* Keya died in 1980, most likely of liver failure.[21] I spoke with his younger brother, Mariko, and he sadly described Keya as a "skinny young man with yellow eyes"[22] whose behavior had weighed heavily on their mother. Like Muliru's mother, she felt humiliated as members of her community repeatedly witnessed her son's drunkenness. Of course, only mothers with sons who lived in Maragoli were likely to undergo this kind of shame; those whose sons worked in faraway places did not have to face such humiliation on a daily basis—though their sons too may have been drinking alcohol excessively (this manner of socializing was even more common in the towns and cities of East Africa).[23] Most likely, the city sons also kept multiple sexual partners.[24]

Since Keya spent most of his money on alcohol, he was unable to buy his mother anything. As Katarina Libese watched wives and other widows like her begin to enjoy the new consumer goods that their husbands and sons bought for them, she felt understandably wretched. She had undoubtedly hoped that her son, whom she had struggled hard to educate, would take over the responsibilities of his father and would also buy her the soap, clothes, butter, and other luxury items that women with dutiful sons or husbands now enjoyed. According to Janet Iravoga, Keya's sister, "My mother simply watched as women with husbands ate bread and Blue Band and rice and wore nice clothes that their husbands bought them. She also wished that she had someone to bring her these things, but Keya drank all his money."[25]

The lamentations sung by Libese reveal her misery at having no one to provide for her:

Umusungu wange goi
Umuyanze wange goi
Umusungu wange goi
Umuyanze wange goi
Nangorendi goi?
Ngumbi kukivi goi
Vyaha nanguli isukari, amajani, isabuni?

My white man
My loved one
What will I do?
I am in trouble
Who will buy me sugar, tea leaves, and soap?[26]

Keya's mother referred to her deceased husband as "white man" because she viewed him as her provider, who, if he had not died, would have been able to buy her these commodities. In other words, her husband was analogous to a white man because they were both considered the source of the new goods—albeit in different ways. Even more significant is the fact that the lamentation hints figuratively at her son's inability to replace his father in the role of a providing "white man." Widows, afraid of being ridiculed by members of their communities, became acutely sensitive to the everyday

actions of the sons who remained in the village. "People talked and sometimes liked to see bad things happen to you," one informant told me.[27]

⋅◌◌◌⋅

How, then, might we explain the misapprehensions between men like Avugwi,
Ndanyi, Mutiva, and Muliru and their mothers? Why did sons insist on ap-
pearing like "men of means" when, in reality, they were barely making ends
meet? Why was it hard for mothers to comprehend their sons' attempts to
please them? These misunderstandings can be at least partly attributed to a
mix-up between their mothers' and colonial officials' interpretation of progressive education. Teaching and clerkship were the two opportunities open
to educated African men at the time. Since clerical jobs were usually located
in the emerging cities of East Africa—in Nairobi, Kampala, Mombasa, and
Dar es Salaam—the young men who became clerks had to migrate to these
cities, where they lived in decidedly modest conditions that were nowhere
near those of the modern "progressive" man imagined by their mothers.[28]

Furthermore, the colonial officials were deeply immersed in their 1920s
rhetoric—that is, the rhetoric that espoused the return of educated Africans
to their villages to do manual work—and they refused to pay these men enough
money to live a decent life in the city. Indeed, the officials believed that the
workers did not need much money because they assumed that their families in the rural areas were self-sufficient.[29] Little did they realize that the
workers' rural families expected support from them—more than support, in
fact: they were expected to substantiate their elevated position and bring
honor upon their families by freely bestowing money and gifts. But apparently these familial duties were beyond the grasp of colonial officials; in
reality, they tended to resent educated Africans like Avugwi, Mutiva, and
Ndanyi who could read, write, and speak English, and as we have seen, they
often looked down upon them, deriding them as "semi-illiterate" men who
refused to "keep their place" or perform "any honest toil in their lives."[30]
So the Africans never got the respect they had earned or the high wages they
deserved. To make matters worse, the low salaries made it hard for sons to
meet their mothers' expectations, and this in turn generated considerable
tension between them and their mothers—so much so that some of the sons
apparently took refuge in drink.

Unfortunately, many of the sons found it difficult to tell their mothers
the truth of their situation, because the gender codes in Maragoli required
that they continually prove their strength and superiority by providing for
women. In many cases, sons adopted a survival strategy that allowed only

infrequent visits home and only for short periods. By making their visits brief they could minimize expenses and still keep up the pretense of being well-off, "progressive" men; but the short visits saddened their widowed mothers, increasing their *kehenda mwoyo*, their "worries of the heart." In many ways, then, the generational conflicts here did not necessarily arise, as is often the case, because younger and older generations had different beliefs and expectations.[31] Clearly, many of the young men we have encountered agreed with their widowed mothers' expectations and sought to become "proper" men and to be seen as men of "civilization" and of "means." They simply lacked the resources to achieve these goals. And the degrading colonial policies played a major role in creating the problem. So unfortunately, the "proper" and "progressive" son hoped for by the widows, the man who could meet all their social and economic needs, who could provide for and protect a wife and children, marry just once, avoid *changaa*, and give generously at funerals—such a man was hard to come by. Somehow widows had to learn how to live with their sons in spite of their weaknesses, in spite of the humiliations their sons endured and sometimes forced them to endure.

᪥

CHAPTER TEN

Cash, Cows, and Bridewealth

In 1942, a widow by the name of Jane Egendi married her daughter, Mary Musimbi, to a Maragoli man serving in World War II who was a member of the King's African Rifle (KAR).[1] Egendi and her team of bridewealth negotiators, which included one of her sons, two brothers-in-law, and three male elders, asked for four cows and two hundred shillings. According to Egendi, this was a high price: a son of hers who had married three years before had paid half of that. But she was convinced that her son-in-law agreed to pay the high amount because he had no time for drawn-out negotiations; as she put it, "he had the money and was expected to return to the KAR the following week."

When the first installment of one cow and one hundred shillings arrived a month later, Egendi gave the cow to her son and kept the money—"I gave him the cow because it was physically there, and he could see it, but I kept the cash for myself." Egendi continued to boast of her newly married daughter, how "good" she was, how she had studied at the Girls Boarding School (GBS), and how well she herself would be taken care of as a widow.[2] Likewise, she praised her son-in-law for being a "real" man, for understanding her needs as a widow, and for paying her a "good amount" of bridewealth.[3]

Grace Isha, who also married a KAR man in 1942, spoke proudly of the high bridewealth her widowed mother had received for her marriage: 180 shillings and four cows. No one, according to Isha, had ever received that much before. Her own mother, who had married in the 1920s, received one cow and a hoe, and Isha's older sister, who had married a clerk in 1937, had gotten only twenty-five shillings and one cow. So Isha was proud of her extraordinary bridewealth; she talked endlessly about how she was "a real good daughter" and how her mother was proud of her. "It was very important to her. I had gone to school, you know, to the GBS. Hey! In those days only *wastaarabu*[4] [modern girls] like me went to the GBS. And we were good girls, good girls that everybody wanted to marry—not like the girls of nowadays."[5]

Melissa Otiende, whose mother was widowed in the late 1930s, echoed Isha's pride. Noting that the competition for wives was quite stiff because of the introduction of KAR money, she told me how she herself had married a KAR man and how her husband had paid dowry "right away, right away," and bought her "KAR *shamba* [land]" a few kilometers down the river. He had paid her mother two hundred shillings, which her mother set quietly aside for herself: "She kept it, kept it all, and no one—not even my brother— knew that she had received all that money."[6] No doubt many mattresses were made lumpy by the cash covertly withheld from daughters.

Bridewealth became a favorite topic of conversation in the early 1940s largely because of the events triggered by World War II. In western Kenya, recruitment for the war had brought about the largest emigration of men from the villages in the history of the area. According to the North Kavirondo annual report, a total of about 6,000 men were recruited for the military, another 7,500 for civil industry, and 3,400 for voluntary civil labor on contracts in western Kenya. A majority of these men came from the southern parts of the district, from Maragoli and Bunyore.[7] They represented a huge increase in the number of wage-earning men and also a large increase in the amount of wages earned, receiving far more than clerks and far more than the men who had worked in the Kakamega mines in the 1930s.[8] Now, better off than they had ever been and eager to marry before they had to return to their military duties, the recruits felt little need to bargain, so bridewealth went up accordingly. It was a sellers' market, so to speak, and the future wives knew it.

Widows in particular benefited from the increased bridewealth because, for the first time, more of the marriage price was paid in cash and less in livestock. This was a significant—and liberating—change from the past, when most bridewealth had been paid in the form of goats, cattle, and sheep. For one thing, cash was less gendered and more democratic, since livestock was usually considered male property and therefore a widow's brothers-in-law or sons tended to have exclusive rights to it. Moreover, cash was easier to care for than a cow, and it had the advantage of being compact and concealable. In the early 1940s, then, as some of their "progressive" sons let them down by failing to provide for them as they would like, widows increasingly turned to their daughters' lucrative marriages to make up for the shortfall.

The women who commanded the highest bridewealth were often those who had received rudimentary education in domestic science at the GBS in Kaimosi.[9] The GBS had begun in 1921 as a school for orphans.[10] Managed under the auspices of the Friends African Mission, its first location was in

Vihiga, Maragoli. However, in 1923 the school was moved to Kaimosi, making it one of the largest components of the missionary center. Then in 1930, the missionaries opened the GBS to nonorphans in order to "universalize" domestic education. The school trained girls from grades six to eight.

Most parents were, however, opposed to sending their daughters to the newly established school, arguing that education ruined the girls' chances of marrying. My conversations with older men and women revealed that parents believed that higher education for daughters was useless because daughters, unlike sons, could never become teachers or clerks. Henry Kilivia, a retired clerk, recalled the doubtful attitude: "People used to say, 'So-and-so is sending their girls to school; how and where will they become clerks?'" Other parents argued that girls with too much education would find it hard to marry because men felt that such women were too "independent," that education "spoiled the brain of women," and that it made them "learn how to think and argue" so that they became "less docile and submissive."[11]

Ironically, most of women's education in western Kenya, as in other parts of Africa, was geared toward domesticity and, especially, toward ensuring that girls became competent mothers and submissive wives.[12] The core curriculum at the GBS was specifically intended to help girls fine-tune these skills. Knitting, hygiene, cooking, and child care were the main subjects, and whatever basic reading, writing, and arithmetic the girls learned was simply meant to facilitate their education in domesticity. One would think that most parents would have been pleased to provide their daughters with this kind of education, but the classrooms at the elementary schools, let alone the GBS, contained very few girls in the 1930s.

In 1933, for instance, there were in Maragoli six subelementary schools for standards one and two, and three elementary schools for grades three through five, yet only sixty girls were enrolled in the elementary schools.[13] So low, in fact, was the enrollment that the principal of the GBS complained that there were not enough qualified students to admit to the school. "It is difficult," she grumbled, "to get Africans interested in education for its own sake, rather than for some coveted reward," and she observed that parents did not see any financial return in educating girls, let alone the advantage of training them as "Christian homemakers who know how to raise healthy, happy children."[14]

Given this apparent hostility toward the education of girls in the 1930s, it was mostly orphans or the girls whose parents were Christians who attended the school. Many of the GBS alumni with whom I spoke bragged that Christianity enabled their parents to spearhead the movement toward *ustaarabu* (modern civilization). "I came from a *good* family, a family of

maendeleo [progress], and that is why I did well," said Grace Isha.[15] Then
again, Melissa Otiende noted that her mother had sent her to the GBS because she wanted the school to "help raise her," to relieve her mother of
the responsibility of feeding her. Her father had worked for the missionaries
and they had paid her fees; when he died, she was considered an orphan
and the missionaries continued to support her.[16] Mary Musimbi was also
considered an orphan, and so the missionaries paid her school fees as well.[17]
But Rose Mwenesi, another GBS alumna, added an interesting reason that
some girls ended up at the GBS in the 1930s. She told me that her uncle sent
his daughter to the GBS because she was rude: "she was a bad girl and she
had defeated her parents." In other words, her cousin was sent "to the GBS
to be taught a lesson."[18] We can conclude, then, that the GBS was viewed as
a place for marginalized girls—for the "disobedient" or orphaned, including
the daughters of widows, whose quasi-orphaned status qualified them for
the new school. This latter group constituted a fairly large percentage of the
girls who attended the GBS.

With time, more and more educated men began to consider these women
desirable, chiefly because the men believed GBS graduates would keep modern households and enhance their sense of respectability. As we have seen,
the men were willing to pay high cash bridewealth for them. According to
Otiende, "You could not marry a poor man if you had been educated. . . . If
you were a good girl and were educated," she reiterated, "you always married a man who tried to pay a high bridewealth. You see, every girl who went
to the GBS was seen as a *mstaarabu*, and such a girl often married a modern
man with money."[19]

Men understood this, too. "In those days," Henry Kilivia, who married
in the 1940s, told me, "you paid a lot of money because you had to act like
a man. You had to show that you could take care of a wife, and this responsibility began with paying a good bridewealth." He insisted that as long as
a man knew he was getting a "good," well-mannered, educated wife, he did
not hesitate to pay. "Alternatively," he noted, "you could marry a primitive girl, and that didn't cost that much. But," he shook his head disapprov-
ingly, "that was not good."[20]

Despite the apparent benefits of the rise in bridewealth payments, there
were inevitable conflicts.[21] While some were eager to take advantage of this
influx to marry off their daughters, others were concerned with how to prevent the influx of money from inflating bridewealth and thereby preventing
poorer men from marrying. Not all young men had joined the military or
found work in the new industries, and these men were of course unable
to compete with the wealthy KAR men. To them the competition was not

fair, and some demonstrated their objections by writing forlorn letters to colonial officials complaining of the prohibitive cost of brides and asking them to intervene on their behalf or at least begin to regulate the payment of bridewealth.[22]

Charles Oyuki, for instance, wrote to the PC of Nyanza Province in August 1942 insisting that the PC do something to help reduce the amount of bridewealth being paid. He complained that after paying four cows and two hundred shillings for his wife, he had nothing left with which to feed her; he also bemoaned his wife's nagging: "Wapi chai? Wapi nguo? Wapi sabuni?" (Where is tea? Where are clothes? Where is soap?). There was no way he could compete with the beneficence of the cash-rich military men, and so, in a novel and rather self-serving interpretation of the government's inaction, he concluded that he would simply stop trying; he would just pay the high bridewealth and forget about trying to modernize his family. Thus, his rhetorical outburst: "Do you want us to go naked like in the old days, not to send our children to school? If so, tell us, and we will abandon all modern things. We will go back to the old ways."[23]

Even more caustic, more scathing, was Shem Musira's letter to the LNC. Musira accused the members of the LNC of being "self-interested" and "letting the people suffer while they benefited from the war." He demanded that the LNC use the power "the government had given them to help him": "Was not the LNC supposed to help us wanainchi [citizens]?" he asked bluntly. Musira's primary complaint was that the father of the woman he had arranged to marry had married her to someone who was willing to pay more money. What most upset him was the cash aspect of bridewealth. He stated that it was mostly the KAR men who could afford to pay and that he and other men who stayed behind were simply masikini tu, masikini tu (just paupers, real paupers). He asked that the LNC somehow manage to fix the amount of bridewealth asked for and paid and also ensure that the chiefs enforce the limits by fining anyone who attempted to pay more.[24]

Peter Jumba called for similar measures to be taken by the LNC, and he wrote to the council saying that he was appalled that the parents of his fiancée were asking three cows and 190 shillings, almost double the amount his brother had paid for his wife three years earlier. He wondered how he could pay that much for mwanamke mmoja, mwanamke mmoja, tu (just one wife, just one wife only), and he decried his mkono tupu (broke) status. Jumba insisted that unlike the KAR men, he did not have money to throw around. Like Oyuki, he wondered whether the LNC was aware that he needed the money to meet the requirements of mambo ya kisasa (the modern world) such as school and medical fees. "How can we deal with the modern world if we have to continue to pay such high bridewealth?" he asked.[25] The demands for high bridewealth had become for him an obstacle to an enlightened future; it had become a "throwback," a sign of "backwardness," because it prevented him—and those like him—from joining the march into modernity.

Basically, the officials did not know how to control bridewealth.[26] They had tried to eliminate it altogether in the 1930s but had failed; in fact, bridewealth was a custom that officials considered to be "one of the greatest obstacles in the way of the advancement of the native peoples."[27] To officials it more or less represented a "sale or purchase with the result that a father is apt to 'sell' his daughter to the highest bidder rather than marry her to a suitable husband," and it was therefore "repugnant to morality," like female circumcision or forced marriage.[28] Officials had at one time toyed with the idea of abolishing bridewealth altogether through legislation, but they had quickly realized that they could not succeed; the payment of bridewealth was deeply rooted in African culture. Their inability to control marriage payments forced them to find ways to rationalize its significance—and so bridewealth, they determined, was important because it helped prevent women from becoming promiscuous. Or, as one official piously intoned, "bridewealth among pagan polygamists is a fundamental condition of regularized union, it is a sign of respectability and to some extent a guarantee of fidelity."[29] Given its significance, the officials concluded that the custom had to be "tolerated for the time being." They discovered, in fact, that any attempt at legislation would simply "write bride price firmly into the law crystallizing the custom and making it difficult, if not impossible, for it to die out."[30] The officials hoped that the "repugnant" custom would become "obsolete with the progress of education and civilization."[31]

To rationalize their nonaction, officials turned to research, primarily by anthropologists, and tried to uncover some explanation that might reduce some of their discomfort with marriage payments. Ironically, in the 1930s the officials concluded that bridewealth payments would eventually weaken family ties—ties that they were determined to safeguard so that Africans might avoid any potential corruption that "civilization" might bring with it.[32] Of course, they found themselves at an impasse: bridewealth payments were morally repugnant to them, but eliminating them might make Africans vulnerable to the corrupting influences of "civilization." They concluded, pragmatically, that a little moral repugnance would have to be tolerated for the sake of civilization. And if they still found the inconsistency too much to bear, they could always recast the problem. Bridewealth, they rationalized, was actually based on intergroup or interfamily exchange, the giving of property by one group or family in exchange for a woman from another group or family.[33] Compensation received in the form of livestock, officials claimed, could be useful only if the whole family was put to work caring for it; in addition, livestock provided the means whereby the group or family that had given up a girl to marriage would have the resources to pay bridewealth when one of their sons wanted to marry. In other words, the payment of bridewealth was therefore not simply a matter between individuals; it was really a process of exchange that involved the whole family, even the whole village, and therefore did not necessarily have to be seen as the selling of a daughter.[34]

Still, for officials, the use of cash for bridewealth was an annoying development. It tainted the meaning of the exchange, and it did not quite fit into their neat rationalization. As one PC groused, "If the bride price is actually paid in cash, the beneficial influences of the system and the traditional religious significance of the marriage, which are the only grounds on which the custom is defensible, disappear, and the marriage becomes a commercial transaction."[35] That is, if a father takes the cash and uses it as he likes, the PC argued, he is in essence simply selling his daughters. Clearly, this was not acceptable, so in one way or another the use of cash had to be stopped, legitimized, or explained away. Colonial officials usually ended up choosing the last. As one PC prudently surmised, once Africans began using cash, the bridewealth system lost its utility; "the system dies; it is no longer useful"—no longer useful, apparently, because it does not serve the needs of the whole family or village.[36] Evidently, when it ceased to serve everyone's needs, the PC believed, bridewealth would disappear; an "evolution" would have occurred. (The logic was impeccable: tolerance of bridewealth was justifiable because it was not really an exchange between individuals; when the introduction of cash made it an exchange between individuals, it would somehow lose its usefulness and simply vanish. That is, either it was not what it seemed or, if it was, it would not last.)

This process of evolution was, however, painfully slow—it could take years, even decades. Something else had to be done in the meantime. The payment of bridewealth had to be regulated. Throughout the mid-1930s, the PC of Nyanza circulated memos to DCs and members of the LNCs in which he noted the urgent need to control the amount of bridewealth. To justify his concern, he detailed the ways in which high bridewealth was responsible for overstocking and for land degradation, he expressed his worry that the "natives waste a lot of time in lawsuits over it," and he accused the Africans of being "lazy" as well as "inherently litigious."[37]

Even more worrisome, indeed abhorrent, to the PC was the general belief in colonial circles that the increase in bridewealth was leading to prostitution. Because young men could not afford to marry, argued the PC, women who would otherwise have become their wives turned to prostitution to support themselves. And just as appalling to the PC was the fact that the demand for high bridewealth led to an increase in polygamy among older men. Since older men had more livestock than young men, they could afford to marry more than one wife, further stiffening the competition for wives among young men. "It is true that rich old men collect wives and like to collect young ones," the Nyanza PC wrote in a confidential dispatch to all PCs and DCs. Unfortunately, limiting the amount of bridewealth would not help young men. As the PC carefully pointed out, "If a rich old man can now afford ten wives at ten heads of cattle per wife he could afford (and would collect) thirty three if the price were reduced to three heads and the position of young men would be worse rather than better."[38] Clearly, this was not an easy problem to solve.

They tried another solution, one more locally engineered. Instead of setting an amount of bridewealth to apply to a whole district, the PC decided that the chief of each location would determine a suitable amount of bridewealth for his area and then record the amount paid by each person. Should the amount exceed the limit, the chief and his retinue of young African clerks were to go to the individual's house and withdraw the excess bridewealth. Of course, this plan failed. The confiscated cattle were often stealthily returned to the bride's home at night, and after the cattle had been moved back and forth several times, the clerks gave up the pursuit, arguing that the process was not efficient.[39]

And in fact it was not. Imagine the scene: two young clerks, nicely dressed in shirts and trousers, sweating beneath the angry sun and towing two indifferent cows behind them. As they sluggishly walk the cows back to the groom's house, perhaps six, seven, or eight miles away, they console each other, knowing full well that at the end of this trek, the father of the groom will most likely receive them with mixed feelings. On the one hand, he will be happy that justice is being done and the greedy parents of his daughter-in-law are finally getting what they deserve; on the other hand, he will probably feel a sense of obligation to pay what he promised.[40] So in the evening, after sunset, he just might recruit a couple of young boys to return the cows—though they have to do this carefully so they are not spotted and reported to the local chief, who might prematurely end their trip. Exhausted and hungry, the boys arrive with the cows in the middle of the night, and no doubt the parents of his daughter-in-law are happy to receive them. They offer the boys water, *ugali*, and vegetables, and after they eat, the boys are given sisal mats to sleep on. Awakened by a crowing rooster, they rub their eyes open, bid farewell to their hosts, and start walking back home.[41] With luck, they will not have to do it again.

By the end of the 1930s, officials had given up any hope that legislation could control the amount of bridewealth—let alone stop its payment altogether. Again, they left the custom to complete its own "evolution."

⦿

When, in the early and mid-1940s, officials began to receive letters from people like Oyuki, Musira, and Jumba insisting that the amounts of bridewealth be limited, they were utterly delighted. Imagining that the concerns expressed in the letters represented those of the general public, they saw the letters as a glimmer of hope and were determined to believe that "evolution" was taking its course. Nevertheless, they still thought they might prod it along. In fact, the PC was so delighted with Oyuki's letter that he responded immediately, congratulating him for "having given the subject of brideprice a lot of thought." He called it a "vexed" habit that could not be regulated by government and noted that the high bride-prices would continue "until such time as the people themselves get together and with one voice say that they will no longer have them, and all agree to do away with bride price or reduce it to a reasonable figure.... When the majority of people in any area can see the difficulty as you have done, then surely they will all gather together and say, 'Why do we go on with this custom, which is like a stone round our necks? We must stop it.' Then will be the time to say to the government, we want a law to help us carry out what is our majority opinion, and the government will be able to help, to see that one or two bad men do not offend against the opinion of the majority."[42]

The PC sent a copy of Oyuki's letter to all the DCs and LNCs in Nyanza Province and insisted that it be read at LNC meetings so that the members could "get people to start thinking how true Oyuki's words were."[43] He wrote to all the DCs in Nyanza Province asking them to gauge the "public opinion" in their various districts. Most of the findings were, however, disappointing to the overly optimistic PC. The LNCs indicated that while many people publicly opposed the increase in bridewealth, they condoned it when they were the ones who had marriageable daughters. As a matter of fact, the LNC's reports stated that there had been an increase in private bargaining and "conditional" bridewealth, whereby those involved hoped to renegotiate for a higher price at some point in the future.[44]

In many ways, then, the PC's understanding of "public opinion" was illusory. Parents of brides continued to demand high bridewealth for their daughters, and those who could afford to pay, men like those in the military, happily paid lest they miss out on wives. Feeling defeated, the LNC members decided that the only possible solution was to ask the chiefs to record the amount paid by each bridegroom. They hoped that such a record would at least help them keep track of the increases and might make people more self-conscious when demanding or paying enormous amounts. But that was, as it turned out, simply wishful thinking.

CHAPTER ELEVEN

Domestic Education at the Girls Boarding School

In the 1940s, widows and other parents in Maragoli actively sought to educate their daughters, primarily because they had seen girls educated in the 1930s garner higher bridewealth for their mothers. They turned to the GBS. Ironically, as more and more parents began to send their daughters to the school for an advanced education in domesticity, the school not only expanded but also became more exclusive. Over the previous decade, the GBS had acquired immense cachet as the colonial government, in its effort to bolster manual education among Africans, began to subsidize its upkeep.[1] The government funds made it possible for the missionaries to erect new buildings: an expanded and improved kitchen with more efficient stoves was constructed in 1938, and a new brick dormitory and dining hall were built in 1942. In that same year, two new missionary teachers joined the school. By the mid-1940s the GBS was admitting between sixty and sixty-four girls each year, training them through standard (grade) eight, the highest level of education that girls could attain in Kenya at the time. Though the school drew students from all over western Kenya, most of them came from Maragoli.[2]

Among other things, the new facilities and new teachers instantly boosted the reputation of the GBS and made admission to the school extremely competitive. "It is our unhappy job to refuse hundreds of girls the opportunity of coming here to school, and there are many tears shed," wrote the principal of the GBS about the admission process. "I will never forget the six hours spent conversationing [sic] students to select from the hundreds of applicants. The intense eagerness was evident by the quivering nerves, shaking knees, working fingers, tense facial and throat muscles, and often tear-filled eyes as the student endured the agony of suspense and questioning."[3] Only those with a zealous desire to marry well would put themselves through an experience so critically demanding. And the girls who survived the process were not afraid to say so, nor were they afraid to congratulate themselves.

For instance, Mary Jendeka, a GBS alumna, displayed no timidity in boasting of her admission to the GBS, saying that it was not a place "for ordinary girls." She happily cataloged the ways in which the GBS girls were exceptional: "We were *wastaarabu*, really good girls, we respected our teachers and parents, and we married civilized husbands."[4] Stella Mbecha, another proud alumna, gloated, "I was one of the pioneers in civilization. You see, I went to the GBS. And that is where *ustaarabu* [modernity] started. No one, no one in North Maragoli had a house full of *ustaarabu* like mine." She also informed me that people used to come to her house to examine the doilies she had made for her chairs and tables, and other visitors, she affirmed, came exclusively to "admire my vegetable garden," which was sensibly planted with "cabbages and carrots in neat, straight rows."[5]

Mbecha was unique. While most of the GBS girls were undoubtedly proud of their achievements, they were not as overbearing as Mbecha. She was intense, imperious, and proud. Though in her late sixties, she was in constant motion, waving her hands, stamping her feet in the dirt, jumping up to offer passionate opinions—or to make another cup of *chai*. Recently widowed, she did not dwell on her loss but instead spent hours talking about her contribution to the women's movement in western Kenya. One of her recent pet projects was a widows' support group—a group of eight widows who pooled small sums of money to give to one of the members every other month to buy whatever she wanted. The members reasoned that the lump sum would allow them to invest in long-term ventures such as school fees for their children or grandchildren.

Mbecha's energy was also evident in the exuberant manner in which she welcomed people to her house. Neighbors often stopped by to borrow salt, sugar, or matchsticks or just to chat or gossip. Her house had become a major clearinghouse for local news, and Mbecha herself was an infamous gossip. So wide was her reputation that local secondary school students who had read Ezekiel Mphalele's *Down Second Avenue* in preparation for their exams nicknamed her Malebona, after the novel's notorious gossip. I was never quite sure whether Mbecha was genuinely interested in helping others or simply welcomed people to her house to flaunt her wealth.

And she was quite well-to-do by local standards. Mbecha and her husband had taken advantage of the agricultural loans offered by the government in the 1970s and had used the money to plant coffee and tea, which earned them a significant profit. They then proceeded to invest the money in real estate in the neighboring town of Kakamega; it was a wise investment that enabled her to collect rent money from her real estate when, in the mid-1990s, cash crops were no longer lucrative. On occasion Mbecha's enthusiasm could be annoying, but it was also refreshing in a village disheartened by misfortune, a village in which the poverty of many people was painfully visible and opportunity glaringly absent. Mbecha's cheerful spirit often inspired me to fill my diary with her stories and exploits, and I unintentionally found myself added to the list of people who frequented her clean brick house. She made me laugh. And somehow she made me less conscious of my own well-to-do status (even if, later at home, I subjected myself to a much-needed soul-searching). I could always count on a cup of tea, a comfortable chair—neatly covered with doilies—and a good gossip with her other regulars as we admired the neatly planted flowerbeds of bougainvillea and white daisies. How much closer could one get to *ustaarabu*? To civilization? To practical Christianity?

Even as the GBS alumnae like Mbecha and Jendeka gloried in their success, they also acknowledged the hardships they had endured while attending the institution. They often mentioned the school's high fees as one of the major difficulties they encountered—in the 1940s the fees were about thirty shillings per term. Wage earners in Kenya, most of them teachers and clerks, earned about sixty shillings per month—except, of course, for military men.[6] As we have seen, widowed mothers in particular found it difficult to come up with so much cash. In fact, Mbecha told me that her mother usually became despondent at the beginning of each school term because she lacked the money for her fees.[7] Keran Vusha noted that her mother sold everything she owned to pay the fees: "She sold all her maize and chickens to send me to school."[8]

Such sacrifice was common, yet most widows still found it necessary to turn to the male members of their families for help, since it was mainly men who worked jobs for cash wages. Once again, this required that the women rely upon their status as grieving widows.[9] For instance, Mary Jendeka related to me the gendered rhetoric—*kehenda mwoyo*—her mother had felt the need to use in order to get the school fees from Jendeka's uncle. "My mother begged and begged my uncle for the money," she noted. "She put her hands on her head [an indication of mourning] and told him all about her *kehenda mwoyo*, about how as a widow she felt alone, how she was poor and needed to be pitied and sympathized with. My uncle listened to her, and he assisted her even though he did not have much money. My mother's pleadings were so powerful that he could not ignore her. He was obliged to take care of her as a 'real' adult man should."[10]

Her uncle was long dead, so I did not have the opportunity to ask him why he had helped Jendeka's mother. However, I did pose the same question to Matayo Jumba, a retired clerk who was in his late sixties and who had known Jendeka's uncle. Jumba told me that he had to help his sister-in-law because "as a real man he could not neglect his widowed sister-in-law." But of course, he was careful to add, Jendeka's uncle might have offered assistance because he knew that Jendeka would "marry well" and he would receive a share of her bridewealth.[11]

Stella Mbecha also recalled for me how her mother had invoked her *kehenda mwoyo* in order to get Mbecha's brother, who worked for a white farmer in the Rift Valley area, to help out with Mbecha's school fees. Her mother would visit him and vigorously "tell him all her problems, all her suffering, all her *kehenda mwoyo*," and, according to Mbecha, "he listened and gave her some money—even though the money was not enough to cover all the school fees." To make up the difference, her mother still had to part with a chicken or goat. Although it was always hard for her brother, who had a large family of his own, to come up with the money, he had "acted as a man and offered help. He never complained."[12]

Keran Vusha's mother was not so lucky. Her male relatives turned a deaf ear to her pleadings, offering elaborate excuses about their own need for money. However, these men did not get off easily. Vusha's mother ended up castigating them in public: "she told everybody, everybody, about her relatives' indifference to her problems. And people listened carefully, taking note of the men's bad behavior, their refusal to act like men and offer help." I asked Vusha why her mother felt the need to share her disappointments so doggedly and so publicly. There was no hesitance in her reply: "My mother wanted other people to know that her relatives had treated her badly as a widow. She wanted them to know because this would make her relatives look bad. People would say they are not 'men.'" Luckily, the white missionary principal of the GBS made it easier for her mother by allowing her to pay her school fees in installments; and Vusha was quick to praise the principal for having recognized that she was an "orphan" and having shown compassion toward her mother.[13]

Yet even if the obstacle of the fees could be cleverly surmounted, there still were other impediments to earning a standard eight diploma from the GBS. Daily routines at the school were exceedingly harsh and rigid. They could unnerve all but the most dedicated. Elizabeth Haviland, principal of the GBS between 1938 and 1946, described one of the easier days, a Saturday morning: "Every girl is very busy this half-cloudy Saturday morning. Some are carrying water or getting wood or preparing lunch of cornmeal gruel.

Others are giving the plates, cups, and spoons their weekly scouring. Others are washing windows. The floors have been cleaned already. The rest are cleaning the backyard, sweeping all paths and open spaces. When these things are done, the girls will look over their flowerbeds and woe to any weeds there.... Saturday," she continued, "is enjoyed in spite of the many tasks. It is rather different from other days with the mile trip to Gologoli Creek to wash their clothes, the general cleaning, and the free afternoon and evening." Schooldays were composed of a much harder routine.

> On Monday through Friday, the daily cleaning must be done quickly. A short rest at breakfast and then the morning in regular class work (reading, writing, arithmetic, language, etc). The afternoons are given to sewing, knitting, cooking, and gardening. Then they say grace, "For food and health and happy days we praise thy name, O Lord." Then the clatter of eating utensils begins.... Another bell rings. It is time for study or prayer. A golden ball beams. The day at Kaimosi is done. The girls do not need a lantern to show the way to their dormitories. They go with shouting, singing, and laughter as the full moon rides higher and higher.[14]

By offering these details Haviland obviously intended her readers in America to know that she was instilling a strict sense of discipline into her students and that the GBS girls, unlike their counterparts in the village, were "civilized." They were considered civilized largely because they worked with their hands, "sewing, knitting, cooking, and gardening"; and they were civilized because they "kept time" and knew when to pray and when to study. If they were not aware of what time it was, a ringing bell always reminded them, and they responded accordingly, moving on to their next activity. The developing awareness of time and routine, so the principal believed, provided structure and discipline and helped prepare the girls for their future role as Christian wives and mothers.[15] Moreover, the missionaries reasoned that the exclusivity of the boarding school, like that of Christian villages, protected the girls from becoming tainted with "heathen" practices.

Many of the girls, however, bemoaned the strict routines to which they adhered. They remembered with special displeasure the school's notorious cold baths at 5:30 in the morning; many of the graduates I spoke with still remember how the frigid water "pierced" their bodies like "syringes" and of how their fear of water was mocked by their seniors. Yet the girls did not dare forgo the baths, because their teachers inspected their bodies and clothes daily. Keran Vusha recalled it this way: "We normally woke up at 5:30 in the morning and took the bucket of water we had fetched the day before to

Domestic education at the Girls Boarding School, 1938 (Friends Collection and Archives, Earlham College)

the bathing area [usually a shed made of maize straw]. You stood there for a long time, afraid to pour water on your body. The older girls who had been at the school before you stared at you mockingly. They were used to the water. But you weren't. You removed your clothes one by one, slowly, slowly." She paused, looked to me for commiseration, and then continued, "Finally you flushed some water on your feet, then legs, then buttocks, then you waited again because you were afraid that the cold water would get in contact with your torso (you know that is where the cold was felt the most). Ehe! It was not easy. It took you almost thirty minutes to just figure out ways to bathe without feeling much pain or cold."[16]

While the mandatory cold baths were clearly a shock to new students, the compulsory use of a fork and knife was equally trying. "The principals would embarrass you," Mary Imbuhira told me. "You had never used a knife and fork at home, so this was your first time, yet the teachers expected you to master its use. You were embarrassed because the older girls stared at you while you were being reprimanded and that made you feel like you were primitive. You put the fork in the right hand instead of the left, and you were so embarrassed."[17]

And if embarrassment and discomfort were not enough to test their mettle, there was also homesickness. Routinely, the girls talked about how they missed their families, their siblings, their mothers' cooking, and how they longed for the relative freedom that their lives at home had afforded them. At home, they could at least sleep a little later than 5:30 in the morning. They could even wear dirty clothes (and many of them did so). Certainly they would not be expected to use a knife and fork or to bathe every day. In spite of their complaints, however, many of my informants were generally glad that they had a certificate from the school. And of course their widowed mothers were proud of them. They, like most parents, had anticipated that their daughters would turn out to be "good" girls and "marry well."

The girls who did not make it to the GBS often settled for an elementary education in domesticity. Though such an education was not as prestigious as a GBS certificate, many girls still enrolled in the elementary schools hoping at least to learn the basics. In 1945, C. H. Williams, the DC of North Kavirondo, commented on the increased number of girls in the classrooms of local elementary schools. He related that "real progress in girls' education is being made, particularly on the domestic side, where the standard of achievement is often very good." He commented further on how female education had become a popular subject of discussion at the LNC meetings: "There is no doubt that the education of girls arouses greater interest among the natives than any other subject. Girls are attending school because most educated men now prefer to marry educated women. Parents now see the benefits of educating daughters as these young women earn them high dowries."[18]

As a matter of fact, "homecraft" education became pervasive in the rural areas in the 1940s and 1950s. In Maragoli, as in other parts of Kenya, this type of education was increasingly promoted by Maendeleo ya Wanawake (Advancement of Women), a voluntary association largely initiated by wives of colonial officials. The purpose of Maendeleo ya Wanawake was to set up community development programs to train women in home science.[19] In these programs young women were taught how to bake and sew, to employ more efficient methods of child care, and to maintain cleanliness in the home.[20] In August 1950, for example, Mrs. Owour, the supervisor of Vihiga Homecraft Training Center, wrote, "This month has been devoted to washing, ironing and care of family clothes. . . . We are emphasizing better feeding, and simple budgeting of family income. We also try to show films on childbirth, weaving, crocheting, proper maintenance of homes, and efficient forms of farming."[21] Mrs. Owour also remarked contentedly on the high interest in learning "modern ways of living"—and she was justified: as many as fifty women were attending the classes, and many more women had to be turned away due to lack of space.

The education of girls had clearly become crucial in the "civilizing" process. In addition to the bridewealth these young women might command, there was a general attitude of pride in having a wife or daughter who had mastered domestic science. In the 1940s and 1950s, most young men educated at the missions had become increasingly preoccupied with marrying women educated in modern domesticity, women who could run their household in modern ways that incorporated both Christian and Western habits of living.[22] Such homes garnered for the men a good share of social respectability; they were highly visible markers of well-being, of being civilized, and of "having made it." "An educated man felt proud when his wife was a *mstaarabu*," James Kinziri, a World War II veteran who came of age in the 1940s, told me. "And when the Bora Afya [Ministry of Health] people came to his house he was not embarrassed, because his wife would have cleaned the house and put beautifully crocheted cloths on tables and chairs. If his wife did these things, it reflected well on the man. People respected him; they said that he was keeping a modern home."[23]

Another proud husband, Joshua Shego, an ex–agricultural officer, talked about the importance of not marrying an "ignorant" woman. "It was important," he told me, "that you married a woman who was educated and knew more about agriculture, because in those days we used to teach people modern ways of doing agriculture." He went on to remark that "if you married an educated woman, she knew agriculture and she made sure that she planted her maize in straight lines, instead of sowing it like the ignorant women. So when your land was nicely planted and weeded, you became proud because your wife was setting a good example."[24]

Missionary reports consistently emphasized the ways in which public respectability for men was at least partly contingent on how well their wives drew upon a formal education in domestic science and carried out the private responsibilities of the household. The public sphere was becoming closely intertwined with the private sphere.[25] For example, Dorothy Pitman, one of the teachers at the GBS, was happy "to watch some of the Normal Training School boys scrutinizing the girls' sewing and other school work, which has been on display at different times in the year." She went on to proudly claim that "many of the boys have already realized that they can have happier homes if they can secure wives who have learned some hygiene, childcare, sewing, cooking."[26]

Pitman was not alone in her enthusiasm for domestic education. Many of the GBS teachers were thrilled when one of their "girls" married one of the boys from the boys' school across the road—Kaimosi Boys School. News of such marriages almost always made it into the *Friends Missionary Advocate*. The missionaries wrote with genuine satisfaction of how "our girls" had learned the finer points of modern weddings and then gone on to establish "homes where Christ is known and revered," homes that were so "spic and span" that they were emulated by other women. In describing one such

A modern Christian wedding (Friends Collection and Archives, Earlham College)

wedding, Dorothy Pitman detailed the bride's white dress: "The dress was long and flowing with small pleats around the shoulder, and the bride's neck stood majestically through it." The bride, Debra Madegwa, was "a very capable girl who was good at house work"; she was marrying Shem Nolega, a graduate of the Boys Normal Training School, who now worked in the mission's Industrial Department. Madegwa's attendants also wore white dresses. As they walked gracefully down the church aisle, they were preceded by a flower girl, who "shyly and meticulously dropped flower petals along the way." Roberta Allen, one of the missionaries, dutifully played the wedding march on an organ belonging to a Mr. Wilbur Beeson and brought in especially for the occasion. After the ceremony, the guests were treated to a feast of rice, chicken, potatoes, and carrots, followed by bread and tea. Local girls, all neatly dressed in blue uniforms, served the food.[27]

Such modern couples were expected to bear children soon and to live happily ever after in clean square houses. And if ill fortune befell them—if, for example, one of their children died in infancy (a very common occurrence)—they were expected to be strong and pray to God for guidance. So when such a fate befell Rachel and Simeon Lidzanga, "a sweet and shy modern couple," they "did not sit about in their soiled clothes or fail to trim their hair and take interest in things about them for weeks" while mourning the death of their child. That would have been uncivilized. Instead, they adopted an enlightened Christian stoicism: "Standing beside the corpse, Rachel smiled

A modern Christian family (Friends Collection and Archives, Earlham College)

through her tears. She believed that it was God's will to take the child." According to Alta Hoyt, Rachel quickly busied herself by attending the women's meeting—where they appropriately discussed the question "Why do God's people have to suffer?" Hoyt remembered that all the women at the meeting were impressed by the courage with which Rachel bore her grief. According to Hoyt, she "showed more courage than any of them had shown in similar bereavement."[28]

These were the kinds of practices and attitudes that widows like Truphena Chore hoped their children would embrace. It was their way up in the world—and their mothers'. Chore's daughter, Mary Imbuhira, told me that her mother struggled to send her to the GBS because she wanted her to emulate her cousin, who had attended school in the 1930s and later married a "rich military man," a dresser in the Middle East Platoon. According to Imbuhira, her mother agreed to send her to the GBS for admittedly mercenary reasons: "I would be profitable to her when I got married and earn her a big dowry like my cousin, whose mother was also a widow."[29] And her mother succeeded—for Imbuhira went on to describe to me her "big" wedding, one that every "important person attended," and the enormous amounts of food that were served, how the "chicken, rice, and meat were overflowing." The occasion had made her mother "very proud, so proud that she talked about the wedding for years." The same was true of Esteri Vugutsa, who also sent her daughter, Edith Kisivura, to the GBS so that she could marry well. She wanted the missionaries to teach her daughter "civilized" manners, and she remarked that Kisivura was clever and a good worker and, because of this, would make a good wife. Domestic education had made it possible for her to "fear and respect" her husband, Vugutsa told me—"education turned young girls into "docile, amiable, and obedient women."[30] No wonder, then, that a respectable Maragoli man wanted to marry a Maragoli trophy wife like those produced at the GBS. And no wonder that the men were willing to pay high dowries for such women, or that the results made the widows happy. But how long would these men stay respectable? How long would the women cheerfully practice the up-to-date domestic sciences and yet still remain docile, amiable, and obedient?

CHAPTER TWELVE

Moral Panic

In 1940, Caitano L. Lineiri, a cook for a Ms. Pretty, a white settler in
Eldoret town, wrote to the president of the North Kavirondo LNC saying
that he had seen "Kavirondo prostitutes" in Eldoret, and he was worried that
some of them might be people's wives. He also reported that young women
were beginning to *tangatanga huku na huku*, that is, "sashay about" provoc-
atively in the towns of Nairobi, Nakuru, Eldoret, and Kitale. Worried that
prostitution had increased tremendously during *siku hizi za hatari*, "the
days of war" (World War II), he suggested that the government institute a
"pass law" barring women from towns.[1]

Lineiri was a member of the Kavirondo Welfare Association, a group of
western Kenyan men who were concerned about the well-being of immi-
grants from western Kenya. Scattered throughout towns all over Kenya,
these welfare associations were prominent in the major cities of East Africa,
and they became increasingly vocal in the 1940s.[2] Members of these associations usually dealt with the concerns of town-dwelling Africans, such as
fundraising for funerals and providing entertainment for male migrants, but
it was their role in controlling women that particularly interested colonial
officials. For example, in 1943, the DC of North Kavirondo was "very impressed" with Hezron Lubang'a, the president of the Maragoli Welfare Association in Kakamega, who had written to the North Kavirondo LNC a frantic
letter, pleading with its members to do something to stop the young girls
from his tribe from "leading wayward lives in town." "Umalaya umezidi
sana sana" (prostitution has increased tremendously) in Kakamega town, he
reported.[3]

Indeed, fears of the supposed waywardness of young women had started
to circulate widely among African men. Members of the North Kavirondo
LNC imagined the existence of brothels not just in towns but in the small

villages as well: as the minutes of the August 1941 meeting indicate, "where any headman is satisfied that any dwellings or other premises are being used for the purpose of a brothel or a house of ill fame, or for other purpose which is prejudicial to morality of public peace, such a headman may, and is hereby empowered to order the owner or occupier to take such action as such a headman may consider necessary for preventing the use thereof for any such purpose."[4] As the minutes make clear, there was no presumption of innocence: "If the person does not respect the headman, he/she is guilty of offence." The situation could not have seemed more serious.

Yet though the members of the LNC debated the issue and hastily passed laws to eliminate the village brothels, it appears now that there were no such places. Every one of my oral sources indicated to me that no "houses of ill fame" existed in Maragoli—and so, unless we accept the unlikely argument of a historical cover-up, it seems we will have to acknowledge that the brothels were nothing but the products of anxious imaginations.[5] Regardless, the LNC needed only to hear rumors of the dreaded houses of ill repute to spur them into action.

Talk about the presumably "wayward" women was quickly picked up and circulated by colonial officials.[6] Responding to reports in the early 1940s about the presence of western Kenyan women in Eldoret town, for example, the DC of Uasin Gishu, western Kenya, wrote to the PC arguing that "in recent years there has arisen a problem of controlling the movement of young girls who, rather than stay at home, raise a little money and, unknown to their parents, come out of the Reserve and follow their male friends who work as casual labourers on European farms.... Some of the women come to towns and soon drift into bad ways." The DC worried that these women would "consort with troops" passing through Eldoret, and he wrote repeatedly about the growing phenomenon of the "Kavirondo prostitutes"; he also fretted about the women who "tempted men" and the men who "ate" it up. His remedy was simple: get rid of the women. In his letter to the PC, he noted that there was a "widespread *feeling* in this district that the movement of women out of the North Kavirondo district should be controlled in order to check the growing propensity amongst Kavirondo girls to move into towns, to live freer lives, and eventually to become prostitutes." Since the free movement of women naturally led to prostitution, he proposed that the LNC make it an offense for any person to transport a woman without permission from a local chief.[7]

Similar exaggerations were heard in the villages—by the hearths, by the water wells, and in the *shambas*—as many of the older Maragoli women joined with African men and colonial officials in expressing growing anxiety about young women's morality. Older women began scrutinizing the bodies of young women for signs of waywardness; women who put on weight were suspected of having become pregnant out of wedlock; those with pimples on their faces were alleged to have contracted venereal disease; and, of course, the women who ventured into town unchaperoned were automatically labeled prostitutes.[8] All of these "symptoms" of waywardness—whether imagined or real—fed into a generalized apprehension over the immorality of women in western Kenya during World War II.

The moral scare was not confined to western Kenya, however. Colonial officials and African men in other parts of Kenya were also concerned about the behavior of young women in their jurisdictions.[9] And their discussions were usually conducted with the same insistent hyperbole as discussions in western Kenya. In 1942, for example, the chairman of Kikuyu Mercy Union in Kisumu, a welfare association, wrote to the DC of Kisumu saying that there had been an "overflow" of Kikuyu women in Kisumu (though he went on, rather anticlimactically, to say that "although it is not a big flow it should be stopped so that it does not become an incitement to others who may hear that such ladies were in Kisumu"). Since "these types of women" were not allowed in Nairobi, Nakuru, and Mombasa townships, he concluded that "they probably have in mind that Kisumu is a town to accommodate prostitutes"—and he demanded that the women be arrested and returned to their homes with a "police escort."[10] The overflow of wicked ladies turned out to be *two* women from Molo: Wangare and Muthoni.

The anxiety over young women was particularly distressing to many widowed mothers, especially for those who had struggled to educate and raise well-behaved daughters who they hoped would marry well. Widows again felt particularly vulnerable because they lacked husbands to help discipline their daughters—only husbands had the real power to do so. "*Omwene hango* [the owner of the home]," as one widow noted, "is the only person with *true* authority to discipline children. So when your husband died, the authority of *omwene hango* died with him, and you were left alone without the authority to even discipline your daughters."[11] The sudden outbreak of moral anxiety had undeniable, and often unfortunate, consequences for widows and their families.

⁘

Throughout the early 1940s, as the anxiety over young women increased, a number of LNC meetings were devoted to figuring out ways to control them. The members' initial suggestion was to send a deputation of elders to the towns to shame the girls into leading respectable lives. After several discussions about the logistics, however, they decided that this tactic would not succeed. Some of the girls, they argued, were "already beyond shaming," and a deputation would be the subject of "undignified derision." Instead, they agreed on "repatriation" and immediately began the careful planning of details.[12] When they found that actually repatriating a wayward woman was too complicated, the members were forced to adopt two rather ad hoc methods: either they did the repatriations randomly when the opportunity arose, or they enlisted the help of the families involved.

To organize a repatriation, the parents or parents-in-law would locate their daughter or daughter-in-law and then file a formal request with the chief, asking him to help return the woman. If the chief agreed, he would usually send three of the village elders, accompanied by two or three strong young men, to the nearby towns of Kisumu, Kakamega, and Eldoret, where they would sit patiently waiting for the arrival of the bus from Maragoli. If they spotted a suspicious woman, they would grab her, pull her aside into some out-of-the-way corner or alleyway, and begin interrogating her about her business in town. Almost always, the intimidated young woman would surrender without a struggle; if she resisted, the "strong young men" would body-punch her until she relented.[13] If she did not give what they felt was a "satisfactory answer," or if the men remained suspicious of her motives, they would strip her and roughly drape a coarse burlap bag over her naked body; she would then be dragged by her accusers onto the crowded bus and forced to sit silent, sullen, and sore until she was deposited in the village to be paraded around for all the villagers to ogle and insult her.[14]

Such spectacles of humiliation inevitably drew crowds, as, typically, the whole village would have been informed of the estimated time the repatriated woman was likely to arrive at the bus stop. The villagers—young and old, men and women—would gather, sometimes waiting for the culprit for several hours. As the emissaries hauled the abducted woman out of the bus, the villagers would be quickly instructed by the elders to make a queue so that everyone could have a good view and to ensure that they could more efficiently spit at her bare feet and pelt her with insults. Thereafter, the woman would be made to traverse the narrow paths that meandered through the village to provide those who could not make it to the bus stop the opportunity to humiliate her—as, all the while, the excited crowd from the bus stop trailed behind, embellishing the tale of the supposed adulteress's capture and boasting of their righteous discipline.

After about an hour of this shameful exposure, the victim was finally led to the chief's office. Again, the crowd would be in tow. To commence the pseudotrial, the presiding disciplinarians would meticulously relate to the chief the details of their successful seizure, how they had found the run-away woman, how she had responded to their presence, and how they had finally gotten her onto the bus. The chief would thank them, ask for the villagers' applause, and then immediately launch into his "sermon" to the woman, railing against her for her inexplicable behavior and warning her of an even worse fate (most likely imprisonment) if she ever tried to run away again. Then, addressing both the young men and the young women in the crowd, the chief would speak more generally about the increasing amount of waywardness among the "youth of these days" and urge everybody to report to him if they suspected anyone else of such behavior. Once she had been sufficiently berated for her moral trespass, and once the young men and women had been warned of the dangers of a dissolute life, the woman was handed over to her family, still clad in a burlap bag. Savoring every detail, the villagers would slowly disperse.[15]

There were actually very few repatriations, perhaps two or three per year, according to the men and women who lived through this period of moral fervor.[16] In spite of the small number, however, the sensational manner in which villagers discussed repatriation gave the impression that it was common. "Even children lined up along the narrow village paths to insult the 'woman in a burlap bag,'" Marita Vugutsa told me, and they "would spit at her" and "call her rotten names." Like the others, Vugutsa regarded such a woman as "filthy," "rotten," and "evil" and felt she should be considered a "prostitute"—it "didn't matter what you called her."[17] Another informant, Melissa Otiende, remembered that people talked about a single repatriation for days and months, often dramatizing—and no doubt embroidering—the events each time they told the story. To represent the woman's fearful state, for instance, the narrator might make "grotesquely tense facial expressions or walk clumsily, like a wounded animal," she recalled.[18] Other people, ashamed of the woman's behavior, "clicked their tongues, shook their heads, and cursed the woman." Still others "worried about what the younger generations were up to, folded their arms across their chests, and seriously contemplated what to do about the situation."[19] It was all part of an honorable and rectifying exhibit, according to Petero Kisia, and "the wearing of a burlap bag and the issuing of potent insults were supposed to teach the woman a lesson, to shame her into living a decent life." Kisia insisted that the process of shaming served to discourage other girls who might be "tempted into such indecent behavior."[20]

Unfortunately, though, repatriations often had a greater impact than officials and elders had envisioned. They may have served as a deterrent, as intended, but the enthralling image of a woman staggering around the village in an old coffee bag amid a swarm of zealous villagers shouting slurs not only was shameful and alarming but also gave the misleading impression that gangs of young women were running away and becoming wayward or, at the very least, that young women were inordinately susceptible to such depravity. So rather than mitigating the problem (such as it was), the repatriations tended to generate more moral panic; and the more attention was given to the spectacle of repatriations, the more women's morality became the occasion for righteous hysteria—and a vicious cycle was created. Husbands and parents, especially widowed mothers, worried that their daughters would stray or that they would be accused of straying—and that they could do nothing about it. Mary Emema, the daughter of one such widow, asked, "You tell me, who would help such a widow—you tell me, who would help her? And she was alone."[21]

The worries of widowed mothers were not completely unfounded. The women I spoke with were quick to recall the heightened peril of being labeled a prostitute. Belisi Musira, who was a teenager in the mid-1940s, noted how difficult it was for girls to go anywhere or to talk innocently with boys. If they did, they were immediately labeled as wayward: "People would say, 'So-and-so's girl is bad, she is not good.'"[22] She remembered how some people assumed that any girl who put on weight was pregnant, and they would utter, sarcastically, "Hmm, so-and-so's daughter looks healthy. Where does she *eat*?" And because some of the girls who were accused of having "eaten" ended up not producing a child after nine months, accusations of infanticide and abortion followed. Some of my informants told me of rumors that circulated about young girls throwing their newborn infants in pit latrines or drinking potent herbs in order to abort.[23]

As talk of increased sexual activity among youth—of their "eating too much"—began to infiltrate Maragoli homesteads and the offices of the LNC, colonial officials began to worry about the spread of venereal disease. Women were quickly blamed for spreading the diseases—an accusation women could not escape because, after all, venereal diseases were *urukutsu lwa vakari*, "women's diseases."[24] The erroneous belief that only women could cause infection originated in the early 1920s, when some Maragoli men who went to work on European farms became infected with gonorrhea and syphilis.[25] While sexually transmitted diseases had surely occurred before, the relatively large outbreak was increasingly associated with women since it was from contact with these "other" women—the supposed prostitutes—that the migrants had become infected. So venereal diseases became women's diseases, and the belief that women were a potent source of venereal disease continued to hold sway even after people began to understand that men were just as likely to infect women as be infected by them.

Concerns over sexually transmitted diseases became common in other parts of Kenya as well, so in 1941 the health officer in Nairobi embarked on a countrywide campaign to control their spread.[26] He passed a law making it illegal for anyone to infect (either intentionally or otherwise) another with these diseases.[27] How one determined the source of such a disease was not specified, but given the prevailing lore concerning their origins, it is not surprising that it was mostly women who were incriminated. Inevitably, then, throughout the 1940s, many women in western Kenya (as in other parts of Kenya) were tried in public courts for supposedly spreading sexually transmitted diseases. The accused were often subjected to mandatory examinations in clinics set aside by the LNC exclusively for this purpose.[28] Moreover, couples who intended to marry formally, either in church or in a traditional ceremony, were required to be tested for venereal diseases. This law sometimes produced uncomfortable scenarios. In 1944, for instance, Tafroza Ebeywa and her KAR husband made arrangements to get married in the local Friends church, and, as required, they went to one of the nearby government clinics to get tested. For some reason they did not receive their results immediately. On the wedding day, with all the guests present, the results of their tests arrived. Ebeywa's was positive. She was shocked. She had never been with a man before. "I was a virgin through and through," Ebeywa told me as she waved both her hands in the air in amazement.[29]

"So what did you do?" I asked.

"I protested and asked to test again at a different clinic," Ebeywa replied.

But the wedding was called off, and the guests simply took the food along with them and walked away "shaking their heads. . . . Nobody stayed around. Everybody was embarrassed and simply walked away."

Ebeywa did get a second test, and this time it was negative. The wedding was rescheduled; friends and relatives gathered again to celebrate, and the pastor of their church blessed the couple and sent them off as husband and wife. Unfortunately for Ebeywa, her first four children died in infancy, and, true to form, some people speculated that the children's health was affected by the strange circumstances at their wedding. "The marriage was cursed from the beginning," said some, with evident schadenfreude; others believed, however, that the children had died because Ebeywa's husband had, while serving in the army, "stepped in the footsteps of a crocodile."[30] The crocodile, the explanation goes, is considered to be a source of bad luck.

The intensified surveillance given to young women only increased the hysteria over their morals. In fact, the women I spoke with remarked that whenever they got sick, they were immediately suspected of having venereal disease. "You know," Mary Jendeka recalled, "in those days, if your stomach ached, sometimes it was just menstruation that caused it, and you lay around for a few days. But some people would start gossiping, saying that you had a woman's disease. . . . So you endured the accusations until you became well."[31] Another informant, Belisi Musira, told me that, "if you were a young girl and broke out with a rash, people would point and say, 'Look at her face, she looks like she has women's disease.'" She explained the pimples by saying, "You know, when you were getting to be a mature girl and you got your period, sometimes your face was not nice. People would think that because you were maturing you desired men and that left you susceptible to women's diseases."[32]

Unfortunately, rumors of "wayward" women soon began to reach men in the KAR, even in places as far away as Burma and Palestine. For example, Hezron Angiro of the First Battalion, East Africa Pioneers, in Burma, wrote to the PC of Nyanza with concerns about his wife's behavior: "It is with the greatest pleasure that I write to you to inform you that my elder brother wrote to me telling me that Jotham Oliech is persuading my wife whom I have suffered for. Secondly he spoke awkward words to her telling her that those who were sent to the army are already dead."[33] Angiro intended no irony in his use of the phrase "greatest pleasure"; this was a standard phrase used by those learning to write letters, whether the news being conveyed had any pleasure in it or not. His letter reveals the kinds of vicious gossip that were circulating. Of course, we will never know whether Oliech actually "persuaded" Angiro's wife to do anything untoward, or even if he "spoke awkward words" to her. We, however, do have firm evidence of the violent beatings wives received for evidently being "persuaded." As we will see, when husbands returned from military service, there were consequences.

∽

Whatever the consequences, this perception of western Kenyan women as immoral was certainly a new development. In the previous decade, officials had believed that women from western Kenya were sexually naive and actually needed to be protected from philandering men in the towns. For instance, when men from Nyanza Province working in Thika, near Nairobi, complained that their wives had become unfaithful, the PC of Nyeri responded by defending the women, saying that their moral outlook was "notoriously" naive and made them "easy prey" to any "out-of-work *Don Juan* from Nairobi."[34] Of course, his response may not have calmed the husbands' jealous fears, but it certainly places the blame on predatory men, not wanton women.

In any case, the PC was expressing what had been the characteristic attitude. During much of the 1930s many of the LNC discussions that dealt with "runaway" girls or wives usually blamed the men whom the women had run away with, not the women. In a meeting held in August 1932, for example, several cases were read which described how unmarried men working in towns or on settlers' farms had returned to the villages and abducted "young girls," some of whom were "minors [and] for whom bride price may have been practically paid by an intended husband."[35] In discussing these cases, the all-male members of the LNC viewed the girls as innocent victims and genuinely sought to protect them; the men in such cases were seen as "seducers" or "abductors."[36] In that same meeting the members of the LNC even suggested instituting a law making it an "offence for any man to take an unmarried girl from the custody of her parents or guardians without their consent." The consent had to be given in the "form of a permit issued by a Headman and countersigned by a District Officer."[37]

How, then, had Kavirondo girls managed to transform themselves from humble and naive women to would-be prostitutes in less than a decade? How real was the perceived threat of prostitution? And more important, how many wayward and wanton Kavirondo girls were actually in the towns? Without a doubt, there were some women in the major towns of East Africa who prostituted themselves with the troops.[38] But were there enough of them to generate the "widespread feeling" of moral panic or to give rise to the frightful specter of "the Kavirondo prostitute"?

To answer these questions we need to go back to the beginning of the war; we need to pause and imagine the anxiety felt by men leaving their wives behind.[39] To begin with, most of the men barely knew their wives. They had little sense of their personalities and whether they could be trusted to remain faithful—even though they had paid considerable bridewealth for them. For better or worse, they considered the women to be "investments." And they were being forced to leave these investments behind for a significant—and indefinite—amount of time. Imagine their apprehension and their fear. Would their wives remain faithful? Would they obey them as the head of the household when they returned? Would they still respect them as their husband, or would they adopt new ideas and attitudes? These were urgent questions, and as might be expected, the KAR men had expressed them to their employers before they left for their military duties— and they received strong assurances from the officials that they would watch out for the women.[40] "On our engagement," wrote Angiro, "the Provincial

Commissioner strictly spoke to us how no one can take neither your wife nor your cattle."[41]

Such reassurances were of course partly intended to give conscripts the impression that the officials were taking their responsibilities for their wives—and their cattle—seriously: they would guard the young women and ensure that they would not stray. The men could leave without worries. But ironically, the inflated rhetoric and the staged repatriations gave both those in the villages and the recruits exactly the opposite impression: the stronger the assurances that the wives would be watched, the more they apparently needed watching. Regrettably, the recruits began to believe that officials had not been effective in restraining their wives and that, in fact, their wives had been let loose. Once aroused, their jealousy was hard to contain, and they let themselves conclude that the matrimonial cages had been opened and their wives had escaped their rule—surely they were on the run, openly cavorting with abandon in places like Eldoret and Kisumu. "Were the PC's speeches only *mere* [empty promises]?" Angiro asked. Goaded by the green-eyed monster, he made a list for the PC of all the men rumored to have helped Oliech "persuade" his wife into sin, and he wondered whether the government had "ordered that all the men who did not come to the army can take the soldier's women."[42] Unfortunately, when men like Angiro returned from their military service, they brought their suspicions home with them. It was mostly the wives who paid, sometimes with their lives, for the vicious rumors spread while their husbands were away.

CHAPTER THIRTEEN

Wife Beating

K AR marriages created a whole new set of problems. Many of these marriages were tormented by emotional and physical conflict, and it was
woefully hard for the young couples to maintain a marriage in the absence of
the men during World War II. Usually the brides, particularly those who were
daughters of widowed mothers, suffered the most. The experience of Mary
Musimbi, the young woman whose mother had been so proud of her high
bridewealth, is representative of that of many KAR brides. Musimbi's husband, Jafeti Agufwa, married her in 1942 while on a brief furlough from his
military duties. After the marriage proposal had been accepted and the brideprice agreed upon, Musimbi was escorted to Agufwa's house by her aunt,
cousin, and mother. They had no time to arrange for a wedding, as Agufwa
was soon expected to return to Mombasa, where he was stationed for the du-
ration of the war. The women left Musimbi's house early in the morning and
arrived at Agufwa's around midday, having walked about eight miles. They
were warmly received, given some refreshments, and after visiting with their
hosts for a few hours, returned home that same day, leaving Musimbi behind.
That night she slept with her new husband in the *idisi*, the little mud hut for
young men, located in the homestead of Agufwa's parents. Early the next day
Agufwa left for Mombasa. Musimbi shyly bade him good-bye, not knowing
when he would return.[1]

During the next four days, the honeymoon days, Musimbi behaved de-
murely, sitting quietly in the homestead, as was expected of newlyweds. She
was waited on by her sisters-in-law and mother-in-law, who brought her meals
and carried water for her bath. Then, as soon as the honeymoon days were over,
Musimbi was confronted with the reality of her status as daughter-in-law:
work, work, and more work, day and night, week after week. For the two long
years that her husband was away, Musimbi was required to wake up early

each morning, fetch water from the river, cook breakfast for everyone in the household, and do the planting and weeding in the *shamba*, until she returned home in the late afternoon to prepare the evening meal by gathering firewood to cook the vegetables and grinding millet for *ugali*.[2] After the meal, after the whole family had eaten their fill, she went to bed exhausted, sleeping alone in the *idisi*. But she was not always able to sleep. Some nights she lay awake with, as the Maragoli saying goes, anger boiling in her stomach.

Her story gets even bleaker. In 1945 Agufwa was released from his KAR duties, and according to Musimbi, he returned a changed man—he now "carried around radiograms and spoke English through the nose like white people. He was quite proud of his accomplishments and did not think that I was good enough for him." His conduct was made worse, Musimbi claimed, by the fact that people "spoke bad words" to her husband, telling him that she had slept with other men in the *idisi* while he was away. So he beat her and demanded that she go back to "her own people." This went on for six months, until Agufwa found a job as a dresser/nurse in Nakuru. The time that Agufwa lived with her at his parents' homestead was, she remembered sadly, the worst months of her marriage, worse even than the two years of thankless labor: "He beat me constantly, constantly, and I persevered," said Musimbi. When his parents intervened, he stopped beating her for a while; sometimes, when they could not help, she slipped off to her mother's to escape the beatings for a few days. Sooner or later, though, she had to return "because I wanted to give my marriage a chance; I didn't want to be a 'chased-away' [divorced] woman, so I kept coming back to Agufwa's hoping that things would get better."[3]

When Agufwa finally left for Nakuru, he was not heard from for five months, until one afternoon he unexpectedly showed up at the homestead for a monthlong leave. And again he beat her. This time, because Musimbi had not conceived a child, he accused her of having contracted a venereal disease, and so he beat her some more, once striking her so hard that he broke her tooth and, another time, punching her in the face so hard that her eye remained swollen shut for days. "Alinipiga karibu kufa [He beat me until near death]," Musimbi said in Swahili (we had been speaking in Luragoli) because the Swahili expression was one commonly used by women who sued their husbands for wife beating in the 1990s.[4]

Eventually Musimbi packed her belongings and went back to her mother's house, where she stayed for a month. After two weeks of waiting, hoping their daughter-in-law would return, Agufwa's parents decided to go fetch her and ask her mother for forgiveness on their son's behalf. But her mother, Jane

Egendi, refused to forgive him and angrily told them that her daughter would not go back until Agufwa himself came to get her—at which time he would have to apologize before the local elders and swear never to beat her daughter again.

Agufwa honored the summons. He apologized. Everybody forgave everybody else. They shook hands with each other and even drank water from the same bowl (to signal their unity), and Musimbi went back to her husband's homestead to give her marriage another chance. They then resumed their usual routines: Agufwa went back to his job in Nakuru, and Musimbi went back to the endless routine of a daughter-in-law's work, followed by bitter, sleepless nights alone in the *idisi*. Now her inability to conceive was added to her list of frustrations: "My in-laws used to talk about my infertility all the time, saying that I was diseased and that I had been cursed."[5] And so her life continued until, once again, Agufwa returned home without notice, got drunk, and beat her until she bled. Again, Musimbi returned to her mother's homestead, and this time her mother immediately took her to Mbale court and asked that the judge grant her daughter a divorce.

I was able to find the records of this case and of at least a thousand similar cases from the 1940s and 1950s in the Kakamega Provincial Record Center. In Musimbi's file, the clerk, in clear, neat handwriting, wrote, "Plaintiff, Jane Egendi, widow of Matayo Ariso, wants Jafeti Agufwa to divorce her daughter because he beats her all the time.... Jane Egendi wants Jafeti Agufwa to disown her daughter in public the same way he married her in public." Yet even though the request was made through the court, Agufwa refused to divorce her, stubbornly claiming that "Musimbi is my wife, and I married her in public."[6] He got what he wanted; they were not granted a divorce. The *hukumu*, or "judgment," by the president of the court reads, "President na wazee wamepeleleza kesi hii pande zote" (the president and the male elders have investigated this case from both sides); and it concluded that "wameona wasiwachane kwa sababu Agufwa hataki" (because Agufwa has confessed in public that he does not want to leave his wife, the court has decided not to issue a divorce).[7] Musimbi was forced to return to Agufwa's homestead. Nevertheless, the court apparently accomplished one thing: Agufwa never beat her again. Much to her disadvantage, he also stopped supporting her. But all had turned out well, at least according to her mother, Egendi, who was clearly relieved that her daughter had been made to remain with her husband; marriage, after all, was a respectable state and divorce was not. For Musimbi, however, the difficulty had not really been resolved: "Where could I go as an infertile nonvirgin? Who would want to marry me?"[8]

Unfortunately, Musimbi's dilemma was fairly common among the so-called KAR wives, that is, women who had hastily married soldier husbands and who had been paid handsomely in bridewealth. Melissa Otiende had a story much like Musimbi's: she had hurriedly married Petero Mutiva, another KAR man, before he left for the war, and she had also stayed at his family's homestead and tried to be a dutiful daughter-in-law. Because her mother-in-law felt somewhat embarrassed that her son had paid so much bridewealth for her, she made Otiende work hard, harder even than Musimbi. "I would work the whole day, with no rest time, but when my mother-in-law returned from the market in the evening, she went to the garden and measured me a section of the land she wanted me to dig. I would dig it until very late, until seven o'clock at night, when the chickens began to return home." "I tell you," she continued, "daughter-in-lawhood was really *trying* in those days, but women still *tried* to be good daughters-in-law."[9] Her husband, like Musimbi's, worked in a distant city (Mombasa) and returned home only for brief visits—and on one of these visits in 1943, according to Otiende, he infected her with venereal disease. She had no choice but to go to the clinic for treatment, but when her in-laws found out, they spread rumors that she was sick because she was sleeping with other men. When and where she had the opportunity to do so they did not reveal—all they knew was that their son could not have been the cause of the infection.

Mutiva's behavior when he returned from the war was sadly predictable: he accused her of adultery and began to beat her. But Otiende persevered in the marriage anyway, and when I asked her why she had continued to stay in so violent a relationship, she responded, "I wanted to give my marriage a chance." On one occasion, however, Mutiva beat Otiende so badly that she ran off to her mother's house. Horrified at her condition, her mother took her to Mbale court, where she hoped to expose and humiliate her son-in-law. And it worked—to a point: Mutiva publicly agreed to stop beating his wife, and he recommitted himself to her. In her case file, the clerk wrote, "Mutiva refuses to divorce his wife, Melissa Otiende, saying that 'Otiende is my wife and I married her in public.'" After this, Mutiva never beat her again, but like Musimbi's husband, he refused to give her any further financial support—partly because, as it turned out, he was living with another woman in Nairobi.

This no doubt upset Otiende, and most likely she wanted to leave her husband again, but as she told me resignedly, she was willing to put up with the marriage because she had four children with Mutiva. "Where does a woman with four children go? You tell me." Otiende hoped that her status as a first wife would at least earn her some respect within Mutiva's family. And it did. Everyone continued to recognize her as Mutiva's wife, and when Mutiva died in 1978, she was given the honor of burying him as a first wife. Otiende's health was failing when I talked with her in the mid-1990s, and she hoped that when she died she would be buried next to her husband. Her wishes were honored in 1997.[10]

In 1952, another widow, Daina Semo, filed a similar suit for divorce against her military husband, Saisi Liavuli, claiming that he "beat me and bit me until I bled."[11] Semo also alleged that her husband never bought her food or clothes and, as a result, she was often hungry and disgraced; she also accused her husband of infecting her with venereal disease. She did not really want a divorce—after all, she had five children with Liavuli. But she insisted in her testimony before the court that she would remain married only if her husband stopped beating her. Liavuli admitted to having beaten Semo "a few times" because he heard that she had had sexual relations with other men while he was away in the army. However, he, like the others, refused to divorce her, contending that "Semo is my wife, and we have five children together." Again, the president of Mbale court and the other presiding elders chose not to grant them a divorce, saying, "Liavuli amekubali ati Liavuli ni bibi yake kamili [Liavuli assures us of his commitment to his wife]."[12]

The men's refusal to grant their wives a divorce was fairly common. To give yet another example, Matayo Jumba, Grace Irihema's husband, refused to divorce her in spite of the fact that he felt it necessary to beat her so terribly that he chased her away. In 1954, her widowed mother, Jane Visiru, sued Jumba for beating her daughter. Like the other KAR wives, Irihema had married Jumba in 1943 while he was on holiday break from the military, and again, like the others, she had been a dutiful daughter-in-law and had successfully carried out the backbreaking routines of daughter-in-lawhood.[13] Yet we still hear the same story: when her husband returned from the military, her in-laws spread rumors that she had slept with other men, and her husband started beating her. "He used to follow me when I went to the river to fetch water," said Irihema, "and if he saw me talking to a man, he would beat me and also threaten to beat that man."[14] In 1952, Jumba finally drove her away, to stay with her widowed mother, and he left to marry another woman in Nairobi. A couple years later, in 1954, her mother assisted her in filing for divorce before the Mbale court—not necessarily because she wanted her daughter to be granted a divorce but because she wanted her daughter's husband to "disown her in public just as he had married her in public."[15] Not surprisingly, once in court Jumba refused to agree to a divorce, arguing, "She

is my wife, and I want to keep her."[16] The president of the court advised
Irihema to return to Jumba's house and insisted that she report back to the
court if Jumba beat her again. But she never received another blow.

What seems most surprising in these cases is that the widowed mothers
saw the courts as allied to their interests, despite the fact that they usually
ruled against their daughters' petitions for divorce. The reason is relatively
simple. When a couple did manage to divorce, the bride's parents were normally expected to return the bridewealth they had received at the time of the
marriage. Rarely could the widows afford this. And so, as we might expect,
the court records reveal that most widowed mothers hoped for reconcilia-
tion between their daughter and son-in-law because they did not have the
money to return the inflated bridewealth that had been paid. Consequently,
when Semo's mother bowed humbly and earnestly before the men presiding
over the court, she begged them not to grant Semo a divorce. Referring to
them reverently as "trusted men," she confessed that she had used up all
the money she had received as bridewealth for her daughter and had nothing
left to give back to Liavuli. There was little that Semo could do. She was
utterly frank with me: "Even if I found a man to marry me, he could not
afford to pay the bridewealth Liavuli had paid for me. And as a nonvirgin
and a divorced woman, I was not worth much. So I had no choice but to stay
married to Liavuli. Where would I have gone?"[17]

∞

In the 1940s and 1950s, divorced women in Africa, as elsewhere, were often
castigated by their society.[18] Western Kenya was no exception. Both oral and
archival sources indicate that the Maragoli did not approve of divorce, and so
most women tried their best to remain married—even to the point that they
were willing to let their husbands mistreat them rather than face the stigma
attached to divorce.[19] But the disgrace of divorce could work both ways;
it could affect the husband's standing in the community as well. Husbands
were not simply permitted to dispose of their wives as they pleased, and they
also felt the pressure to meet expectations. "Ideal" husbands were obliged to
respect their wife and work hard to keep their marriage intact. If they failed,
there were practical repercussions—of sorts. For instance, if a couple decided
that the conflict between them was irreconcilable, the husband could resort
to polygamy (which allowed him to marry another wife without divorcing the
first wife), but the husband was still expected to take care of his first wife's
social and economic needs. The Maragoli did not grant a respectable man the
liberty to casually disown his wife, at least in any kind of public way.[20]

Widowed mothers also wanted their daughters to stay married because they believed in the respectability of the institution of marriage.[21] For the widows, marriage bestowed status on their daughter; it gave her access to property—to land, houses, banana trees, and so on—that she could not have as a divorced woman. So even when they publicly condemned their son-in-law in the courts, they often did so in order to save their daughter's marriage. What they wanted was for the man to stop beating their daughter, and they counted on the power of public humiliation in the courts to force the husband to recommit himself to his marriage. After all, a drawn-out trial conducted in public would certainly have been shameful for the man, since public testimony concerning his abusive behavior would have been considered an irreparable disgrace—not necessarily because it revealed him to be a brute but because it demonstrated that he had failed to "control" his wife, to instill in her the values of deference, respect, duty, and obedience expected of women in this patriarchal society.[22] "Real" men were expected to protect women, not beat them. "Real" men were to be listened to and obeyed by their wives, not defied in any way that might cause the men to become violent. No man wanted to be seen as ineffectual in regard to women—and no man, God forbid, wanted his failure made public.

There were, however, exceptions to this belief in the all-absolving benefits of marriage. In instances of extreme brutality, widowed mothers were ardently determined to get their daughter out of the abusive relationship, even if divorce meant sacrificing a degree of honor and respectability and a huge amount of bridewealth. In 1956, for example, Janet Zilika took her husband, Simion Imbayi, whom she had married in 1944, to court, asking for a divorce because he beat her severely and frequently.[23] She had reported the beatings before, to the African court in Eldoret town, and the magistrate had fined her husband thirty shillings. But the fine had had little effect, so she went back to court, this time in Mbale. During this appearance Zilika informed the court members that her husband, who was an alcoholic, had knocked out her front teeth—a fact quite easy to demonstrate and hard to ignore. Still, nothing was accomplished, except to make Imbayi feel even more embarrassed and dishonored. His response was foreseeable: he became angrier, more ferocious, until at last he stripped Zilika of all her belongings, beat her so brutally she went blind in one eye, and chased her off the homestead. When Mary Migitsu, Zilika's mother, was brought in to testify at Mbale court, she begged the court president to grant her daughter a divorce because she was afraid that Imbayi would beat her to death.

"That kind of brutal violence by a husband toward his wife was bad. In fact, it was a sign that the man was insane," Migitsu told me. "If a husband

Mary Migitsu with the author, 1995 (photo by author)

slapped his wife once or twice on her face, that was not bad because you knew that his wife must have disobeyed him. You knew that the wife deserved it because she was rude or something. . . . And if your daughter complained to you about such a slap, you told her to go back to her husband and obey him. But Zilika's husband was insane and almost killed her."[24] The divorce was granted.

In a similar case, a widow by the name of Respah Mungore, whose daughter had married John Kagai and earned her 250 shillings in bridewealth, regretted the marriage once her daughter's husband returned from the army. Mungore believed that being in the army had driven Kagai mad, and she related how he would often stand in the middle of the living room, in silence, for a whole day.[25] Kagai then began to smoke marijuana and to beat her daughter, but her daughter endured the beating and continued to live with him until, one day, Kagai beat her and stabbed her with a knife. Mungore took her daughter to Mbale court and asked that her daughter be granted a divorce. Once again presented with evidence that could not be ignored, the president of Mbale court supported her. "My biggest *kehenda mwoyo*," she recalled, "was that the president of the court would not listen to me, but he did because he realized that I was alone [widowed]. After I held the Bible and told him all my problems, he listened and let me go home with my daughter." To Mungore the men in charge of the courts were "good men."[26]

Widows like Migitsu and Mungore were—perhaps quite shrewdly—willing to distinguish between "a slap on the face for disobedient wives" and extreme physical violence involving weapons or ending in permanent physical disabilities. In the latter cases, these widows were certainly not taking the abusive son-in-law to court so that he could undergo a first-class public humiliation and then recommit himself to the marriage. The widows wanted their daughter out of such a marriage. In many of these extreme cases, the judges in the courts were willing to respect the wishes of the widow.

∞

What was it, then, that made it comfortable for widows to speak out, to "look men in the eye" and tell them their problems? Was there something more than the severity of the beatings that made them take their troubles to the courts? How were the 1940s courts different from those of the 1930s, when widows had sued their in-laws for denying them rights over their land and where they were expected to "speak silently"?[27] One factor was the court reforms launched by the colonial government in the mid-1940s, which made public tribunals accessible to women. The reforms gave widows a stake in the system and let them feel they could speak out for their daughter without discrediting themselves. A specific court reform that revolutionized trial procedures and outcomes was the requirement that all elders, clerks, and other court servers take an oath before presiding over a case. Similarly, the rule that all witnesses hold either a Bible (for the Christians) or a pot (for the nonbelievers) and swear to tell the truth was a seemingly modest reform, but it profoundly helped build trust in the courts.[28] Maragoli men and women took these procedures very seriously, and many believed they would die if they lied under oath.[29] So strong, in fact, was their belief in the oath that sociologist Arthur Phillips's report on native tribunals in 1945 noted that once the government introduced the oath, all the people who worked in courts asked for salary raises because they were afraid to take bribes as they had previously done.[30] The fear of God's—or the ancestors'—wrath was apparently greater than the fear of poverty.

In any case, these new procedures helped reduce corruption and nepotism and allowed court officials to listen to women and judge their cases with relative fairness and objectivity. And the women were now more than willing to present their cases. Note Visiru's recollection of her daughter's court case: "So I held the Bible and told the judge what I felt. 'Where would my daughter go with four children? And she had married by wedding.' But Jumba could not have disowned her in public because people would have said that she is the one ruining his house, and that would have looked very bad for him." Once satisfied that the court had sufficiently disgraced her daughter's husband, she had a profound sense of vindication: "When I left the courtroom, I experienced an unusual amount of strength. The government had instilled in me power. From the court, my daughter and I went straight to my house, picked up her four children, and straightaway left for Jumba's. It was a great moment of victory because I wanted my daughter to maintain her house [remain married]."[31] Unfortunately, the couple did not quite live happily ever after, even though Jumba had stopped the beatings. He had, it turns out, married a second wife and was living with her in Nairobi, and he rarely sent money home to his first wife. "But that was okay," Visiru told me; "at least he didn't chase her away."

Erika Lisimbu, yet another widowed mother, was grateful to the court officials for helping denounce her son-in-law in public. Her daughter, Nora Kasaya, had also married a KAR man who had accused her of adultery and beat her repeatedly. Yet Lisimbu remarked with pride, "As a widow it was very important that the court officials listened to you because they knew you did not have anyone [husband] to help you. The *teminari* [tribunal] also trusted your words when you courageously took an oath, because people were scared of the oath. But if you took it courageously and told the court that your son-in-law was beating your daughter, the testimony made him look very bad, and he stopped beating your daughter because he did not want to be taken to court again and continuously make himself look bad. He could not deny your daughter in public."[32]

⚬⚬⚬

The testimony of widows and their daughters indicates that the technical reforms introduced in African courts, combined with the sympathetic character of individual African judges presiding over their cases, helped turn courtrooms into arenas where resolution of marital conflicts could take place. Moreover, the courtrooms became one of the few places where women could speak out, where they could dare look men in the eye and ask them for help. In fact, widows came to consider the African men who assumed responsibility in the new court system of the 1940s and 1950s "real men" who were upholding the model of Maragoli masculinity; they felt that men in the courts had assumed familiar, and proper, gender roles—though of course in a new guise. And the courts had the complementary effect of exposing the errant husbands' failures to live up to ideal masculinity by exposing their brutality to the public. Perhaps even more significant, the widows' goals were accomplished in a public forum, a place where the widows no longer had to defer to the whims of individual men. So however alien the courts may have seemed at first, they eventually provided a (relatively) disinterested tribunal where the women could negotiate their claims and secure their rights. Now they could employ the new colonial court system to fight wrongdoing in their society, in much the same way they had relied on their male relatives in the past—and whatever the outcome of the particular case, the women could at least look upon the court as a supportive institution.

PART THREE

Postcolonial Promises

Citizenship and Land Rights
in Postcolonial Kenya

O n September 15, 1964, President Jomo Kenyatta gave what has become known as the "Back to the Land" speech to a crowd of proud Kenyans tightly packed in Jamhuri Stadium, Nairobi.[1] The occasion was Jamhuri Day, the first anniversary of Kenya's independence from Britain. Everywhere the stadium was decorated with Kenya's new flag of black, green, and red stripes with a black Masai shield in the center. Each color and item on the flag was highly symbolic: green stood for land, black for the color of the people who occupied the land, and red for the blood that Kenyans had shed to defend their land. The land was now the new nation of Kenya, a nation whose protection lay in the strength of a shield. Jamhuri Day was a special day; it was a day to celebrate with joy and optimism, a day to reflect on the strength of Kenyans, who had recently toppled the colonial government, a day to ponder future plans for the new nation. All *wanainchi* (citizens) were entitled to a day off from work so they could board one of the free government buses to travel to the stadium to hear the new president, the Mzee or father of the nation, give his speech. Kenyatta's speech began thus: "Our greatest asset in Kenya is our land. This is the heritage we received from our forefathers. In land lies our salvation and survival. It is in this knowledge that we fought for the freedom of our country. Whatever our plans for the future, they must spring from a resolve to put our land to maximum production, however small the acreage we may possess."[2]

Numerous versions of this speech were heard all over Kenya on that mid-September day as each district, division, and municipality observed its own Jamhuri Day celebration and the newly elected black leaders—members of Parliament and councilors—gave speeches in which they proudly reassured Kenyans of their status as *wanainchi*. Some of these leaders had either directly or indirectly fought hard to rid Kenya of the colonial regime. In this acutely euphoric moment, they believed that their newly acquired freedom and power made them capable of achieving anything, including the economic development of their country. Like Kenyatta, the speakers reminded all Kenyans of the "importance of land to the development of the Nation."[3] Since Kenya was largely an agricultural economy, the leaders were keen to prioritize improvements in peasant farming; their immediate concern was for peasants to carry out land consolidation and registration to enhance agricultural production.[4] The government hoped to make the peasants, especially those in the overpopulated areas of Western, Central, and Nyanza provinces, consolidate their landholdings by exchanging fragments with or selling fragments to their neighbors so that all of each peasant's properties would be adjacent to one another; then the peasant would secure a title deed by registering the unified landholdings with the Ministry of Lands and Settlements office. Only a farmer with a title deed would be allowed to grow lucrative cash crops such as tea and coffee, the country's major agricultural exports.[5]

To achieve these ends the new leaders did not want to use force, as colonial officials had done in most of their dealings with the peasants, including widows.[6] Rather, they hoped that the political rhetoric would work, that peasants, as true patriots, as men and women who loved their new nation, would carry out the changes willingly.[7] After all, the peasants were now touted as *citizens* as opposed to the subjects they had been under British rule, and as citizens, they had to feel and act as such. Indeed, as citizens the peasants were expected to accept their obligations as well as their rights—and their main obligation was to work hard and through *harambee,* or cooperation, to build the economy of their new nation. In turn, the new black leaders promised to protect and provide for them. So, in essence, a new compact was being made: you do your part, said the government, and we will do ours; you work hard for the common good, and we will protect your individual rights as citizens of our new nation. Politicians reiterated some version of this unwritten agreement in almost all their public speeches, especially during holidays like Jamhuri. With the new attitude of cooperation, everyone was to benefit.

Such grand promises of mutual support were no doubt seductive, and they became tremendously significant in the first years of independence. But, perhaps inevitably, the promises could not be fulfilled.[8] Many new citizens, especially widows, discovered that their rights were not as secure as promised; and at least in one respect, many even saw their individual rights as citizens violated—particularly when they tried to carry out the consolidation and registration of their land that the new government had mandated.

The sensationalized rhetoric of rights and obligations was elaborated officially in a constitutionlike document called Kenyan Sessional Papers of 1965. One of the most popular articles in the papers, and one that became a staple in the speeches of the new leaders, asserted that "the government would ensure equal opportunities to all *citizens* [my emphasis], eliminate exploitation and discrimination, and provide needed social services such as education, medical care and social security."[9] Throughout the 1960s and 1970s politicians invoked versions of this article to convince their constituencies to vote for them. Its progressive, egalitarian message became a part of almost every politician's stump speech. "Those fortunate enough to have incomes above average," noted Tom Mboya, the first minister of Economic Planning and Development, in a speech to the general Kenyan public, "must share their incomes with the very poor through the tax system so that the government can provide education and training, health services and other forms of assistance to the needy and underprivileged *citizens* [my emphasis] of this new nation."[10]

Peter Kibisu, the member of Parliament (MP) of Maragoli, was particularly earnest in a speech given at a fundraising meeting for a new school in Maragoli. "In order to develop this nation of ours that we fought very hard for," Kibisu told an attentive crowd of Maragoli men and women, "we must try to be trustworthy amongst ourselves and in matters of state and commerce." And he confidently assured his audience, "If we work closely with the government the government will protect us as *citizens* [my emphasis] of this nation." The duty of the new government, he reiterated, "is to ensure that the poor and needy are taken care of. But to do so, the government needs your cooperation. Our slogan is cooperation through the spirit of *Harambee*."[11]

The daily newspaper also became an important channel for dispersing the language of citizenship and development. Throughout Kenya the newspapers continually published excerpts from the officials' speeches, emphasizing emotive phrases like "our precious nation," "our humble and hardworking citizens," and "the fruits of *uhuru* [independence]." Patriotic and propagandistic headlines shouted sentiments that readers could not ignore: "The Maragoli Urged to Make Freedom Real," "Harambee Will Carry Us Through," "Let Us Build Our Nation," and "Hurrah African Socialism."

In the euphoric climate of independence, the reading public naturally— and perhaps naively—came to believe the leaders' rhetoric.[12] Ordinary men and women wrote letters to the editors of the leading Kenyan dailies in which they expressed their excitement to be citizens, their willingness to "contribute to the development of the nation," their anticipation of "reaping the fruits of *uhuru*, or independence," and their "dedication to African roots."[13]

Throughout the 1960s and 1970s, then, many of these men and women generously contributed funds to build schools and hospitals and to supply other basic amenities, such as piped water, to the less well-off. Indeed, one of the most common features of the newly independent Kenya was the Harambee school, which was a secondary school built with donations from ordinary citizens.[14] The schools, with their rows of square brick buildings and roofs of corrugated iron sheets, dotted rural and urban landscapes everywhere and gave even the casual passerby an upbeat impression of the country's commitment to universal education. For many, optimism and confidence were the order of the day.

Women, in particular, were filled with a solemn desire to contribute their own good deeds to such strikingly universal causes. Many of them formed organizations like Maendeleo ya Wanawake (Advancement of Women) and worked tirelessly to set up craft centers where they made and sold handcrafts to earn money, some of which they contributed to build new secondary schools and improve public amenities.[15] And peasants, including widows, in places like Maragoli and other overpopulated regions of Central and Nyanza provinces, struggled to carry out land consolidation and registration, hoping that their efforts would yield more crops and earn them money and thereby help contribute to the general growth of their country's economy. On the whole, citizens worked hard to cooperate among themselves and fulfill their obligations, striving along the way for greater self-sufficiency.

By the late 1960s, many of the self-help projects had begun to produce positive results. "The people," Tom Mboya happily noted in one of his speeches in Parliament, "have responded vigorously to the call and spirit of *Harambee*, and are putting much money and effort into self-help projects." After tracing the history of the concept of self-help in "African tradition," he concluded that such ideas had "strong African roots" and demonstrated an "important potential for our development."[16]

⁘

Mboya's exuberance and contentment were, unfortunately, not shared by many peasants, especially not by many widows, who felt that their rights as citizens had not been respected and that the new leaders had not, in fact, kept many of their promises.[17] The trouble arose over issues of land ownership: because, according to customary law, women's rights to land were only temporary, widows were allowed only to temporarily register land under their name as a way of safeguarding it for their sons. Consequently, it was easy for their male relatives or neighbors to challenge these rights.

This was the situation that Elima Mademba faced. On the evening of April 13, 1971, Mademba, an elderly widow, returned home from the market to find her pots, plates, chairs, clothes, bedding, and other household belongings dumped, soaking wet, in her backyard.[18] She naturally ran to her nearest neighbor to find out what had occurred. Unfortunately, the neighbor happened to be her brother-in-law, Kitigala, the man who had cast her possessions into the rain. He had evicted her.

At once insolent and impassive, Kitigala led Mademba into his house and tossed a land registration certificate before her. Mademba did not know how to read; however, judging from his harsh reception of her, she knew that it did not bear good news. Kitigala announced to her that the government officers in Kakamega had allowed him to register—under his name—the land that she occupied; he then told her he had sold the land to someone else. Aghast, she wondered where her brother-in-law expected her to go; she had no sons to turn to, and besides, she needed her land now more than ever because one of her daughters, whose marriage had failed, was living with her and using the land to support herself. Mademba and Kitigala began to quarrel. Cruelly, he wondered out loud why she was not "already dead since she was too old and not good for much"; he called her daughter a prostitute and demanded that she return to the home of her husband. Wounded and desperate, Mademba wept.

Afraid that Kitigala might physically harm her and her daughter if they stayed in their house, she begged one of her other neighbors to put them up for the night. The next day, Mademba asked her host, who happened to be literate in English, to write a letter on her behalf to the district magistrate in Kakamega. "My Honour," she dictated, "due to my poverty, widowed status, and age and to the fact that Kitigala had told me that he would look after my interests, I did not check on the registering officer, and only came to know of it when Kitigala kicked me off the land and house." She noted that Kitigala had gone ahead and sold the land to someone else. "My Honour," she pleaded, "as a widow and *a loyal citizen* [my emphasis] of this Nation, I kindly ask you to intervene the transfer and exempt me from court fees in my filling [*sic*] a civil suit against Kitigala."[19]

Nothing ever came of Mademba's plea, and even though Kitigala allowed her to return to her house, the land remained registered under his name, and she was not allowed to cultivate it and grow crops for herself. Until her death four years later, she remained dependent on her younger brother's family.[20]

In spite of her failure to get her land back, it is important to note that unlike many of the widows we have met in this book, Mademba called herself a "loyal citizen" instead of a "poor suffering widow" beset with worries of the heart. She was not alone. More and more, widows in the period immediately after independence drew upon the new language of citizenship to meet their needs, just as they had once drawn on the presentation of their worries of the heart. By invoking the new language of patriotic selfhood, widows were doing exactly what the new leaders expected them to do: viewing themselves as Kenyan citizens and not as members of separate ethnic groups like the Maragoli. Widows had come to believe that the new politicized language, rather than that of the worries of the heart, would oblige the new leaders to live up to their promises and fulfill their rights as citizens. Indeed, widows had no other choice but to invoke this language since land consolidation required that they deal more regularly with officials in new government offices, such as the Ministry of Lands and Settlements. Moreover, the officials were often from other parts of Kenya and did not know the local languages, and as "foreigners" they were not necessarily bound by Maragoli patriarchal expectations necessitated by the worries of the heart discourse. (This shuffling of people was also part of the new government's plan to form a unified nation of Kenyans out of distinct ethnic groups.)[21] The officers were, however, obliged to treat all the local people as citizens. So the widows were forced to articulate their grievances in terms of the less personal and more political new language of citizenship.

On January 17, 1974, Jedida Muthembi, a poor and illiterate widow on the verge of homelessness, asked one of her neighbors to use this new politicized language to write a letter to the permanent secretary in the Ministry of Lands and Settlements in Nairobi to report that one of her neighbors had stolen her piece of land. In the letter she related her futile attempts to get help from officials at the district level, from the local elders, and from the arbitration committee in charge of helping peasants swap their land.[22] Muthembi complained that the local leaders had allowed her neighbor, Alfred Abunza, to steal her land and register it under his name. She also revealed that after her husband's death twenty years ago, Abunza (her husband's cousin) had "promised to take care of her" as a widow—in others words, he intended to inherit her as a wife. But as it turns out, Abunza, like many of the other male "inheritors" whom we have come across, was more interested in acquiring her deceased husband's property than in acquiring a new wife.[23] He had tried to swindle her land from her once before, in 1968, but she had managed to sue him in court and get it back. However, this time, in March 1973, Abunza had reported her to the police, claiming that Muthembi was using his land illegally; she was arrested, taken to the police station, and released only after she produced documents showing that the land was hers. The following month, Muthembi recalled, Abunza bribed members of the arbitration committee, who then agreed to write a letter to the land registration officer in Kakamega asking him to register her land under his name. It worked. Muthembi was stunned by the malicious treatment she had received from all the men in her community: "Your Honour," she implored the permanent secretary, "I am a widow twenty years now, poor, and have been a *dutiful citizen* [my emphasis]; I have no one to help me in this matter except you."[24]

Sabeti Inyangala's case also reveals the blatant discrimination practiced against poor and illiterate widows by some of the male elders in their communities. In a letter to the DC of Kakamega, Inyangala stated that her brother-in-law, Zakayo Mwenesi, had altered the boundary that separated his land from hers by moving the hedges onto her land. He was, in effect, stealing a large portion of her land and trying to secure it by planting bananas and eucalyptus trees (such trees were commonly used as permanent markers of land ownership).[25] Her brother-in-law, like Abunza in the previous story, had "promised to take care" of his deceased brother's wife. But again, as was the case in many of these remarriages, Mwenesi was far more interested in his deceased brother's property than in Inyangala as a wife. Nevertheless, the Maragoli elders recognized this new, illegal boundary and allowed him to register his land as such—after receiving a significant cash bribe. Using her most eloquent Swahili, Inyangala's scribe told the DC that it was a shame that she was being denied *haki yake kwa inchi yetu* (her rights in our new nation). The letter noted that the local officials lacked *huruma* (sympathy) for widows like Inyangala. "Sina mtu mwegine anaweza kunisaidia" (I do not have anybody else to help me), the letter concluded.

≪∘≫

I came across nearly two hundred such letters from widows to the district officers and to the Ministry of Lands and Settlements, all of which expressed their strong dissatisfaction with land consolidation and registration.[26] The process was obviously not working out as intended—partly because bribery and corruption hindered the fair and equitable distribution of land, but also because the intensive labor involved in cultivating the larger plots made it difficult for widows to achieve any success.

The first step in land consolidation required that clansmen select among themselves about ten men who supposedly knew all the facts about local land ownership and whom they could trust to arbitrate, in a fair manner, the claims of all the members. The men were then joined by the chief and subchief of the area. Together they formed an arbitration committee, whose task was to help each member of their clan pool his or her scattered pieces of land by exchange with or sale to his or her neighbors; in this way, each small landholder could consolidate his or her land into one larger piece. Thereafter, the committee would request a land surveyor from the district headquarters to visit their area, measure the size of the property, and determine the nature of the soil to ascertain whether the exchange or sale was fair. The farmer was then expected to enclose his or her holding with live hedges to mark the permanency of the exchange. He or she was required to visit the nearest Ministry of Lands and Settlements office, usually located at the district headquarters in Kakamega, to get an official title to the land. The next step was for the farmer to go to the nearest agricultural department to request that an officer be sent to inspect the land again for its size and soil fertility (to be allowed to grow the new cash crops and to secure a government loan for this purpose, one had to have at least two acres). Then the struggle for membership at the nearest farmers' cooperative commenced (membership in a cooperative was crucial, because only cooperatives provided seeds and marketed the cash crops).[27] Overall, the whole process was so long and tedious that even under the most ideal conditions it took a farmer at least three to five years to get his or her land registered.

The conditions were usually far less than ideal for widows. In fact, widows' problems were particularly complicated—for instance, the issue of their husband's grave. Previously, graves had tended to erode quickly due to heavy rains, so that in a matter of a few years, after all the burial rituals were completed and the graves had been leveled, it was assumed that the spirits had been put to rest and would not come back to haunt the living. This freed people to move around easily from one piece of land to the next.[28] But beginning in the 1940s, as more Maragolis began to convert to Christianity, the population increased, and more and more people started to build permanent houses, the converts began cementing over the men's graves. This practice now made it difficult for widows to exchange their land, as many feared that the spirits of the dead continued to inhabit the intact graves. To leave the land, then, was to abandon one's ancestors.

Christian converts had begun to view the souls of the dead not as something to be feared but instead as something special to be preserved and remembered. A permanent grave helped to keep alive the memories of the dead, and so, in many cases, widows were ambivalent about exchanging their land with someone else for fear of blaspheming the memory of their husband.[29] Further, as we have seen, the gravesite had been important to widows because it was there that the hair-shaving ceremony (olovego) and the prayers for the bereaved (lisara) were performed.[30] It was at the gravesite that a widow composed and performed lamentations, singing loudly as she walked around the grave to remind members of her community that she was a widow and needed to be treated with sympathy. Because of the great emotional, economic, religious, and cultural significance of graves for widows, it was often hard for many of them to give up the land where they had buried their husband. Unfortunately, their reluctance contributed to the delays in getting their land inspected and consolidated. In fact, it appears that widows' tendency to delay their decisions gave rich Maragoli men ample time to fabricate situations by which they could steal the widows' land.

The fabrications manifested themselves in several ways. First, the arbitration committee was sometimes not chosen by the clanspeople as anticipated. Instead, the chief and subchiefs simply handpicked cronies whom they could manipulate as they pleased and who had very little knowledge of the history of local land ownership. Second, members of the arbitration committee were not paid a salary, and so they expected to receive bribes as compensation. Third, since the committee was large (at least twelve people), it was hard for its members to reach a consensus quickly, so those who wanted to speed up the adjudication of their land were further enticed to pay bribes. Rich men were able to bribe the officials to get their land registered before it was consolidated, even though the law stipulated that no title deeds could be issued until after land consolidation. Last, since most widows did not know how to read and write, they could be easily duped into thumbprinting documents that actually ended up transferring their land rights to the men. Once the men registered the widows' land under their own names, the widows found it difficult to petition for redress because registration, the last and the most important stage in land consolidation, was considered legally binding and permanent—unless of course one paid a handsome bribe. Beyond question, the corrupt and haphazard manner in which the arbitration committees functioned came to favor rich men over poor widows like Mademba, Muthembi, and Inyangala.[31]

Why did the local Maragoli elders not help out widows as they had done before? And why, we must ask, did widows not try to invoke the discourse of the worries of the heart to get the help they needed? After all, the men on the arbitration committee were Maragoli men familiar with the staging of *kehenda mwoyo* and the negative consequences of not meeting the widows' needs. It appears that the Maragoli elders, much like everyone else in the years immediately following independence, began to believe in the new leaders' rhetoric of rights and obligations; specifically, the elders believed that widows were no longer their sole responsibility, particularly since the government's newly elected black leaders had explicitly stated that it was their duty to help out the needy. That promise, the elders felt, provided them

with a convenient excuse to evade their traditional community responsibilities, and they took it up happily—without feeling guilty that they were elud-
ing their duties or, even more important, that their masculinity was in jeop-
ardy.[32] So now it was justifiable for the elders to ignore widows and instead
assist the well-off men who offered them bribes; furthermore, the elders
needed the money to meet their economic needs, since they did not receive
a salary from the government.

Unfortunately, then, one of the unintended consequences of the shift toward "national unity" was to break up small communities, weakening them
in ways that were detrimental to poor citizens like widows—citizens whom
the new government claimed it was going to protect.

⟨∞⟩

Because widows took the newly elected leaders at their word, the remedy
for their land problems was self-evident. Let down by local leaders and other
officers at the district level, they turned to the members of Parliament and
councilors for help.[33] At the very least, the elected officials owed them an
explanation. After all, during their campaigns they had promised to protect
and care for the poor as citizens if they carried out land consolidation and
registration as instructed. Quite legitimately, then, the widows felt that the
elected officials should take drastic action to help them; besides, these leaders depended on the votes of ordinary people for their jobs, unlike appointed
officials and the local elders the widows had been dealing with.

One morning in 1972, Maria Jemo, Erika Afandi, and Esteri Vugutsa, all of
whom had lost their land to unscrupulous brothers-in-law, set off on a three-
mile walk to their councilor's office in Vihiga to tell him their problems.
"We told him about all our worries of the heart with the chiefs and subchiefs,
how they were not treating us like widows or citizens. And we asked him
for help with land registration," said Afandi.[34] With a calm and reflective
voice, she related how Otiende, the councilor, had called all three of them
into his office and asked them to take turns and tell him their problems.
Their predicaments were similar to those of Mademba, Muthembi, and Inyangala; that is, they had become victims of forged title deeds, trespass, and
even blatant evictions, perpetrated by men who had professed protection.
In fact, Afandi told me that she had met numerous other widows who, like
herself, had visited the councilor's office complaining about corruption in
land consolidation and registration. "Ehhh!" she shrugged, "land consolidation was a terrible thing for widows," and she flicked her hand as if brushing
away flies. I asked her what the councilor had said to them. "He promised

that he would call a *baraza* [meeting of chiefs, subchiefs, and local elders] and also write a letter to the Ministry of Lands in Nairobi."

I had come across the councilor's letter in the archives, and he had indeed kept his promises to Afandi and her fellow widows; he had written a letter to the minister of Lands and Settlements in which he suggested that an "independent council be appointed to look into the kinds of corruption that the widows, the poor, and the illiterate were facing in western Kenya." "The method employed in land consolidation," he wrote, "is far from satisfactory." And, he added, "the most humiliating climax of malpractice is that widows, disabled, poor, and absentee persons have lost their land."[35] Believing that something could actually be done to help the widows, the councilor copied the letter to the PC of Western Kenya. Of course, the minister did not respond. The councilor's letter was, unfortunately, one among thousands of letters that the minister received from people all over Kenya, and he ignored the councilor's plea just as he had ignored previous letters on the topic.

I asked Afandi about the *baraza*. Her account was detailed: "The councilor spoke very shallowly about the need to stop corruption and said no more." The speech, she noted, "was very disappointing, because we widows who were facing land problems came to the meeting because we wanted him to address our specific problems. But he talked around the matter. He was a weak man and was not about to condemn the chiefs and subchiefs in front of everybody. So that is how land consolidation was a bad thing. You could not trust anyone. Everybody was corrupt."

Afandi kept emphasizing, disdainfully, that the councilor was a "weakling" because he lacked influence in higher circles. "See, the councilor did not know how to be a leader. When we elected him we thought he would use his influence to help us, but he never did. He did not do well for his family either." Strangely, part of her disappointment had to do with the fact that the councilor was not as "corrupt as other people and because of that he died a poor man, a very poor man; his family could not even afford money for his coffin; he was not interested in development." Apparently, the situation had become so bad that only the corrupt could be counted on.

To some degree, however, corruption had been forced upon them. More often than not, the new government's haphazard and random allocation of economic resources forced its officials to be aggressive if they hoped to secure some of the resources for members of their constituency. Crudely put, they had to be greedy and take as much as they could.[36] Looting, as Afandi bitterly instructed me, "was the way things worked."[37] And those who could not do it, people like Councilor Otiende, paid for it dearly. "I did not vote for him," Afandi confessed, "because he did not treat us well; he did not treat us like citizens." As it turns out, Afandi was not alone in thinking this way; the councilor did not get the opportunity to serve another term—he lost the next election.

Knowing that the councilor was "weak," the more determined of the widows sought help from the influential and wealthy MP Peter Kibisu. Kibisu, unlike Otiende, was a charismatic and well-to-do man. As an MP, Kibisu also had more connections and more ways to obtain economic resources than the councilor. And this influence was revealed in his high standard of living. His home in Maragoli was a Western-style stucco house equipped with modern amenities like electricity and piped water. He also owned a house in one of the middle-class suburbs of Nairobi where he stayed when attending National Assembly meetings. In addition, he drove a brand-new Peugeot and was always dressed in a natty three-piece suit.[38] Overall, he gave the impression that he was an important and prosperous man who had made it in the new nation, a man who could take good care of the ordinary citizens who had elected him.

Accordingly, when Jedida Karani could not get her land adjudicated because the officers preferred to serve those who had paid them bribes, she asked her daughter to write a letter of complaint to Kibisu. Karani informed him that she felt she was being discriminated against because she was a widow and had no money for bribes. "I am not supposed to bribe, I am a widow, the one who needs to be helped," wrote her daughter. She also told Kibisu that she believed, since Kenyans now lived in a "new world of Africa," that the government should ensure that everyone enjoyed *uhuru* (freedom) and that everybody should be treated as a *"mwanainchi* [citizen] in *inchi ya Kenya* [independent Kenya]."[39] Karani's letter was written in Luragoli, but interestingly, it contained many Swahili words, such as *mwanainchi, inchi ya Kenya,* and *uhuru,* that Karani and her daughter had heard Kibisu use in his public speeches to the Maragoli people. Clearly, Karani employed the Swahili words because she wanted to remind the MP of his promise to take care of ordinary people like herself. Only Swahili words, she believed, could vividly convey the message to Kibisu; only these words could show that she had taken the discourse of citizenship and development seriously.

Others did the same. On June 12, 1973, Elisi Iramema, a forty-five-year-old widow, also used the new language of citizenship when she wrote Kibisu complaining that the chief had allowed her neighbor to register her land under his name. She asked the MP, "How can *Mzee wetu* [our respected father] Jomo Kenyatta ask us to go back to our land if we have no land?" She demanded that the current "good" government, unlike the government of *wabeberu* (colonialists), provide "correct justice" to its *wanainchi* like herself.[40]

Elima Mise, another widow, also emphasized her status as a citizen in her letter to Kibisu. Writing in some of the most eloquent Luragoli I have ever read, Mise told Kibisu that she had been widowed for six years and that no one was helping her with her *kehenda mwoyo*. The local cooperative had even denied her membership and so she had no seeds to plant tea or coffee. She blamed the arbitration committee for her troubles, saying that they tended to interfere with the running of the cooperatives by promoting their own relatives' needs. He should do something: was not everybody entitled to *haki yao* (their rights) in *inchi ya Kenya*? "Is the law intended to serve only people with money and to deny the poor their rights?" she asked, noting that "every poor person was suffering due to the corruption of chiefs, subchiefs, and land officers." Like Iramema and Karani, she demanded that she be treated as a "loyal citizen."[41] Because Kibisu was a Maragoli, Mise believed that by combining the new rhetoric of citizenship with a description of her worries of the heart, she would get his attention. "He was a Maragoli man, and he had to treat us that way even in the new Kenya," Mise told me.[42]

In addition to these letters, several widows visited Kibisu at his home and office in Maragoli to complain about corruption in land consolidation and registration. He responded to their concerns by viciously condemning corruption in his speeches to the Maragoli public. On several occasions, he promised to introduce the matter in the National Assembly so that the president could hear the "troubles of *wanainchi*."[43] Widows and other poor Maragoli peasants applauded the news and looked forward to the time their troubles would be discussed on a national level.[44]

The discussion was overdue. Corruption in land consolidation and registration was not unique to western Kenya; peasants in other parts of Kenya, particularly in Central, Eastern, and Nyanza provinces, faced problems similar to those of Maragoli widows. So when, true to his word, Kibisu did introduce the topic in the National Assembly (in November 1973), the MPs from these other parts of Kenya eagerly joined him in cataloging the instances of corruption and reporting the suffering of the "the less educated people, the widows, the ignorant fellows." The MPs also warned that "the people outside are restless," and they urged the government to listen to what the "members who have been sent by the citizens to come and give the true picture have to say."[45] After weeks of these discussions, often punctuated by hyperbolic rhetoric, the members of the National Assembly voted to appoint a land consolidation commission.

The commission, however, failed to solve this difficult problem. Corruption could not be deciphered easily in a culture with a strong tradition of patron-client relations in which personal and political relationships were intricately connected. Moreover, since the members of the commission were expected to tour several districts, they did not get the chance to speak with many of the peasants who had complaints, so the subchiefs, chiefs, and land officers—the main actors in the corruption—turned out to be the commission's key informants. Predictably, much of the information they gave the commission tended to play down the problems that widows confronted. In the end, the commission's final report, like everything else in land consolidation and registration, tended to favor the local leaders at the expense of the poor and the widowed.

⋅◌⋅

By the end of the 1980s, many widows still did not have their land registered. A national survey showed that fewer than 30 percent of peasants in western Kenya had title deeds.[46] Of these, only about 5 percent could afford to plant the more lucrative crops such as tea or coffee. Jedida Karani was one of the fortunate few who had managed to register her land, and she spoke proudly of her efforts to get the MP to recognize her rights as a citizen. Close to seventy years old, Karani still looked youthful and continued to earn a decent income by growing tea. Many widows were not so lucky. Those unregistered did not qualify for loans, since they had less than two acres of land—the minimum requirement. But even those who met this requirement often decided not to take the loans because they feared (rightly) that the government would confiscate their land if they failed to pay back the loan. (The frequent failure of cooperatives to promptly pay farmers for their produce was a common cause of land confiscation for nonpayment of loans.) In many cases, the widows continued to grow maize for subsistence as they had done in the previous decades. In the end, the government's vision of rural areas dotted with farms growing remunerative cash crops that earned vast revenues for the development of the nation did not materialize. And for most of the widows land consolidation was a distressing failure.

The eloquent Elima Mise and the determined Elisi Iramema had not planted tea, and they regretted the missed opportunity: "corruption had discouraged us." They both mentioned the many tedious and prohibitive steps involved in the land consolidation and registration process: "It was one step after another, and if you did not have anybody to help you, you threw your hands up in the air [gave up]," noted Mise. In addition, both Mise and Iramema ended up speculating that letter writing might not have been the most effective way for widows to communicate their concerns to the MP. "It was very easy," Mise told me, "for the MP to not consider your specific problems as a widow when you wrote him a letter. He could simply say that he did not receive the letter. Then what could you do? What could you do when he spent half of his time in Nairobi?"[47] Clearly, letter writing had not provided answers as immediate and effective as the public and oral discourse of grief had done in previous years.

The widows' claims of citizenship, like the strategy of worries of the heart, allowed them to use the language that was intended to control them to claim their rights—with occasional successes. But as we have seen, it was never simple. Just as they had once achieved mixed results with the discourse of worries of the heart, the widows' reliance on the new language of citizenship was also ambiguous. Much of their success depended on their specific circumstances and on the personalities of the individuals involved—just as in the case of their worries of the heart.

There was one important difference, however. When the widows presented their worries of the heart to the village patriarch, the pleas for help and the pledges of assistance had been implicit. The promises of the postcolonial leaders had not been. They had been explicit, they had encouraged a sense of entitlement, and they had been trusted. So when the inexperienced widows were let down, they felt a stronger sense of betrayal, no doubt because the politicians' promises had been made so unequivocally, so earnestly, and with so much urgency. The appeal of patriotism had been seductive, but when the new officials eventually failed to meet their needs, the widows could not help but feel utterly duped, utterly let down by their own black leaders. They became bitter. And even if we can chalk up part of the confusion to the innocence and euphoria of independence, unfortunately in the following years even more discontentment and disillusionment were to beset the poor and widowed in Maragoli.

CHAPTER FIFTEEN

Rural Widows, City Widows, and the Fight for Inheritance

In 1967, as President Jomo Kenyatta continued his efforts to unify all Kenyans under one nation, he appointed a commission "to consider the existing laws of succession to property on death, the making and providing of wills, and the administration of estates."[1] The final goal of the Commission on the Law of Succession was to discern ways to "combine Hindu, Islamic, European, and customary laws into a single law that would apply to all Kenyans regardless of race, religion, or ethnic group." The goal was certainly ambitious, and throughout much of 1967 the commission, which included a person from each Kenyan ethnic, religious, and racial group, canvassed the rural areas, interviewing ordinary citizens and government officials about succession-related matters.

At the end of the year, the commission presented about 160 recommendations to the government that, sure enough, enthusiastically reiterated many of the points that the executive branch of government wanted to hear. The commissioners, for instance, unanimously agreed on the need to unify all laws of succession. The commission's report also listed several reasons that everyone should have the right to make a will and that there should be a uniform law of intestacy with regard to modern property such as "houses, shops, and other buildings constructed of permanent materials; motor cars and lorries; shares in businesses; life insurance policies; savings bank deposits, etc." Drawing on Britain's Family Provision Act of 1938, the commission urged the Public Trustee's office to exercise some discretion in cases where the deceased "failed to make reasonable provisions for the maintenance of his dependents" and, in such cases, "to ensure that the surviving wives are issued with the personal and household effects of the deceased."[2] As for other relatives of the deceased, the commission suggested that only persons maintained by the deceased prior to his death were entitled to inherit from him.

These were the commission's major recommendations, and they came to form an important part of the Law of Succession Bill and were the principal cause of a heated debate in the National Assembly. The bill also became, unfortunately, one of the major sources of conflict between rural Maragoli widows and other women whom their husbands had married or had affairs with in the cities.

When Charles Njonjo, then attorney general, introduced the commission's recommendations to the National Assembly in 1970 as the Law of Succession Bill, the mostly male members of the assembly "killed" the bill instantly with an almost-unanimous vote. There were two main arguments against the bill: that it inappropriately granted women too much power and that it was a Western import. The statements made against the rights of women were remarkably candid. "It is a great shame," declared one MP, a Mr. Ahmed, "for a law to give a wife an executive power to own property and also to have ten percent of her deceased husband's life interest." Mr. Kase, the assistant minister for Information and Broadcasting, was even more forthright in his complaint: "Ladies [single mothers] will use the Succession Act to inherit property of the deceased person [the father of their children]." This could not be allowed. And furthermore, under the proposed succession act, women would be able to claim an inheritance without even having to go through the trouble of a lawsuit. All of this was so unthinkable that Mrs. Onyango, one of only three female MPs, endorsed the sentiments of the male members. Unlike the men, however, she recognized the general usefulness of the bill; she expressed concern that, without the new act, some husbands would leave expensive properties not covered under customary law—"such as houses in the cities"—to their mistresses, with the result that their children and wives would be left destitute. On the other hand, she also worried that some women would use the act to claim that "two or three men are fathers of one child" and thus help themselves to an inheritance from more than one father.[3] As we will see, her concerns were justified.

The members' objection to the bill on the basis of its Western background was just as sharply vocal. "We do not need foreign customs, which are in this bill, to take care of our people," said Mr. Lotodo, the MP for West Pokot, in a typical dismissal of the bill. Likewise, Mr. Mutiso, the MP for Machakos, remarked that since many Kenyans were illiterate, it was going to be hard for them to write wills. "We are copying the Western way of life. What is wrong with our present system?" he asked, and then declared unconditionally that the bill "must go to hell." Mr. Ahmed also argued vehemently that the bill was irrelevant to a majority of Kenyan people and that the government was simply using the bill to force a foreign law on them. "If anybody wants to go and live under the British law," he announced to the National Assembly, "he should go to England." The bill, he claimed, is a "punishment to our people."[4] Because the MPs opposed the bill so vehemently, and because many ordinary Kenyans voiced similar objections in newspapers and other public forums, the attorney general decided to postpone further discussion of the bill for at least a year.

When the bill was reintroduced to the National Assembly, in July 1972, it was discussed on and off for a couple of months, but again, it was killed. This time, however, the assembly ended up discussing a new version of the bill—one that included all the women with whom a man might have had a significant and lasting relationship. According to the new bill, dependents included not just the wife of the deceased but "the wife or wives, or former wife or wives, and children of the deceased whether or not maintained by the deceased immediately prior to his death."[5] Many members of the National Assembly quickly and summarily dismissed this definition as being too "open" and "broad" and demanded that the attorney general assign a time limit after separation to determine when a wife actually ceased to be a wife.[6] They also wanted the attorney general to make a distinction between former wives staying with their parents and those who remarried, arguing that the latter should not have the right to inherit the property of their ex-husbands. Many of these concerns were fair and valid. Yet no agreement was reached, and again, after days of listening to these objections, some members of the National Assembly suggested that they postpone discussion of the bill and have the attorney general and his committee review the new issues.

Unfortunately, the committee members did not take their assignment seriously—in particular, they refused to determine who actually had the status of a "wife." So when the attorney general once again reintroduced the bill on October 5, 1972, the bill still retained the same vague definition of wife that the members had objected to earlier: it simply pronounced that the term *wife* meant simply what it meant and that it "includes a 'wife' who is separated from her husband." The bill continued to state blandly that the terms "'husband' and 'spouse,' 'widow' and 'widower' shall have a corresponding meaning."[7] There was nothing in the bill about the complicated issues of cowives, cohabitants, or divorcées. And yet this time, interestingly, no one questioned the senseless and vague definitions—except for the MP for Mombasa, Mr. Mwamzandi. When he asked the attorney general to clarify the definition of wife, the answer was even more evasive: the attorney general suggested that no legal definition was needed at the time and re-marked that "in the case of inheriting property the provision of who is to inherit the property is made later on." He also gave bland assurances that the word *wife* would mean here exactly what the bill stated, "but not some-body who has been thrown away for, say, 10 years or more."[8]

With these preposterously vague statements, the members of the Na-tional Assembly put all their questioning to rest and supported the bill, "trusting," as they claimed, that the attorney general would address the issues they had "disagreed on" before presenting the bill to President Kenyatta for his assent. And so on that fifth day of October 1972, the MPs voted almost unanimously to pass the Law of Succession, utterly oblivious to the long-term consequences of their actions for the lives of many Kenyan citizens. To many, their lackadaisical style of governance was shocking, their refusal to discuss the details of the bill disheartening.

The assembly's sudden about-face raises several questions. How could the members so quickly have changed their opinion, given the strength of their initial reservations? How could they come to support wholeheartedly the same law they had vehemently opposed the previous year? What exactly had changed in October 1972? The answer is really quite simple: 1972 was an election year. The most pressing issue was the upcoming national election in October, and the MPs were plainly more interested in wooing the votes of their constituencies than in discussing the details of the succession bill. In-deed, National Assembly records show that members consistently phrased their support for the bill in precisely the same broad terms—of the bill's "progressiveness" and the need to "unify all Kenyans under one nation" and "help families"—that President Kenyatta had employed when he initially sent the commission all over Kenya to drum up support for the bill in 1967. These slogans, as we have seen, reverberated nicely with voters' needs and expectations, more or less because they reflected the patriotic language of the new nation and made Kenyans feel like citizens.[9] By using such emotive phrases, politicians could associate the succession bill with the language of development, and even more important, they could associate the bill with "progress" rather than "Westernization" (the term they had used to reject the first reading of the bill). Unlike progress, Westernization had negative connotations. Not only did it imply copying European habits, but it also suggested abandoning African culture—and obviously, if the bill were the product of the liberal "West," then wives would end up owning property, women would become independent, and worse, families would be divided and national unity compromised—and, of course, no one dared to jeopardize "national unity" in order to uplift the status of women. If the bill was considered "progressive," however, none of this would happen, and the members could use it to get reelected.

The context in which the MPs discussed the bill is also important. When the Law of Succession Bill was first introduced in 1970, it was discussed against the background of the Affiliation Act and the Marriage and Divorce Bill. The Affiliation Act, ratified by colonial officials in 1959, gave women the right to sue the recalcitrant fathers of their children for child support. In 1969, however, the nearly all-male African National Assembly decided to repeal the act, claiming that it tended to exploit men.[10] The Marriage and Divorce Bill, on the other hand, was never passed—perhaps because its main goals had been to give women rights to matrimonial property and to their children in the event of divorce and also to make adultery a criminal offense. The majority of the assembly's male members dismissed the bill's provisions as Western-influenced customs that were, undoubtedly, intended to exploit men.[11] Given this history and the male members' apparent fear of exploitation, it is not surprising that the members of the National Assembly assumed that when the succession bill came up a few years later, it, too, was out to get men. No wonder, then, that the MPs instinctively and offhandedly dismissed it.

But the month of October 1972 had a different feel to it. As the time for reelection campaigns steadily approached, the MPs needed to appear more confident and more in control, and certainly less paranoid. Parliamentary reports for the month of October provide revealing details of the MPs' discussions of the bill, in which they calmly but consistently associated it with slogans of national unity and development. Their rhetoric this time was systematically and strategically tailored to the electorate. The Law of Succession Bill, many of them asserted, would "bring about national unity," "unify all tribes," and "allow men to marry women from other tribes." Even Muslim members, who initially had been against written wills, claiming that such wills interfered with Koranic law (which stipulated that a non-Muslim could not inherit from a Muslim), supported the bill, trusting, strange as it may sound, that the "Attorney General will see to it that there would be no conflict between this bill and the Muslim law." Those who praised the bill for helping families noted that it would help keep away relatives who might grab the deceased's property. Mrs. Gecaga, for example, said that "the majority of our people have been waiting for this bill because it is going to do

a lot of good not only for the women and the children but for the whole society." "The bill," she reiterated, "will prevent dubious relatives from claiming the property of the deceased." Another MP, Mr. Munene, similarly ex-
tolled the virtues of the bill, saying that it would prevent unknown relatives
from claiming that "they are relatives of the deceased and are entitled to
his property and his wife." Not surprisingly, Mr. Kibisu, assistant minister
for Labor and MP for Maragoli, wholeheartedly supported the bill, and he
stood up majestically in Parliament and proclaimed, "The fact that the law
was being introduced showed the progressiveness of Kenyan society and our
struggle for national unity."[12] The MPs applauded him. At long last, the Law
of Succession Bill was voted on, sent to the president, and ratified—and, as
of 1981, became the law of the land.

It soon became clear, however, that the hasty manner in which this law
was passed (as politicians vied for votes) had left unresolved important definitions of wife, child, and dependent—an oversight that was bound to cause
trouble, given the nature of traditional marriage, divorce, remarriage, and
multiple marriages. Politicians had simply pushed aside important issues
as they rushed to exit Parliament and campaign. There was no indication,
for example, of how the changing nature of marriage in rural and urban
areas would be handled. Neither was the issue of the Africans' attitudes
toward written wills considered seriously. And almost certainly, the neglect
of these issues became the cause of the bitter personal tensions that surfaced
between rural Maragoli widows and their urban "cowidows."

Because the succession law was discussed and ratified in such a haphazard
manner, it created all kinds of legal ambiguities. One of the more unusual
consequences was that the court performances of the plaintiffs and the de-
fendants took on a greater significance. Since there were no strictly legal definitions of wife, cowife, or dependent, such status had to be demonstrated—
and so the courtroom often became a stage where one's role was acted out
and one's adversaries dramatically confronted. This was particularly evident
when rural widows had to face their husbands' city widows (or, sometimes,
women their husbands had had affairs with). But the battleground was not
always level. All too often, city women had an edge over rural Maragoli
women. City women were conversant in Swahili and thus could express
themselves more eloquently than rural women (in the urban courts, one
widow told me, "one had to be fluent in Swahili in order to succeed").[13] And

since the contested property of their deceased husband was often located in urban areas, the rural widows were forced to travel long, punishing distances to unknown and alien urban courts.

This was, for example, the case with Beatrice Vusha. In October 1983, her husband, Peter Shego, died in a tragic car accident. Shortly thereafter, Vusha found herself caught up in a bitter conflict with Florence Karia, who had been living with Shego just before his death.[14] Vusha and Shego had been married in 1967 in an ideal Christian wedding that had taken place in the main Friends church in Maragoli. But the couple's Christian vow to remain faithful to each other "until death do us part" was sadly short lived. A few weeks after the wedding, Shego moved to Nairobi to work as a clerk 'at the post office, and a few years later he began a romantic relationship with Karia, a Kikuyu woman. By the time of his death, he had lived with Karia for at least five years, and they had had two children together. In their circle of friends they were viewed as husband and wife—even though Shego had neither paid bride-price nor taken their children to Maragoli to undergo the naming and hair-shaving rituals required of infants. In fact, Shego had kept their relationship a secret, refusing to mention it to either his parents or Vusha. She had had her suspicions—rumor had informed her of her Kikuyu cowife—but since her husband had repeatedly denied the rumors, she had decided to put her prodding to rest. As a teacher at a local primary school in Maragoli, Vusha earned enough money to feed the three children she had had with Shego, and he also sent her a small monthly allowance that enabled her to live relatively comfortably, at least by village standards.

But Vusha was in for a surprise. After she had buried her husband in the village, she left for Nairobi to collect his belongings, which consisted of furniture and other household goods. When she arrived, however, she found the house empty—Karia had taken all the belongings. Vusha immediately sought help and information from Shego's neighbors, and she was soon able to locate Karia. When she confronted the "other woman," she was met with indifference; Karia refused to give up the possessions. When Vusha threatened to sue her, she produced a will that stated that Shego had bequeathed all his Nairobi property to her. Vusha was devastated and immediately filed a case against Karia at Makadara Magistrate Court in Nairobi, but the judge ruled in favor of Karia, based solely on the evidence from the will and on the testimony of Karia and witnesses who verified strongly that Karia had cohabited with Shego for at least five years. In his ruling, the judge noted, "Five years of cohabitation and two children were signs that Shego was very serious about his relationship with Karia—even though they had not taken the necessary official steps to ensure that they were recognized as husband and wife."[15] Vusha painfully retraced her steps back to western Kenya, to her one and only piece of property: a small, defeated old house with mud-plastered walls and an old, rusting iron roof.

In August 1984, another rural widow, Erika Kenderi, faced a situation similar to that of Vusha. Her husband, Shem Onzere, who also worked in Nairobi, willed all his household belongings to his live-in girlfriend, Priscilla Boit. Kenderi and Boit had met only twice during the ten years Boit and Onzere lived together. In September 1983, Onzere became seriously ill, but Boit did not let Kenderi know of the illness. Instead, she single-handedly took care of Onzere until his death in July 1984. Angry and bereaved, Kenderi protested the will and proceeded to sue Boit in Makadara Magistrate Court in Nairobi. The judge, as in Vusha's case, ruled in favor of Boit, the girlfriend in the city. He noted that Boit was entitled to the property in Nairobi since she and Onzere had lived together for ten years and had had four children together. Arguing that Onzere and Boit's relationship was *kamili* (indisputable), the judge accepted the contents of the will as valid.[16]

In urban courts like Makadara, the urban women certainly had an advantage over the rural widows. Many of these courts were indeed intimidating for the rural women, and Makadara is a particularly unwelcoming place. Located just outside Nairobi's city center, in an area surrounded by several long rows of dilapidated, one-room cubicles that house railway workers and their families, Makadara Magistrate Court is a frightening place even for those accustomed to the city. Enormous piles of trash and open sewers affront the eye and assault the nose; vendors selling used clothing, fruit, and fried corn occupy makeshift stalls and noisily solicit customers with shouts that compete in vain with the roaring buses and *matatus* that swarm the nearby bus station. Beggars and turnboys sing discordantly to attract attention, adding to the unrelenting clamor, filth, and tension.[17]

The courthouse was built in the late 1940s when colonial officials decided that Africans who lived in urban areas needed a place to settle their disputes instead of returning to the countryside.[18] Like most courtrooms, it can be a very tense place. Nervous litigants sit on rough wooden benches surrounded by walls that were once white but are now brown with neglect. Occasional shouting matches or fistfights break out between men and women who cannot reconcile themselves to a judge's verdict. Rarely does one see a lawyer—perhaps because most of the people cannot afford one; more often than not, the judge simply decides cases based on the testimonies of the litigants and their witnesses. Swahili is the lingua franca.

Kenderi, Vusha, and at least ten other widows I spoke with who had confronted their urban "cowidows" in Makadara believed that they lost their cases because they were not nearly as aggressive as the city women and because they did not speak fluent Swahili. "My Swahili was the stammering kind, so I just mumbled through the court, and that is why that woman won the case," said Berita Mwariru, a fairly talkative and upbeat woman.[19] Her husband had died in a car accident, like Vusha's husband, but he had left no will. Marita Muteve, yet another widow whose husband had died in a *matatu* wreck, reported, "I did not know how to act in the court." Since her husband had failed to make out a will, Muteve was forced to face her cowidow (or "that woman," as she put it) in Makadara. Muteve elaborated on her ordeal in Nairobi, carefully reporting how everything, especially navigating the city, was intimidating to her since she had visited her husband's Nairobi residence only twice. "I waited for a long time before I could cross the road; the speeding cars, the crowded streets of people pushing you back and forth, scared me. Eeeh! It was not easy!"[20]

Vusha confirmed some of the experiences that Muteve and Mwariru had encountered. "My Swahili was the stammering kind," Vusha told me. "It was not good Swahili, so I think that is why I lost my case; I think that is why the judge sided with Karia." Tall and heavyset with strikingly big beautiful eyes that she used effectively, Vusha was in her late fifties when I talked with her in the mid-1990s. Here in the village at least she appeared imperious, and sitting next to her made me feel as if I should keep an eye on the nearest exit in case I uttered something she did not agree with. Yet even she was frightened by the harsh atmosphere in Makadara. "When I entered the courthouse," Vusha noted, "I realized that I had already lost my case before it even began. The Makadara court was a very foreign place for me, and so that is why I lost my case." She was convinced that the judge did not adhere to the new law of succession: "If the judge had followed the law," Vusha told me, "I would have won because the law would not have recognized that woman as a wife." In addition to her inability to express herself clearly in Swahili and her feeling of being out of place, Vusha felt she had also lost her case because the "Kikuyu judge was full of *ukabila* [tribalism] and did not treat me as a citizen."[21]

Kenderi believed that she lost her case to Boit for the same reasons. Like Vusha, she was in her late fifties when I interviewed her in the mid-1990s. She had a much quieter demeanor than Vusha but appeared in many ways to be more savvy. "You know, my Swahili was the stammering kind, while Boit looked the judge in the eye and spoke so fluently. And the judge understood her. . . . It was hard for me to tell the Kikuyu judge what I felt, what my worries were really about." The Makadara court, she also noted, "was a very foreign place for me, and so that is why I lost my case."[22]

Both Vusha and Kenderi felt that the judges' use of their husbands' wills was unfair. "To me," said Vusha matter-of-factly, "that will was simply a piece of paper; anybody could have written it, so I did not think that the judge would take it seriously. But when the judge acknowledged the will, I realized that the government had turned against me, turned against me completely, and I was no longer a citizen." She went on, incredulously, "How could Shego have known in advance that he was going to die in a car accident?" "Wills," she emphatically concluded, "are not things our people write," and anyway, the *serikali ya vakenya* (government run by Kenyans) should take care of widows like her.[23]

I asked Vusha whether it was indeed so wrong that Karia got the belongings since, after all, she also needed help in raising the children she had had with Shego. A chilly smirk distorted her lips, and she proceeded to instruct me about "illegitimate" children. "Those children," she began, "born out of wedlock, they were not recognized here in Maragoli because they were completely illegitimate. Did she ever bring them here to get their hair shaved or to be given names? See, that is the custom of our people, and Shego did not do this because he did not consider Karia to be his wife. So it was wrong for the judge to give her the property."[24]

Interestingly, questions of "legitimacy" came up even in cases like that of Kenderi, whose husband had taken his second wife to Maragoli and introduced her to his parents. Indeed, Boit, a member of the Nandi tribe, had visited Onzere's parents a few times, and his parents had, during one of those visits, organized a naming and hair-shaving ceremony to legitimize their four grandchildren. Yet according to Kenderi, Boit "was not a legitimate wife because Onzere never paid bridewealth for her, as was expected of legitimate marriages." She then walked me briefly through the history of her gradual acquiescence to her husband's polygamous marriage. "I was very angry when I heard that Onzere was living with her," she began. "Initially, I thought that they were just friends and that he was not that serious about her. But after they had a second child together, then a third, then a fourth, I gave up. I knew I had a cowife. So I stopped being angry. I came to terms with it. I knew I was now in a polygamous marriage, so I asked Onzere to bring Priscilla to Maragoli so that I could meet her. I wanted to meet her properly so that she knew I was around and that I was the senior wife. But I set my eyes on that woman, that Nandi woman, only four times, only four times before Onzere's death."[25]

Kenderi had another major complaint against her cowife. Like many of the women whose husbands lived with their second wife in an urban area, she felt financially deprived because she did not have much access to her husband's earnings: "I always felt like I was a spurned woman. That woman took over my husband completely, completely." It is important to note that the kind of property that widows like Vusha and Kenderi fought over was very different from the rural lands that widows before them had struggled over with their in-laws. Unlike the rather contested rural land, the property held in the city was property to which women had full rights. In the 1970s and 1980s, as many Kenyans began to move into the so-called middle class, they began to invest in "modern" property like sofas and beds, gas cookers, refrigerators, and expensive music systems. As an assistant manager at a bank in Nairobi, Onzere was one such middle-class fellow; he earned a sizable income and lived in the middle-class residential area of Buru Buru. So while Boit enjoyed the comforts of the modern middle class in Nairobi (she was notorious for her expensive wigs and platform shoes), Kenderi eked out a meager living in Maragoli, supporting her six children on her modest *shamba*. Onzere's material possessions were certainly significant, especially by village standards, and Kenderi wanted a share of them: "I knew there would be problems if something happened to Onzere. See, it is not that I did not want Boit to have some of the property, because she had contributed [Boit was a seamstress and owned her own business]. I just wanted us to share. After all, I had more children than she did, and I was the first wife."[26]

Precisely these questions about who is a "legitimate" wife or child and what constitutes a lawful written will had been neglected by the elected leaders of independent Kenya in their debate. The issue of written wills had become especially acrimonious. The main problem was obvious: time after time, propertied men—the middle-class "modern men"—failed to write wills at all. Indeed, wills were so uncommon that when they were presented, they were often viewed with suspicion; they were either automatically disqualified as forged documents or bitterly criticized for sowing ill feeling among kin who felt left out.[27] My queries as to why people did not write wills were usually greeted with comments like "people are ignorant about wills," "if you write a will you are looking for death," "it is not our custom," "wills are cumbersome," or, as Kenderi bluntly put it, wills are simply a "piece of paper." My informants felt so strongly about the difficulties generated by written wills that they often wondered what the fuss was about: "Why write a will? Just let nature take its course." Sadly, this often became a disingenuous way of avoiding the problem, of relegating the difficult decisions about property inheritance to those left behind or to judges using ill-defined laws. This attitude rarely helped widows.

In the colonial period, only African policemen and soldiers had the statutory right to create a will.[28] All other Africans were denied this right, since, according to colonial officials, the indigenous laws were sufficient for Africans handing down property. And it appears that Africans had preferred not to burden themselves with the bureaucracy of written wills when they could simply pass on their property orally. Men (very few women owned property) often made an oral will while on their deathbed.[29] The dying man, in the presence of a couple of elderly men, usually expressed his wishes as to how he wanted his property (usually land and livestock) distributed, and he assumed that the men would execute his will according to his wishes. If, on the other hand, a man died suddenly, his property was distributed based on indigenous law. As we have seen, his widow or widows were usually allowed usufruct rights to his land until his sons were old enough to inherit it. Cattle were often given to the dead man's sons, while goats, chickens, and other small animals remained in the ownership of the widow.

Typically cowidows tended to stay together on their husbands' land, tilling it and raising their children together. In rural settings senior cowidows had authority over younger/junior cowidows and were granted priority in decision making and in distributing property to the junior cowidows. In general, senior cowidows maintained control over domestic matters by, for instance, assigning household chores to their juniors, making key decisions during the initiation rituals of their junior cowidows' female children, and, most importantly, overseeing food distribution for everyone in the polygamous household.[30]

Of course, this arrangement hardly meant that cowidows always lived together in harmony. Sometimes junior cowidows felt that their senior cowidows did not give them a fair share of food or assigned too much work, and such discontent inevitably generated conflict. Competing cowidows usually turned to members of their extended families, especially their parents-in-law, to help solve these conflicts.[31] However, if the cowidows remained unsatisfied with their in-laws' decisions, they had the option of taking their grievances to the local colonial courts, where each could, if she wished, tactically display her worries of the heart to get what she wanted. Generally, though, the senior wife was likely to get a favorable decision, as officials were often careful to observe the gerontocratic rules that prescribed respect for older women.[32]

Just as important to dispute settlement was the fact that marriage customs like bridewealth were generally observed. Marriage was about honoring obligations to other people, including spouses' relatives and the children of the union. When a man married, he was obliged to pay bridewealth to the parents of his bride, which became a legal seal, as well as a social record, of the marriage. Because most men took seriously the steps that legalized marriages, senior wives recognized junior wives as their legal cowives and vice versa. So when the shared husbands died, the cowidows shared the rights to use his land and grow crops to feed their children. Normally, as we have seen, each widow and her children received a piece of land to cultivate and grow crops. However, the senior cowidow got first pick and therefore determined what land her junior cowidows could have access to and consequently what food they might grow on it.

Sometimes, though, children whom the deceased husbands had begotten out of wedlock came into the picture as competing heirs. When a man impregnated a woman out of wedlock, he was obliged to pay a heifer to the father of the woman and also to provide some basic foodstuffs to the mother of his child—at least a basket of maize, a chicken, and a bottle of milk. Since women who bore out-of-wedlock children did not often earn their parents a high bridewealth (they were, in fact, derogatively labeled "used goods"), the gift of the heifer was a way to make up for some of the bridewealth lost.[33] The food was meant to help the new mother regain the strength she had lost through childbirth and to ensure that she could produce enough milk to breast-feed the infant. The pregnancy compensation also implied that the man recognized the child to be his, and this, more or less, legitimized the child in the eyes of his wives. Typically, it was only when the mother of the illegitimate child was ready to marry someone else that she brought the child to live with his or her father. In some cases, the child was actually adopted by the older wife of the father. If the father of a male child died, the senior widow and the dead man's father usually made sure that the child received a piece of the family land to settle on.[34] Some accommodation was almost always made.

As Africans moved to the cities in large numbers after Kenya's independence, however, the practice of these traditions began to decline. One reason was that no one knew what to make of the new urban "wives." When men forged romantic relationships with women in the cities other than their wives, some of them from other ethnic groups, it became difficult to determine what a "legitimate" marriage was, especially because there was no law to turn to. Did marriage depend on the length of cohabitation? Was it the number of children the couple had? Was it the number of visits they made to the rural areas? Was it the payment of bridewealth? To complicate matters, men had begun to acquire modern possessions whose bestowal could not easily be determined by customary law. The new configuration of wives and property was perplexing in the extreme, and yet the members of the National Assembly continued to ignore the issues. Even as late as the mid-1980s, the question of what constituted a legitimate marriage had not been solved, and since there was no law to follow, it was left up to individual judges to determine—largely based on the litigants' performance in court—who was a legitimate spouse and who was not.[35] Most of the time the urban women did a better job of representing themselves because they were better versed in the protocols of the urban courts and could speak Swahili fluently. There was little chance, then, for the "stammering" rural widows who knew little Swahili and nothing of the cities to receive a fair trial.

It is hard not to conclude that the haphazard manner in which the succession bill was discussed and instituted was not significantly different from the manner in which the colonial officers had dealt with the problems they had encountered (remember, for instance, how the morality laws were instituted the 1940s). Ironically, by employing the vague rhetoric of development and national unity to cover up the citizens' real and practical concerns, the new leaders had acted as selfishly and irresponsibly as the colonial rulers before them. By forcing the inexperienced Maragoli widows to defend their rights in callous and indifferent urban courts, the postcolonial rulers were paradoxically beginning to resemble their colonial predecessors. It is difficult to say who was more unaware and indifferent. No matter who was making the decisions, the widows of Maragoli paid dearly.

Perhaps we are always ambivalent about our present circumstances, but the Maragoli men and women I visited were especially so, and they almost all looked back to former times with a stubborn wistfulness: *Maisha ga kare gari amarahi kabisa* (life was better in the colonial days than now). Despite the colonial introduction of warfare that killed many of their grandfathers and great-grandfathers, despite the fact that many of the colonial laws had been as harmful and indifferent to people as those instituted by the leaders of independent Kenya, despite the colonial officials' humiliating "moral" surveillances that had threatened and demeaned many of the widows' daughters, despite the officials' demeaning attitude toward widows' highly educated sons and their refusal to pay them the salaries they deserved, despite the few years of euphoria after gaining independence, despite the fact that widows were now theoretically citizens and not merely the subjects they had been under colonial rule, despite all this and more, most of the widows I spoke with in the mid-1990s felt that their lives and those of their parents had been better under colonial rule. "Avandu vitu vayononyia ivindu kabisa," they exclaimed (our people have ruined things).

I should not have been surprised at this answer, at the unconcealed nostalgia for the colonial years, for this is the kind of rhetoric that had assailed my young ears as I grew up in an independent Kenya. Still, their admiration for the British colonizers bothered me, and I could not rest until I had at least tried to understand how people remembered the two periods, especially those whose parents and grandparents (unlike mine) were not tied to the missionary or colonial enterprise. Surely, I thought, they will tell me what I want to hear; surely they will tell me that they and their parents and grandparents suffered greatly under colonial rule. But instead I heard comments like this: "We had schools and hospitals, and white people took good care of us. The white teachers were serious about teaching—not like the teachers of today, who take naps in the offices and never show up for class." "White people never deceived you; there was no corruption like we have now among our own people."

Of course, I knew about teachers who took naps instead of teaching and about the rampant corruption of public officials—I had experienced both; I also knew that Africa is the only continent on the planet that has gotten poorer in the past twenty-five years; and, of course, I knew from reading shelves of scholarly works that the policies of the new leaders were just as bad as those of their colonial predecessors and that African leaders had essentially stepped into the empty shoes of colonial administrators and governed with the same lack of discernment and compassion.[1] Yet it was hard to understand why my informants in Maragoli still revered their colonial leaders. How could they remember colonialism so fondly? How could they think of them so highly given the harmful and ill-conceived colonial policies that had often made their lives so difficult? I prodded my informants further, hectoring them with question after question until they threw up their hands and told me what exactly they had found so commendable about the colonial days: "We had schools and hospitals and roads, and white people took good care of us; white people never deceived us like our own people do now." They all said the same thing.

Obviously, they were not telling me what I wanted to hear, and I became exasperated—at them, but also at myself for not getting it, and also because I knew their attitudes would be difficult to explain. What I had wanted—and anticipated—was for the Maragoli men and women to tell me about the evils of colonialism, as my high school teachers had done a decade before. I had wanted them to fall in line with all that scholars had verified over and over again: the callous immorality of colonial rule. So why did my informants feel so incensed, so bedeviled, by the Africans leaders and not the colonizers before them? Surely as a fledgling graduate student I could not write a book that concluded with such politically incorrect statements and expect it to be well received.

I had to try a different angle; I changed tactics and began questioning my informants about what exactly they found troubling in their lives since Kenya's independence. I asked them about AIDS, for example, the merciless disease that was killing so many of their children and grandchildren. I had expected to provoke a spirited engagement, but they denied that this was a significant cause of their problems. They would answer somewhat dismissively, "We have heard of AIDS and that it is killing people, but many of

our young people die of TB or malaria, not AIDS." They insisted that the
fault was to be found in their own leaders. "Our people simply don't know
how to govern; they don't work hard and don't take good care of ordinary
people."

Try as I might, I could not get them to respond by bringing up the nation's
current problems, and so I thought I would remind my informants of the
colonial period and the moral panics engineered by colonial officials that
had harmed so many of them. Were not some of these experiences dreadful?
I posed this question to Tafroza Ebeywa, whose marriage, as you may recall,
had been terminated on her wedding day, with her guests forced to walk
away from the reception because her test for venereal disease, a mandatory
test instituted by colonial officials for every African preparing to get married,
was mistakenly found to be positive. Surely that shame was as bad as any
inflicted by the subsequent African administrations.

"Yes, it was hard to go through it," Ebeywa replied. "But I just persevered
and just tried to survive."[2] Now in her late seventies, she had lived almost
three decades in an independent Kenya under African rule.

"But, why," I asked, "can't you persevere under the hardships of the current government the way you did in the 1940s? Why do you judge the black
leaders so harshly?"

"See, it is hard to persevere when our own people are treating us badly,
when they are supposed to take care of us like they are our own people,"
Ebeywa answered vehemently.

I wondered how she could have become so disillusioned, and eventually
I gave up on finding the answers I wanted from my Maragoli informants. I
thought I would track down some of my high school teachers instead. Surely
my old teachers, men who had vociferously instructed us about the evils
of colonial rule (and carefully ignored the fact that Idi Amin had ruthlessly
forced them into exile in Kenya)—surely they would tell me exactly what I
wanted to hear.

"Life is definitely worse now than in the old days," one of them said,
frowning.[3] "Our leaders have failed us," sighed another.[4]

What exactly was wrong with these men? I wondered. Why had they
revised their passionate judgment upon colonial iniquity? Was it merely
personal disappointment, or perhaps the despondency one feels as one an-
ticipates old age, that odd melancholy one feels when youth is gone but old
age has not yet arrived?

Of course, it may have simply been something more tangible. Almost
all of my Maragoli informants, as well as informants from other parts of
rural western Kenya, felt that their living standards had sharply deteriorated

since independence. "Life is very hard in Kenya these days; the white people treated us better," said Mary Otieno, from the neighboring Bunyore ethnic group.[5] "Our leaders don't care about us anymore; at least white people told the truth and were not corrupt," remarked Christopher Musira, another seventy-year-old from Bunyore.[6] Somehow it always came back to failed politicians.

Whoever is to blame, we must not underestimate the Maragoli disappointment in their government and how it has altered their outlook, though it is not exactly clear what we should make of their assessments of colonial and postcolonial rule or what exactly they intended to convey by praising colonialism. They may have simply found in me an opportunity to vent their frustrations—I was, after all, an educated villager who had left for America and who might be able to help. Besides, they would face no repercussions in expounding their problems to me. No doubt some of their longing for the colonial days also arose from the general human tendency to romanticize the past.

And yet I think there is more to it than finding a neutral audience or indulging in simple nostalgia. It is just as likely that exaggerated expectations of postcolonial bliss and the subsequent failure of the new leaders to meet the needs of ordinary citizens influenced the attitudes of many of my informants. It is possible that some of them may have been too forgiving in their judgments of colonial rule precisely because they did not expect much from the colonial rulers and were therefore more grateful than they should have been for the slightest attention. It is also possible, as Mahmood Mamdani has argued about Uganda and South Africa, that the Maragoli understood some of the harsh colonial policies as emanating from the African colonial intermediaries, such as chiefs and local elders, rather than directly from the colonizers themselves, and they therefore felt that colonial rule never affected them directly.[7] Moreover, it may be, as Kwame Anthony Appiah has suggested about Ghana and other parts of West Africa, that the "cognitive and moral traditions" of the Maragoli were powerful enough to ward off the various colonial assaults they faced. In other words, the interdependence of living in small, close-knit communities governed by traditions—like the "worries of the heart" discourse—immunized them from the more adverse effects of colonial rule.[8]

No doubt these explanations can help us understand the memories of colonial rule in Maragoli. But I would also suggest that it is not simply a matter of perception. One of the first things I noticed during my research in the mid-1990s was that the living conditions in rural western Kenya were indeed much poorer than I remembered as a schoolgirl. Many people lacked food, clothing, and clean water. In many ways, the postcolonial period in western Kenya appeared to me now, to borrow Achille Mbembe's description of postcolonial Cameroon, as a "time of unhappiness," a time of "anxious virility" in which the people wanted to assert themselves but were undone by poverty and the impotence of their corrupt government.[9] Indeed, many villagers in rural western Kenya exhibited the same "nervous conditions" that Tsitsi Ndangarembga saw in rural Zimbabwe—and they, too, seemed to have been rendered lethargic and helpless.[10] They had lost the sense of opportunity they had felt while living under the colonial government. Rarely did I hear of the kind of self-determination exhibited by many of those who had lived in the missions, and rarely did anyone express confidence that there were institutions or administrators that could be turned to for assistance. It was also ironically evident that the enthusiastic desire for national unity after independence had eroded the networks of mutual dependency that had helped sustain small communities—and now there was almost no one able or willing to listen to the "worries of the heart." And many, like Tafroza Ebeywa, were not willing to be patient with their black leaders or to recognize, as scholars like Basil Davidson might wish, that these leaders had inherited the many mistakes of their colonial rulers and thus needed time to sort out the problems.[11]

All in all, their spirits seemed to me as low and heavy as the footfall of an elephant, and though there may be countless reasons for their deep disenchantment, I suspect that many of my informants were at least partially motivated to praise the colonizers because they wanted to see change in the new government, not necessarily because they had liked colonial rule. Every one of them wanted the black leaders of independent Kenya to take responsibility for the social and economic problems they faced, and they wanted them at the very least to provide basic social amenities like clean water and schools for their children. Or, as one informant poignantly put it, they wanted their leaders not to "fail" them.

These troubles are not likely to be remedied easily or quickly. Though, in the end, if we really want a deeper understanding of African experiences in both the colonial and the postcolonial periods, I think we have to begin paying as much attention to intra-African relations as we have to the relations between colonizers and colonized. This ultimately calls for a more careful analysis of how local people came to think and believe as they did about the colonizers, the missionaries, the new black leaders, and, for that matter, their own families, neighbors, and communities. Along with the stories they told about their colonizers, we need to hear the stories Africans told among themselves about themselves; we also need to hear firsthand the ways they related to each other at the markets, *shambas*, churches, and watering holes, all the places where they reveal their most intimate expectations, hopes, and disappointments. It would help to listen in on their conversations and take seriously their evaluations of the changes in the twentieth century—even if they contradict our own personal, intellectual, and political thinking.

GLOSSARY

amajini. Mermaids.

amanani. Ogres.

amasahi mahiu. Warm blood.

amasahi mazilu. Cold blood.

avamenya. Refugees.

baraza. Meeting of chiefs, subchiefs, and local elders.

Blue Band. A brand of margarine.

bwana. Boss, master, Mr.

chai. Tea brewed with milk and sugar.

changaa. A potent local alcoholic drink made from millet.

duka. A shop.

fundi. Carpenter.

harambee. Cooperation.

hukumu. Judgment.

idisi. Young men's hut.

iliini. Straight line; Christian villages.

kehenda mwoyo. Worries of the heart.

kesonga. The long pole extending from the ground up through the center of the straw roof of a circular mud house; also used to refer to the whole house.

kokola buvira. Witchcraft.

leso. A piece of cloth that women tie around their waist or head.

lisara. A day of prayer in honor of a deceased person.

maendeleo. Progress; civilization.

masikini. Poor person.

masikini tu. Just poor.

matatu. Minibuses, a widely used form of transportation in Kenya.

mstaarabu. Modern person (plural, *wastaarabu*).

mwanainchi. Citizen (plural, *wanainchi*).

mzungu in Swahili; *msungu* in Margoli. White person.

nyanza. Lake.

olovego. Hair-shaving ceremony performed by the relatives of the deceased after burial; it is intended to be a cleansing ritual.

omwene hango. Owner of a home.

shamba. Garden, land.

teminari. Tribunal; Local Native Council.

tsimbavasi. Sympathy.

ugali. A thick paste made from corn or millet flour that is a staple in western Kenya.

uhuru. Freedom; independence.

ukabila. Tribalism.

ummenya. Refugee.

ustaarabu. Civilization; modernity.

wabeberu. Colonizers; colonialists.

wanainchi. See *mwanainchi.*

wastaarabu. See *mstaarabu.*

yambo. Hello. How do you do?

NOTES

INTRODUCTION

1. The population of Maragoli grew steadily and rapidly throughout the twentieth century. In 1948, for example, the population was estimated at 750 people per square mile, and by 1969, it had nearly doubled to 1271. For details, see Joseph Ssennyonga, "Maragoli's Exceptional Population Dynamics: A Demographic Portrayal," Institute of African Studies Paper 108 (University of Nairobi, 1978).

2. Betty Potash, "Widows in Africa: An Introduction," in *Widows in African Societies: Choices and Constraints,* edited by Betty Potash (Stanford, CA: Stanford University Press, 1986), 1. For recent figures for widowhood rates in Africa, see Maria Cattell, "African Widows: Anthropological and Historical Perspectives," *Journal of Women and Aging* 15, no. 2 (2003): 49–66; Ian Timaeus and Angela Reynar, "Polygynists and Their Wives in Sub-Saharan Africa: An Analysis of Five Demographic and Health Surveys," *Population Studies* 52, no. 1 (2003): 145–62; and Uche Ewelukwa, "Postcolonialism, Gender, and Customary Injustice: Widows in African Societies," *Human Rights Quarterly* 24, no. 2 (2002): 420–57.

3. For examples of ethnographic microhistories, see Landeg White, *Magomero: Portrait of an African Village* (Cambridge: Cambridge University Press, 1987); David W. Cohen and E. S. Atieno Odhiambo, *Siaya: The Historical Anthropology of an African Landscape* (Athens: Ohio University Press, 1989); Nancy Rose Hunt, *A Colonial Lexicon of Birth Ritual, Medicalization, and Mobility in the Congo* (Durham, NC: Duke University Press, 1999); and T. C. McCaskie, *Asante Identities: History and Modernity in an African Village, 1850–1950* (Edinburgh: Edinburgh University Press, 2000).

4. E.g., Rose Mwenesi, Central Maragoli, June 27, 1995; Leah Andiah, North Maragoli, Sept. 14, 1994.

5. Berita Mwariru, South Maragoli, June 12, 1995.

6. For a review of this literature, see Cattell, "African Widows." Specific examples from western Kenya include Edwins Laban Moogi Gwako, "Widow Inheritance among the Maragoli of Western Kenya," *Journal of Anthropological Research* 54, no. 2 (1998): 173–98; and Susan Reynolds Whyte, "The Widow's Dream: Sex and

Death in Western Kenya," in *Personhood and Agency: The Experience of Self and Other in African Cultures,* edited by M. Jackson and I. Karp (Washington, DC: Smithsonian Institution Press, 1990), 56–78.

7. Gwako, "Widow Inheritance among the Maragoli of Western Kenya."

8. Mahmood Mamdani, *Citizen and Subject: Contemporary Africa and the Legacy of Late Colonialism* (Princeton, NJ: Princeton University Press, 1996); Kwame Anthony Appiah, *In My Father's House: Africa in the Philosophy of Culture* (New York: Oxford University Press, 1992); and Achille Mbembe, *On the Postcolony* (Berkeley and Los Angeles: University of California Press, 2001).

9. A. Adu Boahen carried out the seminal research on colonial rule. See his *African Perspectives on Colonialism* (Baltimore: Johns Hopkins University Press, 1987).

CHAPTER ONE

1. C. W. Hobley, *Kenya, from Chartered Company to Crown Colony: Thirty Years of Exploration and Administration in British East Africa,* 2d ed. (London: Frank Cass, 1970), 80.

2. For example, when C. W. Hobley, the first subcommissioner of western Kenya, asked the people in western Kenya what the term *Kavirondo* meant, they replied, "It is the name which the people of the south side of Kavirondo gulf [of Lake Victoria] apply to the people of the north side." However, they told him that it was a term used only when the two groups would meet at "a dance and smoke bhang and sing about old times." Moreover, Hobley was told that the people of the south side used the term *Kavirondo* to refer to those on the north side because they fought them and drove them away; apparently, the term was originally "more or less an epithet or reproach." See C. W. Hobley, "Anthropological Studies in Kavirondo and Nandi," *Journal of the Royal Anthropological Institute* 1, no. 2 (1903): 359.

3. South Kavirondo, on the other hand, was the district south of Lake Victoria, the region inhabited by Luo and Kisii.

4. For a rich ethnography of the Maragoli in the 1930s, see Günter Wagner, *The Bantu of Western Kenya,* 2 vols. in 1 (London: Oxford University Press, 1970). For recent studies of the Maragoli and other related Luyia groups, see Judith Abwunza, *Women's Voices, Women's Power: Dialogues of Resistance from East Africa* (Peterborough, ON: Broadview Press, 1997); and Robert Maxon, *Going Their Separate Ways: Agrarian Transformation in Kenya, 1930–50* (Cranbury, NJ: Associated University Presses, 2003). For a general history of the Luyia people, see Gideon S. Were, *A History of the Abaluyia of Western Kenya, 1500–1930* (Nairobi: East African Publishing House, 1967).

5. Thomson published his impressions of western Kenya in 1885 in *Through Masai Land.*

6. Joseph Thomson, *Through Masai Land,* 3d ed. (London: Frank Cass, 1968), 276, 284, 292.

7. Ibid., 280, 270.

8. Henry Morton Stanley, for example, compared the Masai to the Apaches and Comanches of the United States and argued that any European or American killed while traveling through Masailand should be considered a martyr. See Robert I. Rotberg, introduction to *Through Masai Land*, by Joseph Thomson, 3d ed., vi–vii.

9. For biographies of Thomson, see Rev. J. B. Thomson, *Joseph Thomson: African Explorer* (London: Sampson Low, Marston, 1897); and Robert I. Rotberg, *Joseph Thomson and the Exploration of Africa* (London: Chatto and Windus, 1971).

10. Rotberg, *Joseph Thomson*, 302.

11. For a study of the impact of the Arab/Swahili slave trade on the daily lives of the eastern African people, see Marcia Wright, *Strategies of Slaves and Women: Life-Stories from East/Central Africa* (London: James Currey, 1993). Charles Ambler's *Kenyan Communities in the Age of Imperialism: The Central Region in the Late Nineteenth Century* (New Haven, CT: Yale University Press, 1988) is a marvelous study of eastern Kenya during this period.

12. Kenneth R. Dundas, "The Wawanga and Other Tribes of the Elgon District, British East Africa," *Journal of the Anthropological Institute of Great Britain and Ireland* 43 (1913): 19–75; Eric Barker, *A Short History of Nyanza* (Kampala, Uganda: East African Literature Bureau, 1950), 2–5.

13. Beads were a form of currency.

14. Joseph Thomson, *Through Masai Land*, 284.

15. G. H. Mungeam, *British Rule in Kenya, 1895–1912* (Oxford: Clarendon Press, 1966), 11–17.

16. G. H. Mungeam, introduction to *Kenya, from a Chartered Company to Crown Colony*, by C. W. Hobley, 2d ed. (London, Frank Cass, 1970), v.

17. Hobley, *Kenya*, 67–74.

18. Bruce Berman and John Lonsdale, *Unhappy Valley: Conflict in Kenya and Africa* (Athens, OH: Ohio University Press, 1992), 45–74; and R. Cummings, "A Note on the History of Caravan Porters in East Africa," *Kenya Historical Review* 1, no. 2 (1973): 109–38.

19. Hobley, *Kenya*, 82.

20. Ibid., 83, 85.

21. "Report on the Expedition against the Kitosh, Kabras, and Kikelelwa, by C. W. Hobley, September 13, 1895," in *Kenya: Select Historical Documents, 1884–1923*, by G. H. Mungeam (Nairobi: East African Publishing House, 1976), 121.

22. R. Meinertzhagen, *Kenya Diary, 1902–1906* (London: Longmans, 1957), 60–74; Robert Tignor, *The Colonial Transformation of Kenya: The Kamba, Kikuyu, and Masai from 1900–1939* (Princeton, NJ: Princeton University Press, 1976); and Forbes Munro, *Colonial Rule and the Kamba: Social Change in the Kenya Highlands, 1889–1939* (Oxford: Clarendon Press, 1975).

23. Mungeam, introduction to Hobley, *Kenya*, xii.

24. Hobley's writings include "Eastern Uganda: An Ethnological Survey," *Journal of the Anthropological Institute* 31 (1902): 234–45; "Anthropological Studies in Kavirondo and Nandi"; *The Ethnology of the A-kamba and Other East African Tribes* (London: Frank Cass, 1910); and *Bantu Beliefs and Magic* (London: Frank Cass, 1922).

25. Mungeam, introduction to Hobley, *Kenya*, x.

26. "C. W. Hobley's Attempt to Work through Local Leaders, December 21, 1898," in Mungeam, *Kenya*, 123.

27. "The Philosophy of Force as Expounded by A. H. Hardinge, April, 1897," in Mungeam, *Kenya*, 129.

28. "C. W. Hobley's Views on Punitive Patrols, September 22, 1896," in Mungeam, *Kenya*, 122; and Berman and Lonsdale, *Unhappy Valley*, 54–55.

29. Berman and Lonsdale, *Unhappy Valley*, 156.

30. "C. W. Hobley's Views on Punitive Patrols, September 22, 1896," in Mungeam, *Kenya*, 122.

31. A. T. Matson, *Nandi Resistance to British Rule, 1890–1906* (Nairobi: East African Publishing House, 1972).

32. Hobley, *Kenya*, 110.

33. Ibid., 89.

34. "C. W. Hobley's Views on Punitive Patrols, September 22, 1896," in Mungeam, *Kenya*, 122.

35. Hobley, *Kenya*, 124.

36. Berman and Lonsdale, *Unhappy Valley*, 53.

37. R. I. Rotberg, introduction to *Imperialism, Colonialism, and Hunger: East and Central Africa*, edited by Robert I. Rotberg (Lexington: University of Kentucky Press, 1983), 1–6; J. Ford, *The Role of Trypanosomiases in African Ecology: A Study of the Tsetse Fly Problem* (Oxford: Clarendon Press, 1971); and M. H. Dawson, "Smallpox in Kenya, 1880–1920," *Social Science Medicine* 13B, no. 4 (1979): 245–50.

38. Hobley, *Kenya*, 105.

39. Ibid., 118.

40. Ibid., 104.

41. Norman Leys, *Kenya* (London: Hogarth Press, 1925), 76; and Berman and Lonsdale, *Unhappy Valley*, 23, 25.

42. Hobley, *Kenya*, 42.

43. Ibid., 53.

44. Ibid., 11.

CHAPTER TWO

1. Elton Trueblood, *The People Called Quakers* (New York: Harper and Row, 1966), 122–23, 230; Thomas D. Hamm, *The Transformation of American Quakerism: Orthodox Friends, 1800–1907* (Bloomington: Indiana University Press, 1988).

2. Trueblood, *People Called Quakers*, 123.

3. Willis Hotchkiss, *Sketches from the Dark Continent* (Cleveland: Friends Bible Institute, 1901), 47, 150. See also his *Then and Now in Kenya Colony: Forty Adventurous Years in East Africa* (New York: Fleming H. Revell, 1937), 42–50; and *American Friend* (hereafter *AF*), Nov. 1902, 6.

4. *AF*, Nov. 1902, 6.

5. Earlham College (hereafter EC): *Report of the Friends African Industrial Mission* (1903), 6.

6. Ane Marie Bak Rasmussen, *A History of the Quaker Movement in Africa* (London: British Academic Press, 1995), 46.

7. *AF*, Sept. 1902, 7.

8. Edna Chilson, *Arthur B. Chilson: The Ambassador of the King* (Wichita, KS: privately printed, 1943), 19.

9. Hobley, *Kenya*, 109.

10. EC: letter from Hotchkiss to *AF*, July 16, 1902.

11. Hobley, *Kenya*, 109.

12. EC: letter from Hole to *AF*, Aug. 7, 1902.

13. EC: letter from Hotchkiss to *AF*, July 16, 1902.

14. EC: letter from Hole to *AF*, Aug. 7, 1902.

15. Arthur Chilson's diary, Aug. 10, 1902, in Edna Chilson, *Arthur B. Chilson*, 28.

16. Arthur Chilson's diary, Aug. 17, 1902, in Edna Chilson, *Arthur B. Chilson*, 29.

17. EC: letter from Hotchkiss to *AF*, Dec. 18, 1902.

18. Ibid.

19. EC: letter from Virginia Blackburn to her parents, July 25, 1903.

20. EC: letter from Emory Rees to *Friends Missionary Advocate* (hereafter *FMA*), Apr. 1904, 20.

21. EC: letter from Virginia Blackburn to her parents, Dec. 11, 1905.

22. Edgar H. Stranahan, *Friends African Industrial Mission* (Plainfield, NJ: Quaker Press, 1905), 4.

23. Errol Elliott, *Quakers on the American Frontier: A History of the Westward Migrations, Settlements, and Developments of Friends on the American Continent* (Richmond, IN: Friends United Press, 1969), 45–68.

24. Stranahan, *Friends African Industrial Mission*, 3.

25. *AF*, Nov. 1 1902, 889.

26. *AF*, Dec. 1902, 905.

27. Stranahan, *Friends African Industrial Mission*, 6.

28. *African Report* (hereafter *AR*), Jan. 1906, 3.

29. EC: letter from Virginia Blackburn to her parents, May 2, 1905.

30. EC: letter from Emory Rees to *FMA*, Apr. 1906, 20.

31. *AR*, May 1907, 1–2.

32. *AR*, July 1907, 4.

33. *AR*, May 1906, 3.

34. *AR*, Jan. 1906, 2.

35. For stories of white cannibalism elsewhere in Africa, see Hunt, *Colonial Lexicon*, 118–34.

36. *AR*, Mar. 1905, 1.

37. *FMA*, Mar. 1906, 23.

38. *AR*, Oct. 1906, 3.

39. *AR*, June 1906, 2.

40. *FMA*, June 1906, 3.

41. *AR*, Oct. 1906, 4.

42. *AR*, June 1907, 2.

43. Sept. 12, 1994.

44. EC: Virginia Blackburn's Letters, 1904–10; and *AR*, Jan. 1908, 4.

45. *FMA*, Jan. 1908, 2.

46. *AR*, May 1908, 2; *AR*, Oct. 1908.

47. *AR*, May 1908, 3.

48. John Kefa, West Maragoli, Oct. 12, 1994.

CHAPTER THREE

1. West Maragoli, Oct. 12, 1994.

2. North Maragoli, Oct. 17, 1994.

3. South Maragoli, May 20, 1995.

4. North Maragoli, Dec. 2, 1994.

5. North Maragoli, Apr. 12, 1995.

6. West Maragoli, June 1, 1995.

7. West Maragoli, April 3, 1995.

8. For example, Mary Kakiya, Stella Kisivula, Leah Andiah, and Berita Vugutsa, North Maragoli.

CHAPTER FOUR

1. This theme has also been explored by Keletso Atkins, *The Moon Is Dead! Give Us Our Money! The Cultural Origins of an African Work Ethic, Natal, South Africa, 1843–1900* (Portsmouth, NH: Heinemann Press, 1993); and Jean Comaroff and John Comaroff, *Of Revelation and Revolution: The Dialectics of Modernity on a South African Frontier*, 2 vols. (Chicago: University of Chicago Press, 1991–97).

2. EC: letter from Virginia Blackburn to her parents, June 19, 1904.

3. *AR*, May 1907, 4.

4. Ibid., 2.

5. EC: letter from Virginia Blackburn to her parents, Jan. 15, 1905.

6. See, e.g., Jean Comaroff and John Comaroff, *Of Revelation and Revolution*, 2:274–322.

7. *AR*, July 1907, 2.

8. EC: Virginia Blackburn's letter to her parents, Aug. 26, 1903.

9. EC: Roxie Reeve's diary, May 2, 1918.

10. *AR*, Oct. 1908, 4.

11. *AR*, Jan. and Mar. 1912, 5.

12. *AR*, May 1907, 4.

13. *AR*, Oct. 1908, 4.

14. EC: letter from Virginia Blackburn to her parents, Oct. 14, 1903.

15. Ibid.

16. *AR*, May 1908, 4.

17. Wagner, *Bantu of Western Kenya*, 90–106.

18. *AR*, Jan. 1912, 2.

19. Ibid., 1.

20. *AR*, Feb. 1914, 4.

21. For details of Reeve's experiences in western Kenya, see Samuel Thomas, "Gender and Religion on the Mission Station: Roxie Reeve and the Friends African Mission," *Quaker History* 90, no. 2 (2001): 24–46.

22. EC: letter from Roxie Reeve to friends in Richmond, IN, July 9, 1918.

23. EC: Roxie Stalker's diary, Dec. 25, 1918. It appears that it was female missionaries and, especially, unmarried female missionaries who received such challenges from the converts (or perhaps only female missionaries were willing to write about the tensions between them and the converts). In general, single female missionaries did not always have an easy time, as they were also often mistreated and patronized by male missionaries. For details, see Samuel Thomas, "Gender and Religion on the Mission Station"; Margaret Hope Bacon, "Quaker Women in Overseas Ministry," *Quaker History* 77, no. 2 (1988): 84–99; Nancy Rose Hunt, "'Single Ladies on the Congo': Protestant Missionary Tensions and Voices," *Women Studies International Forum* 13, no. 4 (1990): 370–97.

24. Mira Bond, *FMA*, June 1918, 6.

25. EC: Roxie Stalker's diary, Feb. 13, 1923.

26. Ibid., Sept. 11, 1918.

27. *AR*, Jan. 1919, 2.

28. *AR*, Feb. 1914, 2.

29. Ibid.

30. *AR*, May 1910, 6.

31. EC: letter from Roxie Reeve to home, Jan. 12, 1918.

32. EC: Roxie Stalker's diary, Oct. 12, 1918.

33. Ibid., Aug. 15, 1919.

34. *AR*, Dec. 1919, 2.

35. *AR*, July–Sept. 1919, 3.

36. *AR*, May 1919.

37. *AR*, June 1919, 2.

38. Clifford Giplin, "The Church and the Community: Quakers in Western Kenya, 1902–1963" (PhD diss., Columbia University, 1976), 92–108.

39. *AR*, Mar. 1920, 4.

CHAPTER FIVE

1. North Maragoli, Jan. 12, 1995.

2. A *leso* or *kanga* is a colorful cotton cloth worn by women in many parts of eastern Africa.

3. Wagner, *Bantu of Western Kenya*, 95.

4. West Maragoli, Sept. 26, 1994.

5. South Maragoli, Jan. 15, 1999.

6. West Maragoli, June 30, 1995.

7. Walter H. Sangree, *Age, Prayer, and Politics in Tiriki, Kenya* (New York: Oxford University Press, 1966), 43; John Rowe, "Kaimosi: An Essay in Mission History" (Master's thesis, University of Wisconsin, Madison, 1958).

8. Rose Mutongi, West Maragoli, Sept. 12, 1995.

9. Rose Mutongi, West Maragoli, Feb. 12, 1999; and Fairfax, VA, USA, June 15, 2005.

10. *FMA*, May 1923, 3.

11. Mary Vugutsa, West Maragoli, Jan. 5, 1999; and Matayo Mwenesi, West Maragoli, June 7, 2004.

12. J. W. C. Dougall, *The Village Teacher's Guide: A Book of Guidance for African Teachers* (London: Sheldon Press, 1931), 2–4.

13. Shem Vulimu, South Maragoli, May 6, 1995.

14. Kavetsa Adagala, "Language and Literature in Primary Schools: Lulogoolo ne Tsing'ano Tsya Valogooli," Institute of African Studies, Paper 121 (University of Nairobi, 1979), 7.

15. Elizabeth Munday, "Birth and Death and In-Between: Children in Wanga Society," Institute of African Studies, paper 151 (University of Nairobi, 1983), 16–17.

16. Adagala, "Language and Literature in Primary Schools," 4. Also see Alta Hoyt, *Bantu Folklore Tales of Long Ago* (Wichita, KS: Day's Print Shop, 1951).

17. Mary Muteve, West Maragoli, Apr. 22, 1995; Rose Mutongi, West Maragoli, Jan. 16, 1999.

18. Mary Vusha, South Maragoli, May 5, 1995.

19. Deborah Gaitskell, "Housewives, Maids, or Mothers: Some Contradictions of Domesticity for Christian Women in Johannesburg, 1903–39," *Journal of African History* 24, no. 2 (1983): 241–56; and Deborah Gaitskell, "Devout Domesticity? A Century of African Women's Christianity in South Africa," in *Women and Gender in Southern Africa*, edited by C. Walker (Cape Town: David Phillip, 1990), 89–120.

20. Rose Mutongi, West Maragoli, June 4, 2003.

21. Hoyt, *Bantu Folklore Tales*, 24–25.

22. *FMA*, Feb. 1933.

23. *FMA*, June 1926.

24. James Jumba and Petero Mwaliku, North Maragoli, Sept. 16, 1994.

25. Belisi Mutiva, South Maragoli, Nov. 15, 1994; South Maragoli, Nov. 12, 1994.

26. Wagner, *Bantu of Western Kenya*, 159–66.

27. For more details, see Gwako, "Widow Inheritance among the Maragoli of Western Kenya."

28. *AR*, May 1918, 6.

29. Janet Mwenesi, "Yohanna Amugune of Maragoli, 1878–1960," in *Biographical Essays on Imperialism and Collaboration in Colonial Kenya*, edited by B. E. Kipkorir (Nairobi: Kenya Literature Bureau, 1980), 160–77; and Japhet Amugune, *A Christian Pioneer* (Kaimosi, Kenya: Friends Bible Institute, 1971). For Amugune's obituary (d. June 2, 1960), see *FMA*, Aug. 1960, 14.

30. Ruben Kagai, West Maragoli, Mar. 12, 1995.

31. Shem Vulimu and Belisi Idavo, South Maragoli, May 6, 1995.

32. Marita Muliru, West Maragoli, Jan. 3, 1999.

33. John Majani, North Maragoli, Dec. 21, 1994.

34. Giplin, "Church and the Community," 56–57.

CHAPTER SIX

1. *FMA*, Dec. 1939, 329.

2. Kenya National Archives (hereafter KNA): DC/NN.1/18, Annual Report, 1936.

3. A. D. Roberts, "The Gold Boom of the 1930s in East Africa," *African Affairs* 85 (1986): 32–45.

4. KNA: DC/NN.1/13, Annual Report, 1932.

5. *FMA*, July–Aug. 1933, 200; and *FMA*, Feb. 1933, 57–58.

6. KNA: DC/NN.1/12, Annual Report, 1931.

7. Matayo Mwerema, North Maragoli, Dec. 17, 1994.

8. For a vivid portrayal of a locust-beating scene in the Rift Valley region of Kenya in the 1940s, see Caroline Link's movie *Nowhere in Africa* (2001), which is based on Stefanie Zweig's book by the same name.

9. KNA: DC/NN.1/14, Annual Report, 1933.

10. Ibid.

11. Hugh Fearn, *An African Economy: A Study of the Economic Development of the Nyanza Province of Kenya, 1903–1953* (London: Oxford University Press, 1961), 130, 150.

12. As calculated by A. D. Roberts using statistics given by the Department of Native Affairs Annual Report in 1935. See his "Gold Boom of the 1930s." For a detailed listing of these wages, see Gavin Kitching, *Class and Economic Change in Kenya: The Making of an African Petite Bourgeoisie, 1905–1970* (New Haven, CT: Yale University Press, 1980), 260. Note that those with more experience on the job earned more money than the average wage.

13. As calculated by Kitching in *Class and Economic Change in Kenya*, 255.

14. As quoted in A. D. Roberts, "Gold Boom of the 1930s," 32–45; see also KNA: DC/NN.1/15, Annual Report, 1934.

15. The first volume was published in 1949 and the second volume in 1956 by Oxford University Press.

16. Wagner, *Bantu of Western Kenya*, 10.

17. At least six hundred tons of goods per day were sold in Mbale. See ibid., 169.

18. Ibid., 166.

19. Ibid., 10.

20. Ibid., 174.

21. KNA: DC/NN.1/20, Annual Report, 1937.

22. Wagner, *Bantu of Western Kenya*, 175.

23. KNA: DC/NN.1/20, Annual Report, 1937.

24. Wagner, *Bantu of Western Kenya*, 165.

25. Fearn, *African Economy*, 141.

26. Ibid., 142.

27. West Maragoli, Feb. 20, 1995.

28. Ibid.

29. Wagner, *Bantu of Western Kenya*, 166.

30. Fearn, *African Economy*, 140.

31. Ibid., 147.

32. South Maragoli, Jan. 3, 1995.

33. Wagner, *Bantu of Western Kenya*, 166.

34. West Maragoli, June 4, 1995.

35. *Kesonga* refers specifically to the long pole extending from the ground up through the center of the roof of a round mud hut but is often used to refer to the whole house.

36. West Maragoli, June 4, 1995.

37. For a detailed survey of the literature on these churches, see Terence Ranger, "Religious Movements and Politics in Sub-Saharan Africa," *African Studies Review* 29, no. 2 (1986): 1–69.

38. For a marvelous history of Waroho, see Cynthia Hoehler-Fatton, *Women of Fire and Spirit: History, Faith, and Gender in Roho Religion in Western Kenya* (New York: Oxford University Press, 1996).

39. Ibid., 44.

40. KNA: MSS/21/1, Owen Papers (M937/box 1, acc. 8301-8301/5), letter from Owen to Pitts, Oct. 25, 1933, as quoted in Hoehler-Fatton, *Women of Fire and Spirit*, 44.

41. South Maragoli, July 1, 1995.

42. For details, see Giplin, "Church and the Community"; and S. Kay, "The Southern Abaluyia: The Friends Africa Mission and the Development of Education in Western Kenya, 1902–1965" (PhD diss., University of Wisconsin, 1973).

43. Giplin, "The Church and the Community"; Kay, "Southern Abaluyia"; and John Lonsdale, "Political Associations in Western Kenya," in *Protest and Power in Black Africa*, edited by R. I. Rotberg and A. Mazrui (New York: Oxford University Press, 1970), 120–37.

44. *FMA*, July–Aug. 1933, 200; and *FMA*, Feb. 1933, 57–58.

45. *FMA*, Feb. 1933.

46. KNA: DC/NN.2/20, Handing-Over Reports, 1938.

47. Mary Jendeka and Petero Muteve, North Maragoli, Apr. 12, 1995.

48. Wagner, *Bantu of Western Kenya*, 175.

49. Ibid., 179.

50. Ibid., 9.

CHAPTER SEVEN

1. Tabitha Kanogo, *Squatters and the Roots of Mau Mau, 1905–63* (London: James Currey, 1987); Bruce Berman, *Control and Crisis in Colonial Kenya: The Dialectic of Domination* (Athens, OH: Ohio University Press, 1990); and David Throup, *Economic and Social Origins of Mau Mau, 1945–53* (London: James Currey, 1987).

2. KNA: PC/NZA/1/7 and DC/NN.1/8, Annual Reports, 1912 and 1935. See also Candice Bradley, "The Possibility of Fertility Decline in Maragoli: An Anthropological Approach" (Nairobi: Population Studies Research Institute, University of Nairobi, 1989); Joseph Ssennyonga, "Population Growth and Cultural Inventory: The Maragoli Case" (PhD diss., University of Sussex, 1978); Abwunza, *Women's Voices, Women's Power*, 1–10; and Joyce Lewinger Moock, "The Migration Process and Differential Economic Behavior in South Maragoli, Western Kenya" (PhD diss., Columbia University, 1975).

3. For a reassessment of these debates, see Meredith Turshen, "Population Growth and the Deterioration of Health, Mainland Tanzania, 1920–1960," and Marc Dawson, "Health, Nutrition, and Population in Central Kenya, 1890–1945," both in *African Population and Capitalism: Historical Perspectives*, edited by Dennis D. Cordell and Joel W. Gregory (Madison: University of Wisconsin Press, 1994), 78–92, 187–200.

4. Joseph Ssennyonga, "The Maragoli Population Trends: Experiential Perceptions of the Maragoli Themselves," Institute of African Studies, paper 107 (University of Nairobi, 1978).

5. Erika Egehiza, Elisha Kavihiza, Marita Olovoga, and Joseph Luyari, Central Maragoli, May 7, 1995.

6. Elisha Kavihiza, Central Maragoli, May 2, 1995.

7. *1930 Report of the Committee on Native Land Tenure in the North Kavirondo Reserve* (Nairobi: Government Printer, 1930).

8. Throup, *Economic and Social Origins of Mau Mau*, 56–90.

9. *1930 Native Land Trust Ordinance* (Nairobi: Government Printer, 1930), 10.

10. Kitching, *Class and Economic Change in Kenya*, 188–99; and Lynn Thomas, *The Politics of the Womb: Women, Reproduction, and the State in Kenya* (Berkeley and Los Angeles: University of California Press, 2003), 36–44.

11. KNA: Legislative Council Debates, Dec. 20, 1932, as quoted in Lonsdale, "Political Associations in Western Kenya," 512.

12. Fearn, *African Economy*, 146.

13. *FMA*, Feb. 1937.

14. For details on the NKCA, see Lonsdale, "Political Associations in Western Kenya."

15. KNA: DC/NN.1/13, Annual Report, 1932.

16. KNA: PC/NZA.326/4/4, Safari diary of Major A. W. Sutcliffe, DC, Mar. 24, 1931.

17. Ibid.

18. Fearn, *African Economy*, 145.

19. Ibid., 149.

20. KNA: PC/NZA/2/1/36, minutes of the North Kavirondo LNC meeting, May 29, 1932; KNA: DC/NN.1/13, Annual Report, 1932.

21. KNA: DC/NN.1/13, Annual Report, 1932.

22. For a detailed study of the native tribunals in Kenya, see Arthur Phillips, *Report on Native Tribunals* (Nairobi: Government Printer, 1945).

23. Wagner, *Bantu of Western Kenya*, 98.

24. KNA: PC/NZA/1/1, report by John Ainsworth, PC of Nyanza, 1905. For a brief study of the habits and beliefs of people in western Kenya at the end of the nineteenth century, see Hobley, "Anthropological Studies in Kavirondo and Nandi."

25. *1930 Report of the Committee on Native Land Tenure in the North Kavirondo Reserve*, 12.

26. KNA: PC/NZA/1/4, Annual Report, 1909; and Norman Humphrey, *The Liguru and the Land: Sociological Aspects of Some Agricultural Problems of North Kavirondo* (Nairobi: Government Printer, 1947), 5.

27. Wagner, *Bantu of Western Kenya*, 98.

28. Phillips, *Report on Native Tribunals*, 14.

29. Jacob Omido, South Maragoli, May 12, 1995.

30. Phillips, *Report on Native Tribunals*, 14.

31. Ibid.

32. Ibid, 15.

33. Ibid.

34. Ibid., 21.

35. Ibid., 22.

36. KNA: DC/NN.1/14, Annual Report, 1933.

37. KNA: DC/NN.1/13, Annual Report, 1932.

38. West Maragoli, Mar. 2, 1995.

39. West Maragoli, Mar. 12, 1995.

40. Central Maragoli, Feb. 23, 1995.

41. South Maragoli, May 27, 1995.

42. Kakamega Provincial Record Center (hereafter KPRC): DX/1/5.

43. Truphena Idavo, Central Maragoli, Mar. 2, 1995.

44. KPRC: DX/2/19.

45. Central Maragoli, Jan. 12, 13, 1999.

46. South Maragoli, Jan. 1, 1999.

47. KPRC: DX/1/67.

CHAPTER EIGHT

1. KNA: PC/NZA.3/10/1/9, report of a deputation received by the superintendent of local education and Mr. Webb, inspector of schools, Kisumu, regarding the
opening of a government African school at Maragoli, Feb. 23, 1927. The reference to
"two Maragolis" refers to the fact that Maragoli was divided into two administrative
units: north and south.

2. Supported by the Church Missionary Society, Maseno Boys School not only
was the leading school in western Kenya but also had a major national reputation. See
John Anderson, *The Struggle for the School* (London: Longman, 1970), 43.

3. KNA: PC/NZA.3/10/1/9, Feb. 23, 1927.

4. KNA: PC/NZA.3/10/1/9, letter from Mr. Webb, inspector of schools, to the
DC of North Kavirondo, Aug. 27, 1927.

5. The DC accused Weller of not consulting him early enough. KNA:
PC/NZA.3/10/1/9, letter from DC to Mr. Weller, Aug. 25, 1927.

6. KNA: PC/NZA.3/10/1/9, letter from G. Webb, inspector of schools, to the DC
of North Kavirondo, Nov. 2, 1927.

7. Carol Summers, *Africans' Education in Southern Rhodesia, 1918–1940*
(Portsmouth, NH: Heinemann Press, 2002).

8. Derek Paterson, *Creative Writing: Language and Political Imagination in
Colonial Central Kenya* (Portsmouth, NH: Heinemann Press, 2003).

9. For details on Jones's work in the American South, see Kenneth King, *Pan-
Africanism and Education: A Study of Race Philanthropy and Education in the
Southern States of America and East Africa* (Oxford: Oxford University Press, 1971),
chaps. 2, 4, 5, and 7; "best oriented" phrase is quoted on p. 36.

10. Jones carried out a similar commission in Sierra Leone, Liberia, and South
Africa in 1921–22. See Jesse Jones, *Negro Schools in the Southern States* (New York:
Oxford University Press, 1928), 2–3.

11. Ibid., xvii, 7–9.

12. Harold Jowitt, *The Principles of Education for African Teachers in Training*
(Toronto: Longmans, Green, 1954), 52, 121; Dougall, *Village Teacher's Guide*; and
Giplin, "Church and the Community," 154–63.

13. KNA: Kenya Education Department, Annual Report, 1929.

14. Dougall, *Village Teacher's Guide*, 1–23.

15. Arthur was referring to the popular nationalist movements in the two countries. For details on these movements, see, e.g., Timothy Mitchell, *Colonizing Egypt* (Cambridge: Cambridge University Press, 1988), for Egypt; and Partha Chatterjee, *The Nation and Its Fragments: Colonial and Postcolonial Histories* (Princeton, NJ: Princeton University Press, 1993), for India.

16. "Report on the Kikuyu Conference of January 23–27, 1925," *East African Standard*, Feb. 4, 1925.

17. KNA: PC/NZA.3/10/1/9, Education, North Kavirondo, 1927.

18. KNA: DC/NN.1/9, Annual Report, 1928; "Kavirondo Taxpayers Welfare Association: Crimes of Violence and Tax Collection," *East African Standard*, July 2, 1927; and "Kavirondo Association Memo for the Commission," *East African Standard*, Dec. 31, 1927.

19. Kay, "Southern Abaluyia," 56.

20. For details on the Thuku riots, see Audrey Wipper, "Kikuyu Women and the Harry Thuku Disturbances: Some Uniformities of Female Militancy," *Africa* 56, no. 2 (1977): 23–35; Harry Thuku, *Harry Thuku: An Autobiography* (Nairobi: Oxford University Press, 1970); King, *Pan-Africanism and Education*, 64–94.

21. KNA: DC/NN.1/18, Annual Report, 1936.

22. KNA: PC/NZA/4/7/7, North Kavirondo LNC minutes, 1929.

23. KNA: DC/NN.1/9, Annual Report, 1928.

24. John Anderson, *Struggle for the School*, 1–8.

25. Giplin, "Church and the Community," 175.

26. KNA: DC/NN/1/14, Annual Report, 1932.

27. South Maragoli, Dec. 27, 1994.

28. West Maragoli, Dec. 28, 1994.

29. KNA: PC, LNC minutes, Feb. 28/29, 1940.

30. Ibid.

31. KNA: PC/NZA/4/7/7, North Kavirondo LNC meeting held at Matungu on Feb. 14, 1931. The term "orphan" was used to refer to anyone whose father was dead—even if the mother was still alive.

32. West Maragoli, May 21, 1995.

33. West Maragoli, Oct. 11, 1994.

34. KNA: PC/NZA.3/10/1/9, letter from the inspector of schools, G. E. Webb, to Mr. F. J. Jennings, DC of North Kavirondo, Aug. 27, 1938.

35. KNA: PC/NZA/4/7/7, minutes of the North Kavirondo LNC meeting held at Kakamega, Nov. 16 and 17, 1938.

36. West Maragoli, Dec. 14, 1994.

37. Central Maragoli, Dec. 5, 1994.

38. Respah Mungore and Luka Amugune, Central Maragoli, May 12, 1995. Elias Mandala has described in detail similar patterns of children assisting their parents with household chores in the lower Tchiri Valley in Malawi. See Elias Mandala, *Work and Control in a Peasant Economy: A History of the Lower Tchiri Valley in Malawi, 1859–1960* (Madison: University of Wisconsin Press, 1990).

39. Margaret Jean Hay, "Luo Women and Economic Change during the Colonial Period," in *Women in Africa: Studies in Social and Economic Change*, edited by Nancy J. Hafkin and Edna G. Bay (Stanford, CA: Stanford University Press, 1976).

40. KNA: DC/NN.1/11, Annual Report, 1930.

41. Truphena Idavo, Central Maragoli, Mar. 23, 1995.

42. North Maragoli, Jan. 12, 1995.

43. South Maragoli, Mar. 29, 1995.

CHAPTER NINE

1. Peter Avugwi, West Maragoli, Jan. 7, 1995.

2. Anthony Clayton and D. C. Savage, *Government and Labour in Kenya, 1895–1963* (London: Cass, 1976), 56–90; and Kitching, *Class and Economic Change in Kenya*, 241–79.

3. West Maragoli, Jan. 7, 1995. For a detailed study of life histories of "elite" men in West Africa, see Stephan Miescher, *Making Men in Ghana* (Bloomington: Indiana University Press, 2005).

4. West Maragoli, Jan. 10, 1995.

5. For an interesting study of salaries and similar family expectations in Cameroon, see Mbembe, *On the Postcolony*, 102–40; and Achille Mbembe and Janet Roitman, "Figures of the Subject in Times of Crisis," *Public Culture* 7 (1995): 323–52.

6. Kezia Avugwi, West Maragoli, Jan. 10, 1995.

7. For a study of string (French) beans in West Africa, see Susanne Freidberg, "French Beans for the Masses: A Modern Historical Geography of Food in Burkina Faso," *Journal of Historical Geography* 17 (2004): 23–37; and Susanne Freidberg, "On the Trail of the Global Green Bean: Methodological Considerations in a Multi-site Ethnography," *Global Networks* 1, no. 4 (2001): 12–25.

8. Rose Kitivura, Central Maragoli, Jan. 7, 1999.

9. Kenda Mutongi, "Thugs or Entrepreneurs? Perceptions of *Matatu* Operators in Nairobi, 1970 to the Present," *Africa* 76, no. 4 (2006).

10. Central Maragoli, Apr. 12, 1995.

11. Ronika Ajema, Central Maragoli, May 20, 1995.

12. Central Maragoli, Apr. 12, 1995.

13. Ronika Ajema, Central Maragoli, May 20, 1995.

14. Ibid.

15. North Maragoli, Nov. 14, 1994.

16. North Maragoli, Nov. 20, 1994.

17. Jane Migitsi and Shem Mutiva, North Maragoli, Jan. 15, 1995; Mary Musimbi, Central Maragoli, Jan. 22, 1995.

18. Peter Muliru, West Maragoli, Dec. 1, 1994.

19. Peter Muliru, West Maragoli, Dec. 3, 1994.

20. Linet Muliru, West Maragoli, Dec. 3, 1994.

21. Due to lack of medical attention, most sick people often do not know what is ailing them.

22. West Maragoli, Dec. 4, 1994.

23. Charles Ambler, "Drunks, Brewers, and Chiefs: Alcohol Regulation in Colonial Kenya," in *Drinking: Behavior and Belief in Modern History*, edited by S. Barrows and R. Room (Berkeley and Los Angeles: University of California Press, 1991), 65–83; Emmanuel Akyeampong, *Drink, Power, and Cultural Change: A Social History of Alcohol in Ghana, c. 1800 to Recent Times* (Portsmouth, NH: Heinemann Press, 1996); and Justin Willis, *Potent Brew: A Social History of Alcohol in East Africa, 1850–1999* (Athens, OH: Ohio University Press, 2002).

24. Luise White, *The Comforts of Home: Prostitution in Colonial Nairobi* (Chicago: University of Chicago Press, 1990); and Diana Jeater, *Marriage, Perversion, and Power: The Construction of Moral Discourse in Southern Rhodesia, 1894–1930* (Oxford: Oxford University Press, 1993).

25. West Maragoli, Mar. 5, 1995.

26. West Maragoli, Mar. 8, 1995.

27. Matayo Isigi, South Maragoli, Nov. 16, 1994.

28. For a detailed discussion of African economic grievances during this period, see, e.g., Frederick Cooper, *Decolonization and African Society: The Labor Question in French and British Africa* (Cambridge: Cambridge University Press, 1996), 110–23.

29. For similar assumptions, see Lisa Lindsay, *Working with Gender: Wage Labor and Social Change in Southwestern Nigeria* (Portsmouth, NH: Heinemann Press, 2003); and Frederick Cooper, *On the African Waterfront: Urban Disorder and the Transformation of Work in Colonial Mombasa* (New Haven, CT: Yale University Press, 1987).

30. KNA: PC/NZA.3/10/1/9, Education, North Kavirondo, 1927.

31. Benedict Carton, *Blood from Your Children: The Colonial Origins of Generational Conflict in South Africa* (Charlottesville: University of Virginia Press, 2000); and Meredith McKittrick, *To Dwell Secure: Generation, Christianity, and Colonialism in Ovamboland* (Portsmouth, NH: Heinemann Press, 2002).

CHAPTER TEN

1. The King's African Rifle was a regiment of lightly armed infantry composed of soldiers from British East Africa (Kenya, Uganda, Tanzania, and Malawi). For a detailed study of the KAR, see Timothy Parsons, *The African Rank-and-File: Social Implications of Colonial Military Service in the King's African Rifle, 1902–1964* (Portsmouth, NH: Heinemann Press, 1999).

2. For details on domestic education at the GBS, see Samuel Thomas, "Transforming the Gospel of Domesticity: Luhya Girls and the Friends African Mission, 1917–1926," *African Studies Review* 43, no. 2 (2000): 1–26.

3. North Maragoli, Mar. 16, 1995.

4. The literal meaning of *mstaarabu* (the singular of *wastaarabu*) is "like an Arab."

5. North Maragoli, Jan. 6, 1995.

6. South Maragoli, Feb. 10, 1995.

7. KNA: DC/NN.1/23, Annual Report, 1941.

8. For details on KAR salaries, see Parsons, *African Rank-and-File*, 74–75.

9. KNA: AB/4/12, Community Development Officer's Monthly Report, May 1945.

10. For a history of the GBS, see Samuel Thomas, "Transforming the Gospel of Domesticity"; and Levinas Painter, *The Hill of Vision: The Story of the Quaker Movement in East Africa, 1902–1965* (Kaimosi: East African Yearly Meeting of Friends, 1966).

11. Central Maragoli, Feb. 6, 1995.

12. See, e.g., the essays in Karen Tranberg Hansen, ed., *African Encounters with Domesticity* (New Brunswick, NJ: Rutgers University Press, 1992); Hunt, *Colonial Lexicon*; and Lynn Thomas, *Politics of the Womb*, 52–78.

13. Painter, *Hill of Vision*, 58.

14. *FMA*, Mar. 1934, 3.

15. North Maragoli, May 21, 1995.

16. South Maragoli, Feb. 12, 1995.

17. Central Maragoli, Jan. 22, 1995.

18. Central Maragoli, June 27, 1995.

19. South Maragoli, Mar. 27, 1995.

20. Central Maragoli, Feb. 6, 1995.

21. Parsons, *African Rank-and-File*, 150–51.

22. KNA: PC/NZA/3/18/20.

23. KNA: PC/NZA/3/18/20, "Kwa Bwana Mkubwa wa Nyanza Province," Aug. 5, 1942.

24. KNA: PC/NZA/3/18/20, "Mahari imezidi," May 12, 1941.

25. KNA: PC/NZA/3/18/20, "Maneno ya Mahari," Aug. 3, 1941.

26. Philip Mayer, *Gusii Bridewealth Law and Custom* (Oxford: Livingstone Institute, 1950).

27. KNA: PC/NZA/3/18/20, Kenya Confidential Dispatch no. 151 to the Secretary of State, Oct. 20, 1931.

28. KNA: PC/NZA/3/18/20, memo from H. E. Lambert on limitation of brideprice, Aug. 4, 1948.

29. KNA: PC/NZA/3/18/20, Kenya Confidential Dispatch no. 151 to the Secretary of State, Oct. 20, 1931.

30. KNA: PC/NZA/3/18/20, memo from Chief Secretary in Nairobi to all PCs and DCs, Oct. 29, 1941.

31. Ibid.

32. Berman and Lonsdale, *Unhappy Valley*, 77–92.

33. Most of the officials' knowledge on bridewealth was drawn from government-sponsored studies. See, e.g., Philip Mayer, *Bridewealth Limitation among the Gusii* (Nairobi: Government Printer, 1932).

34. KNA: PC/NZA/3/18/20, memo from Chief Secretary in Nairobi to all PCs and DCs, Oct. 29, 1941.

35. Ibid.

36. Ibid.

37. KNA: PC/NZA/3/18/20, memos from PC of Nyanza to DCs and LNCs, May 2, 1934, July 17, 1935, Jan. 12, 1936.

38. KNA: PC/NZA/3/18/20, Kenya Confidential Dispatch no. 151 to the Secretary of State, Oct. 20, 1931.

39. KNA/PC/3/18/20, Paul Mboya's response to D. O'Hagan and H. E. Lambert, Nov. 4, 1948.

40. Peter Agoi, South Maragoli, May 3, 1995.

41. Ibid.

42. KNA: PC/NZA/3/18/20, letter from Hunter to Oyuki, Sept. 28, 1945.

43. KNA: PC/NZA/3/18/20, letter from PC of Nyanza to DCs and LNCs, Oct. 20, 1942.

44. KNA: PC/NZA/3/18/20, memo from H. E. Lambert on limitation of brideprice, Aug. 4, 1948.

CHAPTER ELEVEN

1. Painter, *Hill of Vision*, 58.

2. *FMA*, Dec. 1942, 5.

3. *FMA*, July and Aug. 1945, 34.

4. North Maragoli, Dec. 12, 1994.

5. North Maragoli, Feb. 4, 1995.

6. KNA: DC/NN.1/25, Annual Report, 1943.

7. North Maragoli, Feb. 7, 1995.

8. South Maragoli, Mar. 2, 1995.

9. James Onzere, Elima Visiru, Janet Jendeka, South Maragoli, Jan. 22, 1995.

10. North Maragoli, Apr. 12, 1995.

11. West Maragoli, June 30, 1995.

12. North Maragoli, Feb. 7, 1995.

13. South Maragoli, Feb. 17, 1995.

14. *FMA*, July 1938, 21.

15. Samuel Thomas, "Transforming the Gospel of Domesticity."

16. South Maragoli, May 3, 1995.

17. South Maragoli, Jan. 23, 1995.

18. KNA: DC/NN.1/30, Annual Report, 1945.

19. Audrey Wipper, "The Maendeleo ya Wanawake Movement: Some Paradoxes and Contradictions," *African Studies Review* 18, no. 3 (1975): 99–120; Audrey Wipper, "Equal Rights for Women in Kenya?" *Journal of Modern African Studies* 9, no. 3 (1971): 429–42: and Audrey Wipper, "The Maendeleo ya Wanawake Movement

in the Colonial Period: The Canadian Connection, Mau Mau, Embroidery, and Agriculture," *Rural Africana* 29 (1975–76): 195–214.

20. KNA: PC/NZA/3/1/30, "Vihiga Sub-station," Feb. 21, 1952. For other parts of Africa, see Timothy Burke, *Lifebuoy Men, Lux Women: Commodification, Consumption, and Cleanliness in Modern Zimbabwe* (Durham, NC: Duke University Press, 1996).

21. KNA: AB/4/117, Community Development Officer's Monthly Report, Aug. 1950.

22. Samuel Thomas, "Transforming the Gospel of Domesticity," 12–15.

23. Central Maragoli, Mar. 22, 23, 1995.

24. Central Maragoli, Mar. 4, 1995.

25. For studies that have made this relation more explicit, see Lindsay, *Working with Gender;* and Leonore Davidoff and Catherine Hall, *Family Fortunes: Men and Women of the English Middle Class, 1780–1850* (Chicago: University of Chicago Press, 1991).

26. *FMA*, May 1940, 45.

27. *FMA*, Dec. 1943, 3.

28. *FMA*, Jan. 1941, 12.

29. South Maragoli, Apr. 2, 1995.

30. South Maragoli, Nov. 12, 1994.

CHAPTER TWELVE

1. KNA: PC/NZA/3/18/21, "Barua kutoka kwa wa Kakamega walio Eldoret kwa President of Local Native Council," Dec. 14, 1940.

2. Luise White, *Comforts of Home*, 190–94.

3. KNA: PC/NZA/3/18/21, "Umalaya umezidi sana," Jan. 12, 1943.

4. KNA: PC/NZA/4/7/7, minutes of the North Kavirondo LNC, 1941.

5. Peter Agoi, South Maragoli, Mar. 22, 1995.

6. For a detailed study of moral scares elsewhere in Africa, see Jeater, *Marriage, Perversion, and Power.*

7. KNA: PC/NZA/3/18/21: letter from the DC of Uasin Gishu to the PC of Nyanza, May 20, 1942.

8. Matayo Kakiya and Mary Shemisi, Central Maragoli, Oct. 20, 1994.

9. Luise White, *Comforts of Home*, 190–94.

10. KNA: PC/NZA/3/18/21, letter from the chairman of the Kikuyu Mercy Union to the DC of Kisumu, Apr. 2, 1942.

11. Maria Jemo, West Maragoli, Mar. 12, 1995.

12. KNA: PC/NZA/4/7/7, minutes of the North Kavirondo LNC meetings, May 12, Sept. 2, and Oct. 5, 1940; May 5, June 2, and July 5, 1941.

13. KNA: PC/NZA/4/7/7, minutes of the North Kavirondo LNC meetings, July 5, 1941.

14. Peter Agoi, South Maragoli, Feb. 24, 1995; Matayo Kakiya, Central Maragoli, Oct. 20, 1994.

15. Mary Imbuhira, South Maragoli, Apr. 2, 1995; Peter Shego and Belisi Musira, North Maragoli, May 12, 13, 1995; Matayo Kakiya, Central Maragoli, Mar. 20, 1995; and Petero Muse, South Maragoli, Mar. 23, 1995.

16. Ibid.

17. South Maragoli, June 12, 13, 1995.

18. South Maragoli, Mar. 26, 1995.

19. Matayo Kakiya, Central Maragoli, Mar. 20, 1995.

20. Central Maragoli, Sept. 30, 1994.

21. West Maragoli, June 23, 1995.

22. North Maragoli, May 13, 1995.

23. Matayo Kakiya, Central Maragoli, Mar. 20, 1995; Philemona Onzere, South Maragoli, Mar. 20, 1995; Mary Jendeka, North Maragoli, Apr. 12, 1995.

24. James Musira, South Maragoli, June 12, 1995.

25. KNA: PC/NZA/2/3, Medical Report for 1909, "An Account of Venereal Diseases in the Naivasha District."

26. Parsons, *African Rank-and-File*, 158–66.

27. KNA: DC/NN.1/25, Annual Report, 1941.

28. KNA: DC/NN.1/26, Annual Report, 1942.

29. West Maragoli, Jan. 12, 1999.

30. Rose Mutongi, Fairfax, Virginia, USA, June 28, 2005.

31. North Maragoli, Apr. 15, 1995.

32. North Maragoli, May 12, 1995.

33. KNA: PC/NZA/3/21, Marriage, Divorce, and Succession file.

34. KNA: PC/NZA/3/18/21, Ref. Minute no. 19 of the District Commissioners of Central Province of 29th and 30th May 1934.

35. KNA: PC/NZA/4/7/7, minutes of the North Kavirondo LNC, 1932.

36. Brett Shadle, "Bridewealth and Female Consent: Marriage Disputes in African Courts, Gusiiland, Kenya," *Journal of African History* 44 (2003): 241–62; and Brett Shadle, "'Girl Cases': Runaway Wives, Eloped Daughters, and Abducted Women in Gusiiland, Kenya, c. 1900–1965" (PhD diss., Northwestern University, 2000).

37. KNA: PC/NZA/4/7/7, minutes of the North Kavirondo LNC, 1932.

38. Luise White, *Comforts of Home*, 147–67; and Parsons, *African Rank-and-File*, 158–66.

39. Hals Brands, "Wartime Recruiting Practices, Martial Identity and Post–World War II Demobilization in Colonial Kenya," *Journal of African History* 46, no. 1 (2005): 103–26; and Parsons, *African Rank-and-File*, 70–91.

40. KNA: PC/NZA/4/7/7, minutes of the North Kavirondo LNC, Sept. 12 and Dec. 2, 1939, Jan. 19, 1940.

41. KNA: PC/NZA/3/21, Marriage, Divorce, and Succession file.

42. Ibid.

CHAPTER THIRTEEN

1. Central Maragoli, Apr. 23, 24, 1995.

2. Cathy Silber has explored similar issues regarding marriage in rural China in the early part of the twentieth century. See her *Writing from the Useless Branch: Text and Practice in Nushu Culture* (forthcoming).

3. Central Maragoli, Apr. 27, 28, 1995.

4. Central Maragoli, Apr. 23, 1995.

5. Ibid.

6. KPRC: NN/3/729, Feb. 3, 1952.

7. Ibid.

8. Central Maragoli, Apr. 23, 24, 1995.

9. South Maragoli, Feb. 13, 17, 1995.

10. James Mutiva, South Maragoli, Dec. 17, 1999.

11. KPRC: NN/3/659, Sept. 1, 1955.

12. Ibid.

13. South Maragoli, Mar. 12, 1995.

14. South Maragoli, Mar. 15, 1995.

15. KPCR: NN/3/899, Jan. 9, 1954.

16. Ibid.

17. Central Maragoli, Mar. 20, 1995.

18. Judith Byfield, "Women, Marriage, Divorce and the Emerging Colonial State in Abeokuta (Nigeria), 1892–1904," *Canadian Journal of African Studies* 30 (1996): 32–51; Luise White, *Comforts of Home*; Claire Robertson, *Trouble Showed the Way: Women, Men, and Trade in the Nairobi Area, 1890–1990* (Bloomington: Indiana University Press, 1997), 190–238; Jean Marie Allman and Victoria Tashjian, *"I Will Not Eat Stone": A Women's History of Colonial Asante* (Portsmouth, NH: Heinemann Press, 2000); and Shadle, "Bridewealth and Female Consent."

19. Matayo Vurimu, West Maragoli, July 4, 1995.

20. Shem Kagai, Jane Iviregwa, and Matroba Luginu, West Maragoli, Mar. 23, 1995.

21. Wagner, *Bantu of Western Kenya*, 379–446; Margot Lovett, "On Power and Powerlessness: Marriage as a Political Metaphor in Colonial Western Tanzania," *International Journal of African Historical Studies* 27, no. 2 (1994): 42–59.

22. Lovett, "On Power and Powerlessness," 48.

23. KPRC: NN/3/1414, July 12, 1956.

24. South Maragoli, June 2, 1995.

25. KPRC: NN/3/1102. Mungore attributed her son-in-law's strange behavior to the ghosts of the people he had killed during the war. Apparently, Kagai had not undergone the cleansing ceremony, which entailed killing a sheep, to appease the ghosts of the dead and to lessen his trauma from violent war experiences.

26. Central Maragoli, May 12, 1995.

27. For examples on how women used the courts in the colonial period, see Shadle, "Bridewealth and Female Consent"; Allman and Tashjian, *"I Will Not Eat Stone"*; and Richard Roberts, "Representation, Structure, and Agency: Divorce in the

French Soudan during the Early Twentieth Century," *Journal of African History* 40 (1999): 389–410.

28. Phillips, *Report on Native Tribunals*, 20–21.

29. Elima Vusha, West Maragoli, Dec. 18, 1994. According to Jacob Omido, who worked as a clerk in six different African courts in North Kavirondo during this period, many people took the swearing very seriously. Omido told me (South Maragoli, Dec. 14, 1994) that men and women would run out of the courtroom once they were given a Bible or a pot because they were afraid of lying under oath.

30. Phillips, *Report on Native Tribunals*, 20–21.

31. South Maragoli, Mar. 11, 1995.

32. West Maragoli, Mar. 15, 1995.

CHAPTER FOURTEEN

1. *East African Standard*, Sept. 15, 1964, 1.

2. The full speech can be found in *Report of Commission on Land Consolidation* (Nairobi: Government Printer, 1964).

3. *East African Standard*, Sept. 15, 1964, 4.

4. Studies of the political and economic culture of independent Kenya include Bethwell A. Ogot and W. R. Ochieng, eds., *Decolonization and Independence in Kenya, 1940–93* (Athens, OH: Ohio University Press, 1995); and Angelique Haugerud, *The Culture of Politics in Modern Kenya* (Cambridge: Cambridge University Press, 1995).

5. The idea of land consolidation originated with the colonial officials; see R. J. M. Swynnerton, *A Plan to Intensify the Development of African Agriculture in Kenya* (Nairobi: Government Printer, 1954). For a detailed study of land consolidation and other land reforms in postcolonial Kenya, see M. P. K. Sorrenson, *Land Reform in the Kikuyu Country: A Study in Government Policy* (London: Oxford University Press, 1967); John Gerhart, *The Diffusion of Hybrid Maize in Western Kenya* (Mexico City: CIMMYT, 1975); and Angelique Haugerud, "Land Tenure and Agrarian Change in Kenya," *Africa* 19, no. 1 (1989): 61–90.

6. For the colonial period, see David Anderson, "Depression, Dust Bowl, Demography, and Drought: The Colonial State and Soil Conservation in East Africa during the 1930s," *African Affairs* 83 (1984): 321–43; David Anderson and David Throup, "Africans and Agricultural Production in Colonial Kenya: The Myth of the War as a Watershed," *Journal of African History* 26 (1985): 327–45; Throup, *Economic and Social Origins of Mau Mau*; Kanogo, *Squatters and the Roots of Mau Mau*; Berman and Lonsdale, *Unhappy Valley*; Fiona Mackenzie, "Political Economy of the Environment, Gender, and Resistance under Colonialism: Murang'a District, Kenya, 1910–50," *Canadian Journal of African Studies* 25, no. 2 (1991): 226–56.

7. For details, see Ogot and Ochieng, *Decolonization and Independence in Kenya*, xi–xviii.

8. For fictional explorations of some of these themes, see Ngugi wa Thiong'o, *Petals of Blood* (Nairobi: Heinemann Press, 1977); Ngugi wa Thiong'o, *A Grain of Wheat* (Nairobi: Heinemann Press, 1967); and M. G. Vassanji, *The In-Between World of Vikram Lall* (New York: Alfred A. Knopf, 2004).

9. "African Socialism and Its Application to Planning in Kenya," Sessional Paper no. 10 (Nairobi: Government Printer, 1965).

10. Tom Mboya, "An Address by Hon. T. J. Mboya, 1965," in *The Challenge of Nationhood: A Collection of Speeches and Writings,* by Tom Mboya (London: Heinemann Press, 1979), 69.

11. *East African Standard,* Jan. 4, 1967, 2.

12. National Radio broadcastings also became more accessible to many more people and provided another venue for dispersing this rhetoric. Mary Musira, North Maragoli, Jan. 4, 1999.

13. For a similar argument, see E. S. Atieno Odhiambo, "*Matunda ya Uhuru,* Fruits of Independence: Seven Theses on Nationalism in Kenya," in *Mau Mau and Nationhood: Arms, Authority, and Narration,* edited by E. S. Atieno Odhiambo and J. Lonsdale (Athens, OH: Ohio University Press, 2003), 37–46.

14. There are numerous studies of Harambee projects in Kenya: e.g., Peter M. Ngau, "Tensions in Empowerment: The Experience of the Harambee (Self-Help) Movement in Kenya," *Economic Development and Cultural Change* 35 (1987): 523–56; L. S. Wilson, "The Harambee Movement and Efficient Public Good Provision in Kenya," *Journal of Public Economics* 48, no. 1 (1992): 1–19; Barbara Thomas-Slayter, "Development through *Harambee:* Who Wins and Who Loses?" *World Development* 15 (1987): 463–81; and Martin J. D. Hill, *The Harambee Movement in Kenya: Self-Help, Development, and Education among the Kamba of Kitui District* (Atlantic Highlands, NJ: Athlone Press, 1991).

15. Wipper, "Maendeleo ya Wanawake Movement"; Wipper, "Equal Rights for Women in Kenya?"; and Wipper, "Maendeleo ya Wanawake Movement in the Colonial Period."

16. Mboya, "Speech in Parliament Introducing the Motion on Kenya Government," in Mboya, *Challenge of Nationhood,* 98.

17. Atieno Odhiambo has characterized the early postcolonial period in Kenya as a time of "competitive politics," when *wanainchi* could engage in political discussions relatively freely without being accused by the government of being seditious. See E. S. Atieno Odhiambo, "Democracy and Ideology of Order in Kenya," in *Democratic Theory and Practice in Africa,* edited by W. O. Oyugi et al. (Portsmouth, NH: Heinemann Press, 1988), 111–39.

18. KPRC: DX/5/63, Land Consolidation—General Correspondences.

19. Ibid.

20. Ibid.

21. For details, see Ogot and Ochieng, *Decolonization and Independence in Kenya,* xi–xviii.

22. KPRC: DX/5/56, Land Consolidation—General Correspondences.

23. This complaint is a common one in studies of widow inheritance in many other parts of Africa. For a summary of this literature, see Cattell, "African Widows"; and Ewelukwa, "Postcolonialism, Gender, and Customary Injustice." Edwins Laban Moogi Gwako has explored this issue more closely in Maragoli. See his "Widow Inheritance among the Maragoli of Western Kenya."

24. KPRC: DX/5/56, Land Consolidation—General Correspondences.

25. KPRC: DX/5/81, Land Consolidation—General Correspondences.

26. KPRC: DX/5/56, Land Consolidation—General Correspondences.

27. KPRC: HB/9/20, Land Registration and Consolidation—General Correspondences.

28. Wagner, *Bantu of Western Kenya*, 159–66.

29. Matayo Kilivia and Maria Vulimu, West Maragoli, May 25, 1995.

30. Wagner, *Bantu of Western Kenya*, 159–66.

31. For details of corruption in Africa, see, e.g., Mbembe, *On the Postcolony*; Jean-François Bayart, *The State in Africa: The Politics of the Belly* (London: Longman, 1996); and Haugerud, *Culture of Politics in Modern Kenya*.

32. Matayo Kilivia and Maria Vulimu, West Maragoli, May 25, 1995.

33. KPRC: HB/9/10, Land Adjudication, Mar. 27, 1972.

34. North Maragoli, June 4, 1995.

35. KPRC: HB/9/10, Land Adjudication, Mar. 27, 1968.

36. For a detailed discussion of the politics of clientelism in other parts of Africa, see Thomas Callaghy, *The State-Society Struggle: Zaire in Contemporary Perspective* (New York: Oxford University Press, 1984); and Bayart, *State in Africa*, chaps. 7–9.

37. North Maragoli, Jun. 4, 1995.

38. Erika Chavulimu, West Maragoli, Dec. 20, 1998.

39. KPRC: DX/5/62, Land Complaints, Mar. 24, 1967.

40. KPRC: DX/5/63, "Poverty Land Case," Feb. 21, 1973.

41. KPRC: HB/9/10, Land Complaints, June 12, 1969.

42. West Maragoli, May 2, 1995.

43. See, e.g., *East African Standard*, June 10, 1969, and Jan. 2, 1970.

44. Jedida Karani, West Maragoli, Jan. 7, 1995.

45. KNA: National Assembly Reports, Nov. 1973.

46. *Report on Land Consolidation* (Nairobi: Government Printer, 1987).

47. West Maragoli, May 2, 1995.

CHAPTER FIFTEEN

1. At the same time, the Commission on Marriage and Divorce was sent out to record existing laws of marriage and divorce and to discern ways to unify these laws. The two commissions were intended to complement each other. For details on the Commission on Marriage and Divorce, see Lynn Thomas, "Contestation,

Construction, and Reconstitution: Public Debates over Marriage Law and Women's Status in Kenya, 1964–1979" (MA thesis, Johns Hopkins University, 1989).

2. Quotations from *Report of the Commission on the Law of Succession* (Nairobi: Government Printer, 1968), 31.

3. Quotations from KNA: National Assembly, Nov. 19, 1970.

4. Quotations from KNA: National Assembly, Nov. 17, 1970.

5. KNA: National Assembly debate, July 10, 1972.

6. Some of the most vocal participants in the debate were Mr. Mwamzandi, Mr. Okero, Mr. Kase, and Mr. Araru.

7. "The Law of Succession Act," *Laws of Kenya* (Nairobi: Government Printer, 1981), chap. 160.

8. KNA: National Assembly debate, Oct. 5, 1972.

9. See chap. 14.

10. Lynn Thomas, *Politics of the Womb*, 135–72.

11. Lynn Thomas, "Contestation, Construction, and Reconstitution," 56–89.

12. Quotations from KNA: National Assembly debate, Oct. 5, 1972.

13. Esteri Kadenge, West Maragoli, Mar. 28, 1995.

14. KNA: *Baraza*, Mar. 15, 1984. I first located the brief version of this case in *Baraza*, a Swahili newspaper published weekly by the East African Standard Company. The newspaper published cases that were decided by Makadara and Kibera, the two main magistrate courts in Nairobi. Beatrice Vusha and Matayo Shego (Peter Shego's brother) related the rest of the story to me on May 6, 1995, in West Maragoli.

15. *Baraza*, Mar. 15, 1984, 7.

16. Kenderi and her mother, Belisi Migitsi, Central Maragoli, Jan. 12, 15, 16, 1995.

17. See Mutongi, "Thugs or Entrepreneurs?" Turnboys are young men who work at bus stops soliciting passengers for buses and minibuses.

18. Yash P. Ghai et al., *Public Law and Political Change in Kenya: A Study of the Legal Framework of Government from Colonial Times to the Present* (Nairobi: Oxford University Press, 1970), 23–40.

19. South Maragoli, June 12, 1995.

20. North Maragoli, Feb. 15, 1995.

21. West Maragoli, May 17, 18, 20, 1995.

22. Central Maragoli, Jan. 15, 1995.

23. West Maragoli, May 6, 1995.

24. West Maragoli, May 17, 1995.

25. Central Maragoli, Jan. 15, 1995.

26. Ibid.

27. David W. Cohen and E. S. Atieno Odhiambo, *Burying SM: The Politics of Knowledge and the Sociology of Power in Africa* (Portsmouth, NH: Heinemann Press, 1992).

28. Phillips, *Report on Native Tribunals*, 306.

29. KNA: RR/8/30, Luyia Law Panel: meetings held at Kakamega on May 15–17, 1962.

30. Matayo Kilivia and Maria Vulimu, West Maragoli, May 25, 1995.

31. Wagner, *Bantu of Western Kenya*, 68.

32. Ibid., 67–80.

33. KNA: RR/8/30, Luyia Law Panel: meetings held at Kakamega on May 15–17, 1962.

34. Ibid.

35. See, e.g., Susan Hirsch, *Pronouncing and Persevering: Gender and the Discourses of Disputing in an African Islamic Court* (Chicago: University of Chicago Press, 1998); and John L. Comaroff and Simon Roberts, *Rules and Processes: The Cultural Logic of Dispute in an African Context* (Chicago: University of Chicago Press, 1981).

CONCLUSION

1. This list is too long, but Frantz Fanon's *The Wretched of the Earth* (New York: Grove Press, 1963) is the seminal work.

2. West Maragoli, June 10, 1995.

3. Shem Kanyamburi, Kakamega, Mar. 14, 1995.

4. Peter Olukula, Kakamega, Mar. 14, 1995.

5. Luanda, Bunyore, June 14, 1995.

6. Luanda, Bunyore, Dec. 6, 1994.

7. Mamdani, *Citizen and Subject*.

8. Appiah, *In My Father's House*, 7.

9. Mbembe, *On the Postcolony*, 238.

10. Tsitsi Ndangarembga, *Nervous Conditions* (New York: Seal, 1988).

11. Basil Davidson, *The Black Man's Burden: Africa and the Curse of the Nation-State* (New York: Times Books, 1992).

BIBLIOGRAPHY

ARCHIVAL SOURCES

This book draws on archival sources from the Public Record Office and the Friends House in London; the Rhodes House in Oxford; Earlham College in Richmond, Indiana; the Kenya National Archives (KNA) in Nairobi; and the Kakamega Provincial Record Center (KPRC) in Kakamega, western Kenya. These sources helped me piece together historical outlines of the main socioeconomic and political events in colonial Kenya. At the Public Record Office, the Colonial Office file was a rich source of reports, correspondence, and discussions of issues that concerned Kenyan policy makers: taxation, marriage, customary law, agriculture, labor, and education. Some of these matters were specific to Kenya; others were also of great concern to the Colonial Office as a whole—many of the issues having come up in other British colonies as well. The Friends House in London and the Friends Collection and Archives at Earlham College contained reports and correspondence concerning the activities of Quaker missionaries in Kenya.

At the KNA, the provincial and district commissioners' annual reports, political record books, and handing-over reports provided raw data that helped me put together ethnographic information for western Kenya. Here I also found the minutes of the North Kavirondo Local Native Council (LNC), which contain rare African voices. Attorneys general files (A-G) at the KNA contained details about all legal ordinances formulated by colonial officials, while the Ministry of African Affairs files (MAA) provided detailed information and surveys of African education, marriage, sanitation and living standards, and the general status of women and family in Kenya. Lastly, the parliamentary, or National Assembly, debates revealed the complex ways in which legislation was crafted and voted on by the members of the assembly.

At the KPRC, I found detailed records of civil cases heard at the African Tribunal Courts in Maragoli. These records, kept since 1934, consisted of more than two thousand cases of land grievances and another two thousand marriage cases that dealt mainly with disputes involving divorce, wife beating, and bridewealth.

Kenya

Kenya National Archives, Nairobi.
Kakamega Provincial Record Center, Kakamega, western Kenya.

Great Britain

Public Record Office, Kew Gardens, London: CO 533 and CO 822.
Church Missionary Society Archives, Friends House, London.
Rhodes House Library, Oxford University.
John Ainsworth, Provincial Commissioner of Nyanza, 1910–17.
C. M. Dobbs, Senior Commissioner of Nyanza, 1926–30.

United States

Friends Collection and Archives, Lilly Library, Earlham College, Richmond, IN.

INTERVIEWS AND CONVERSATIONS

Afandi, Erika, North Maragoli, June 4, 1995.
Agoi, Peter, South Maragoli, Feb. 24; Mar. 22, 24; May 3, 5, 1995.
Ajema, Ronika, Central Maragoli, May 20, 1995.
Amugune, Luka, Central Maragoli, May 12, 15, 1995.
Andiah, Leah, North Maragoli, Sept. 14, 1994.
Avugwi, Kezia, West Maragoli, Jan. 10; May 21, 1995.
Avugwi, Peter, West Maragoli, Oct. 9, 11; Dec. 14, 1994; Jan. 7, 8, 10; Apr. 16; May
    21, 1995.
Azigare, Petero, South Maragoli, Sept. 25, 26; Dec. 23, 25, 27, 1994.
Chavulimu, Erika, West Maragoli, Dec. 20, 1998.
Chavulimu, Joshua, West Maragoli, Dec. 15, 1994; Feb. 2, 4, 5, 20, 1995.
Demesi, Maria, South Maragoli, Jan. 15, 17, 1999.
Doresi, Maria, North Maragoli, Oct. 17, 18, 1994.
Ebeywa, Tafroza, West Maragoli, June 10, 1995; Jan. 12, 1999.
Egehiza, Erika, Central Maragoli, Mar. 11, 12; May 7, 1995.
Egendi, Jane, North Maragoli, Mar. 13, 16, 17, 1995.
Emema, Mary, West Maragoli, June 23, 1995.
Esteri, Kadenge, West Maragoli, Mar. 28, 30, 1995.
Idavo, Belisi, South Maragoli, Dec. 14, 15, 1994; Feb. 25, 27; May 6, 1995;
    June 5, 2003.
Idavo, Truphena, Central Maragoli, Mar. 23, 25, 26, 1995.
Imbuhira, Mary, South Maragoli, Jan. 23; Apr. 2, 1995.
Iravoga, Janet, West Maragoli, Jan. 25, 26; Mar. 2, 5, 8, 12, 23, 25, 1995.
Irihema, Grace, South Maragoli, Mar. 12, 15, 16, 1995.
Isha, Grace, North Maragoli, May 21, 23, 26; Jan. 6, 1995.
Isigi, Matayo, South Maragoli, Nov. 16, 1994.

Iviregwa, Jane, West Maragoli, Mar. 23, 1995.

Jemo, Maria, West Maragoli, Mar. 12, 1995.

Jendeka, Janet, South Maragoli, Jan. 22, 1995.

Jendeka, Mary, North Maragoli, Dec. 12, 1994; Apr. 12, 15, 1995.

Jumba, James, North Maragoli, Sept. 15, 16, 1994.

Jumba, Jonesi, South Maragoli, Feb. 26, 27; May 19, 27, 1995.

Jumba, Matayo, West Maragoli, June 30, 1995.

Kadenge, Esteri, West Maragoli, Mar. 28, 1995.

Kagai, Ruben, West Maragoli, Sept. 23, 26, 1994; Mar. 12, 1995.

Kagai, Shem, West Maragoli, Mar. 23, 1995.

Kakiya, Mary, North Maragoli, Dec. 13, 1994.

Kakiya, Matayo, Central Maragoli, Oct. 20, 1994; Mar. 20, 1995.

Kanyamburi, Shem, Kakamega, Mar. 14, 1995.

Karani, Jedida, West Maragoli, Jan. 7, 1995.

Kasaya, Berita, West Maragoli, May 2, 3; June 1, 1995.

Kavaya, Shem, North Maragoli, Jan. 12, 16; May 22, 24, 1995.

Kavihiza, Elisha, Central Maragoli, May, 1, 2, 7, 1995.

Kazira, James, North Maragoli, Nov. 20, 1994.

Kazira, Janet, North Maragoli, Nov. 20, 1994.

Kefa, John, West Maragoli, Oct. 12, 13, 26, 1994.

Kenderi, Erika, Central Maragoli, Jan. 12, 15, 16, 1995.

Keverenge, James, West Maragoli, Sept. 23, 26, 1994.

Kilivia, Henry, Central Maragoli, Feb. 6, 1995.

Kilivia, Matayo, West Maragoli, May 25, 1995.

Kilivia, Petero, South Maragoli, Jan. 3, 5, 1995.

Kinziri, James, Central Maragoli, Mar. 22, 23, 1995.

Kisala, Petero, Central Maragoli, Jan. 12, 13, 1999.

Kisia, Mariko, South Maragoli, Mar. 2, 3, 6, 1995.

Kisia, Petero, Central Maragoli, Sept. 30, 1994.

Kisivula, Stella, North Maragoli, Sept. 15, 1994.

Kitivura, Rose, Central Maragoli, Jan. 7, 1999.

Libese, Katarina, West Maragoli, Mar. 8, 1995.

Libese, Mariko, West Maragoli, Dec. 4, 1994.

Lisimbu, Erika, West Maragoli, Mar. 14, 15, 1995.

Luginu, Matroba, West Maragoli, Mar. 23, 1995.

Lusiola, Mary, West Maragoli, Apr. 3, 5, 6, 1995.

Luvusi, Mark, North Maragoli, Apr. 12, 16, 1995.

Luyari, Joseph, Central Maragoli, May 7, 1995.

Majani, John, North Maragoli, Dec. 20, 21, 1994.

Mbecha, Stella, North Maragoli, Feb. 4, 6, 7; Mar. 3, 12, 15, 1995.

Migitsi, Belisi, Central Maragoli, Jan. 12, 15, 16, 1995.

Migitsi, Jane, North Maragoli, Jan. 15, 1995.

Migitsu, Mary, South Maragoli, June 2, 1995.

Miremu, Musa, South Maragoli, July 1, 1995.
Mirimu, Jane, West Maragoli, Sept. 12, 1994.
Mise, Elima, West Maragoli, May 2, 1995.
Mukiri, Mariko, South Maragoli, Jan. 1, 3, 1999.
Muliru, Linet, West Maragoli, Dec. 3, 1994.
Muliru, Marita, West Maragoli, Jan. 3, 1999.
Muliru, Peter, West Maragoli, Dec. 1, 3, 1994.
Mungore, Respah, Central Maragoli, May 12, 1995.
Muse, Petero, South Maragoli, Mar. 20, 23, 1995.
Musimbi, Elisi, South Maragoli, Mar. 20, 26, 29, 1995.
Musimbi, Mary, Central Maragoli, Nov. 1, 3, 1994; Jan. 22, 24; Apr. 23, 24, 27, 28,
    1995.
Musimbi, Respah, West Maragoli, June 4, 1995.
Musira, Belisi, North Maragoli, May 12, 13, 1995.
Musira, Christopher, Luanda, Bunyore, Dec. 6, 1994.
Musira, James, South Maragoli, June 12, 1995.
Musira, Mary, North Maragoli, Jan. 4, 1999.
Muteve, Marita, North Maragoli, Feb. 15, 1995.
Muteve, Mary, West Maragoli, Apr. 22, 23, 1995.
Muteve, Petero, North Maragoli, Apr. 11, 12, 20, 1995.
Mutiva, Airen, South Maragoli, Mar. 3, 1995.
Mutiva, Belisi, South Maragoli, Nov. 15, 1994.
Mutiva, James, South Maragoli, Dec. 17, 1999.
Mutiva, Mariko, North Maragoli, Nov. 14, 1994.
Mutiva, Shem, North Maragoli, Jan. 15, 1995.
Mutongi, Rose, West Maragoli, Oct. 22, 23, 1994; Sept. 12, 1995; Jan. 16, Feb. 12,
    1999; June 4, 12, 13, 2003; and Fairfax, VA, USA, June 14, 15, 28, 2005.
Mwaliku, Peter, North Maragoli, Sept. 15, 16, 1994.
Mwariru, Berita, South Maragoli, June 12, 1995.
Mwenesi, Matayo, West Maragoli, June 7, 8, 2004.
Mwenesi, Rose, Central Maragoli, June 27, 1995.
Mwerema, Matayo, North Maragoli, Dec. 17, 1994.
Ndanyi, Yohana, Central Maragoli, Dec, 5, 6, 1994; Mar. 19, 20; Apr. 12,
    1995.
Olovoga, Marita, Central Maragoli, May 7, 1995.
Olovoga, Shem, North Maragoli, Jan. 1, 4, 12, 1995.
Olukula, Peter, Kakamega, Mar. 14, 1995.
Omido, Jacob, South Maragoli, Dec. 14, 16, 1994; Jan. 10, 12, 13; May 1, 7, 12, 18,
    1995.
Onzere, James, South Maragoli, Jan. 22, 1995.
Onzere, Petero, North Maragoli, Nov. 14, 1994.
Onzere, Philemona, South Maragoli, Mar. 20, 1995.
Onzere, Shem, North Maragoli, Jan. 15; June 12, 13, 16, 1995.

Otiende, Melissa, South Maragoli, Feb. 2, 10, 12, 13, 16, 17; Mar. 26, 27, 1995.

Otieno, Mary, Luanda, Bunyore, June 14, 1995.

Semo, Daina, Central Maragoli, Mar. 20, 1995.

Semo, Erika, North Maragoli, Dec. 2, 3, 1994.

Shego, Joshua, Central Maragoli, Mar. 4, 19, 1995.

Shego, Matayo, West Maragoli, May 6, 1995.

Shego, Peter, North Maragoli, May 12, 13, 1995.

Shemegi, Marita, Central Maragoli, Feb. 6, 9, 23, 1995.

Shemisi, Mary, Central Maragoli, Oct. 20, 1994.

Visero, Berita, South Maragoli, May 20, 21, 1995.

Visero, James, West Maragoli, Dec. 20, 28, 1994; Apr. 4, 6, 1995.

Visiru, Elima, South Maragoli, Jan. 22, 1995.

Visiru, Jane, South Maragoli, Mar. 6, 11, 1995.

Vugutsa, Berita, North Maragoli, Dec. 23, 1994.

Vugutsa, Esteri, South Maragoli, Nov. 12, 1994.

Vugutsa, Marita, South Maragoli, June 12, 13, 1995.

Vugutsa, Mary, West Maragoli, Jan. 5, 1999.

Vulimu, Maria, West Maragoli, May 25, 1995.

Vulimu, Shem, South Maragoli, May 4, 6, 1995.

Vurimu, Matayo, West Maragoli, July 4, 1995.

Vusha, Beatrice, West Maragoli, May 6, 17, 18, 20, 1995.

Vusha, Elima, West Maragoli, Dec. 18, 1994.

Vusha, Keran, South Maragoli, Feb. 17; Mar. 2; May 3, 1995.

Vusha, Mary, South Maragoli, May 4, 5, 1995.

Zilika, Janet, South Maragoli, Apr. 2, 4; June 2, 1995.

PERIODICALS

African Report

The American Friend

Baraza

Drum

East African Standard

Friends Missionary Advocate

Nation

True Love

Viva

Weekly Review

KENYAN GOVERNMENT PUBLICATIONS

Native Labor Commission, 1912–13 (1913).

1930 Native Land Trust Ordinance.

1930 Report of the Committee on Native Land Tenure in the North Kavirondo Reserve (1930).

Bridewealth Limitation among the Gusii, by Philip Mayer (1932).

Report of Food Shortage Commission (1943).

Report of the Sub-committee on Post-war Employment of Africans (1943).

Proposals for the Reorganization of the Administration in Kenya (1945).

Report on Native Tribunals, by Arthur Phillips (1945).

General Aspects of the Agrarian Situation in Kenya (1946).

The Agrarian Problem in Kenya (1947).

The Agrarian Problem in Kenya, note by Sir Philip Mitchell (1947).

The Liguru and the Land: Sociological Aspects of Some Agricultural Problems of North Kavirondo, by Norman Humphrey (1947).

African Population of Kenya Colony (1950).

The Pattern of Income and Consumption of African Laborers in Nairobi, October–November 1950 (1951).

A Plan to Intensify the Development of African Agriculture in Kenya, by R. J. M. Swynnerton (1954).

Report of the Committee on African Wages (1954).

Report of Commission on Land Consolidation (1964).

"African Socialism and Its Application to Planning in Kenya," Sessional Paper no. 10 (1965).

Report of the Commission on the Law of Succession (1968).

Report on Land Consolidation (1987).

The Law of Succession Act (1981).

BOOKS, ARTICLES, PAPERS, THESES, AND DISSERTATIONS

Abu-Lughod, Lila. 1990. "The Romance of Resistance: Tracing Transformations of Power through Bedouin Women." *American Ethnologist* 17:41–55.

Abwunza, Judith. 1997. *Women's Voices, Women's Power: Dialogues of Resistance from East Africa.* Peterborough, ON: Broadview Press.

Adagala, Kavetsa. 1979. "Language and Literature in Primary Schools: Lulogoolo ne Tsing'ano Tsya Valogooli." Institute of African Studies Paper 121. Nairobi: University of Nairobi.

———. 1979. "Tsing'ano Tsya Valogooli." Institute of African Studies Paper 121, appendix. Nairobi: University of Nairobi.

Akyeampong, Emmanuel. 1996. *Drink, Power, and Cultural Change: A Social History of Alcohol in Ghana, c. 1800 to Recent Times.* Portsmouth, NH: Heinemann Press.

Allman, Jean Marie, and Victoria Tashjian. 1999. "Rounding Up Spinsters: Gender Chaos and Unmarried Women in Colonial Asante." *Journal of African History* 37, no. 2: 195–214.

———. 2000. *"I Will Not Eat Stone": A Women's History of Colonial Asante.* Portsmouth, NH: Heinemann Press.

Allman, Jean Marie, Susan Geiger, and Nakanyike Musisi, eds. 2002. *Women in African Colonial Histories*. Bloomington: Indiana University Press.

Ambler, Charles. 1988. *Kenyan Communities in the Age of Imperialism: The Central Region in the Late Nineteenth Century*. New Haven, CT: Yale University Press.

———. 1991. "Drunks, Brewers, and Chiefs: Alcohol Regulation in Colonial Kenya." In *Drinking: Behavior and Belief in Modern History*, edited by S. Barrows and R. Room. Berkeley and Los Angeles: University of California Press.

Amugune, Japhet. 1971. *A Christian Pioneer*. Kaimosi, Kenya: Friends Bible Institute.

Anderson, David. 1984. "Depression, Dust Bowl, Demography, and Drought: The Colonial State and Soil Conservation in East Africa during the 1930s." *African Affairs* 83:321–43.

Anderson, David, and David Throup. 1985. "Africans and Agricultural Production in Colonial Kenya: The Myth of the War as a Watershed." *Journal of African History* 26:327–45.

Anderson, John. 1970. *The Struggle for the School*. London: Longman.

Appiah, Kwame Anthony. 1992. *In My Father's House: Africa in the Philosophy of Culture*. New York: Oxford University Press.

Ariès, Philippe. 1962. *Centuries of Childhood: A Social History of Family Life*. Translated by Robert Baldick. New York: Vintage.

Atieno Odhiambo, E. S. 1988. "Democracy and Ideology of Order in Kenya." In *Democratic Theory and Practice in Africa*, edited by W. O. Oyugi et al. Portsmouth, NH: Heinemann Press.

———. 1995. "The Formative Years, 1945–55." In *Decolonization and Independence in Kenya, 1940–93*, edited by B. A. Ogot and W. R. Ochieng. Athens, OH: Ohio University Press.

———. 2003. "*Matunda ya Uhuru*, Fruits of Independence: Seven Theses on Nationalism in Kenya." In *Mau Mau and Nationhood: Arms, Authority, and Narration*, edited by E. S. Atieno Odhiambo and J. Lonsdale. Athens, OH: Ohio University Press.

Atkins, Keletso. 1993. *The Moon Is Dead! Give Us Our Money! The Cultural Origins of an African Work Ethic, Natal, South Africa, 1843–1900*. Portsmouth, NH: Heinemann Press.

Bacon, Margaret Hope. 1988. "Quaker Women in Overseas Ministry." *Quaker History* 77, no. 2: 84–99.

Barker, Eric. 1950. *A Short History of Nyanza*. Kampala, Uganda: East African Literature Bureau.

Barnes, Sandra. 1999. *"We Women Worked So Hard": Gender, Urbanization, and Social Reproduction in Colonial Harare, Zimbabwe, 1930–1956*. Portsmouth, NH: Heinemann Press.

Bayart, Jean-François. 1996. *The State in Africa: The Politics of the Belly*. London: Longman.

Berman, Bruce. 1990. *Control and Crisis in Colonial Kenya: The Dialectic of Domination*. Athens, OH: Ohio University Press.

Berman, Bruce, and John Lonsdale. 1992. *Unhappy Valley: Conflict in Kenya and Africa*. Athens, OH: Ohio University Press.

Boahen, A. Adu. 1987. *African Perspectives on Colonialism*. Baltimore: Johns Hopkins University Press.

Bohannan, Paul. 1960. "Homicide and Suicide in North Kavirondo." In *African Homicide and Suicide*, edited by P. Bohannan. Princeton, NJ: Princeton University Press.

Bozzoli, Belinda (assisted by M. Nkotsoe). 1991. *Women of Phokeng: Consciousness, Life Strategy, and Migrancy in South Africa, 1900–1983*. Portsmouth, NH: Heinemann Press.

Bradley, Candice. 1989. "The Possibility of Fertility Decline in Maragoli: An Anthropological Approach." Nairobi: Population Studies Research Institute, University of Nairobi.

Brands, Hals. 2005. "Wartime Recruiting Practices, Martial Identity and Post–World War II Demobilization in Colonial Kenya." *Journal of African History* 46, no. 1: 103–26.

Burke, Timothy. 1996. *Lifebuoy Men, Lux Women: Commodification, Consumption, and Cleanliness in Modern Zimbabwe*. Durham, NC: Duke University Press.

Burns, Francis. 1910. "Trial by Ordeal among the Bantu Kavirondo." *Anthropos* 5:808.

Byfield, Judith. 1996. "Women, Marriage, Divorce and the Emerging Colonial State in Abeokuta (Nigeria), 1892–1904." *Canadian Journal of African Studies* 30:32–51.

———. 2002. *The Bluest Hands: A Social and Economic History of Women Dyers in Abeokuta (Nigeria), 1890–1940*. Portsmouth, NH: Heinemann Press.

Callaghy, Thomas. 1984. *The State-Society Struggle: Zaire in Contemporary Perspective*. New York: Oxford University Press.

Carton, Benedict. 2000. *Blood from Your Children: The Colonial Origins of Generational Conflict in South Africa*. Charlottesville: University of Virginia Press.

Cattell, Maria. 1992. "Old Age among the Samia of Western Kenya." PhD diss., Bryn Mawr College.

———. 2003. "African Widows: Anthropological and Historical Perspectives." *Journal of Women and Aging* 15, no. 2: 49–66.

Chanock, Martin. 1985. *Law, Custom, and Social Order: The Colonial Experience in Malawi and Zambia*. Cambridge: Cambridge University Press.

Chatterjee, Partha. 1993. *The Nation and Its Fragments: Colonial and Postcolonial Histories*. Princeton, NJ: Princeton University Press.

Chesoni, Z. R. 1966. "Divorce and Succession in Luyia Customary Law." *East African Law Journal* 2:162–78.

Chilson, Edna. 1943. *Arthur B. Chilson: The Ambassador of the King*. Wichita, KS: privately printed.

Clayton, Anthony, and D. C. Savage. 1976. *Government and Labour in Kenya, 1895–1963*. London: Cass.

Cohen, David W. 1985. "Doing Social History from Pim's Doorway." In *Reliving the Past: The Worlds of Social History*, edited by O. Zunz. Chapel Hill: University of North Carolina Press.

Cohen, David W., and E. S. Atieno Odhiambo. 1989. *Siaya: The Historical Anthropology of an African Landscape*. Athens, OH: Ohio University Press.

———. 1992. *Burying SM: The Politics of Knowledge and the Sociology of Power in Africa*. Portsmouth, NH: Heinemann Press.

Cohen, David W., S. Miescher, and Luise White. 2001. "Voices, Words, and African History." In *African Words, African Voices: Critical Practices in Oral History*, edited by D. W. Cohen, S. Miescher, and L. White. Bloomington: Indiana University Press.

Coleman, Wil. 1990. "Doing Masculinity/Doing Theory." In *Men, Masculinities and Social Theory*, edited by J. Hearn and D. H. J. Morgan. London: Unwin Hyman.

Comaroff, Jean, and John Comaroff. 1991–97. *Of Revelation and Revolution: The Dialectics of Modernity on a South African Frontier*. 2 vols. Chicago: University of Chicago Press.

Comaroff, John L., and Simon Roberts. 1981. *Rules and Processes: The Cultural Logic of Dispute in an African Context*. Chicago: University of Chicago Press.

Conklin, Alice. 1997. *A Mission to Civilize: The Republican Idea of Empire in France and West Africa, 1895–1930*. Stanford, CA: Stanford University Press.

Cooper, Barbara. 1997. *Marriage in Maradi: Gender and Culture in a Hausa Society in Niger, 1900–1989*. Portsmouth, NH: Heinemann Press.

Cooper, Frederick. 1983. "Urban Space, Industrial Time, and Wage Labor in Africa." In *Struggle for the City: Migrant Labor, Capital, and the State in Urban Africa*. Beverly Hills, CA: Sage Publications.

———. 1987. *On the African Waterfront: Urban Disorder and the Transformation of Work in Colonial Mombasa*. New Haven, CT: Yale University Press.

———. 1994. "Conflict and Connection: Rethinking African Colonial History." *American Historical Review* 99, no. 5: 1516–45.

———. 1996. *Decolonization and African Society: The Labor Question in French and British Africa*. Cambridge: Cambridge University Press.

Cummings, R. 1973. "A Note on the History of Caravan Porters in East Africa." *Kenya Historical Review* 1, no. 2: 109–38.

Davidoff, Leonore, and Catherine Hall. 1991. *Family Fortunes: Men and Women of the English Middle Class, 1780–1850*. Chicago: University of Chicago Press.

Davidson, Basil. 1992. *The Black Man's Burden: Africa and the Curse of the Nation-State*. New York: Times Books.

Dawson, M. H. 1979. "Smallpox in Kenya, 1880–1920." *Social Science Medicine* 13B, no. 4: 245–50.

Dawson, Marc. 1994. "Health, Nutrition, and Population in Central Kenya, 1890–1945." In *African Population and Capitalism: Historical Perspectives*, edited by Dennis D. Cordell and Joel W. Gregory. Madison: University of Wisconsin Press.

Dougall, J. W. C. 1931. *The Village Teacher's Guide: A Book of Guidance for African Teachers*. London: Sheldon Press.

Du Bois, W. E. B. 1903. "Of Mr. Booker T. Washington and Others." In *The Souls of Black Folk: Essays and Sketches*, by W. E. B. Du Bois. Chicago: University of Chicago Press.

Dundas, Kenneth R. 1913. "The Wawanga and Other Tribes of the Elgon District, British East Africa." *Journal of the Anthropological Institute of Great Britain and Ireland* 43:19–75.

Echenberg, Myron. 1991. *Colonial Conscripts: The Tirailleurs Senegalais in French West Africa, 1857–1960*. Portsmouth, NH: Heinemann Press.

Elliott, Errol. 1969. *Quakers on the American Frontier: A History of the Westward Migrations, Settlements, and Developments of Friends on the American Continent*. Richmond, IN: Friends United Press.

Emerson, Elizabeth. 1958. *Emory J. Rees, Language Pioneer: A Biographical Sketch*. Gowanda, NY: Niagara Frontier Publishing.

Ewelukwa, Uche. 2002. "Postcolonialism, Gender, and Customary Injustice: Widows in African Societies." *Human Rights Quarterly* 24, no. 2: 420–57.

Fair, Laura. 2001. *Pastimes and Politics: Culture, Community, and Identity in Post-abolition Urban Zanzibar*. Athens, OH: Ohio University Press.

Fanon, Frantz. 1963. *The Wretched of the Earth*. New York: Grove Press.

Farge, Arlette, and Jacques Revel. 1991. *The Vanishing Children of Paris: Rumor and Politics before the French Revolution*. Translated by Claudia Mieville. Cambridge: Cambridge University Press.

Fearn, Hugh. 1961. *An African Economy: A Study of the Economic Development of the Nyanza Province of Kenya, 1903–1953*. London: Oxford University Press.

Feierman, Steven. 1990. *Peasant Intellectuals: Anthropology and History in Tanzania*. Madison: University of Wisconsin Press.

Ford, J. 1971. *The Role of Trypanosomiases in African Ecology: A Study of the Tsetse Fly Problem*. Oxford: Clarendon Press.

Freidberg, Susanne. 2001. "On the Trail of the Global Green Bean: Methodological Considerations in a Multi-site Ethnography." *Global Networks* 1, no. 4: 12–25.

———. 2004. "French Beans for the Masses: A Modern Historical Geography of Food in Burkina Faso." *Journal of Historical Geography* 17:23–37.

Gaitskell, Deborah. 1983. "Housewives, Maids, or Mothers: Some Contradictions of Domesticity for Christian Women in Johannesburg, 1903–39." *Journal of African History* 24, no. 2: 241–56.

———. 1990. "Devout Domesticity? A Century of African Women's Christianity in South Africa." In *Women and Gender in Southern Africa*, edited by C. Walker. Cape Town: David Phillip.

Gerhart, John. 1975. *The Diffusion of Hybrid Maize in Western Kenya*. Mexico City: CIMMYT.

Ghai, Yash P., et al. 1970. *Public Law and Political Change in Kenya: A Study of the Legal Framework of Government from Colonial Times to the Present*. Nairobi: Oxford University Press.

Giplin, Clifford. 1976. "The Church and the Community: Quakers in Western Kenya, 1902–1963." PhD diss., Columbia University.

Gould, W. T. S. 1989. "Technical Education and Migration in Tiriki, Western Kenya, 1902–1987." *African Affairs* 88, no. 351: 253–71.

Gutto, Shadrack. 1976. "The Status of Women in Kenya: A Study of Paternalism, Inequality, and Underprivilege." Nairobi: Institute for Development Studies, University of Nairobi.

Guyer, Jane. 1981. "Household and Community in African Studies." *African Studies Review* 24, nos. 2–3: 87–137.

———, ed. 1995. *Money Matters: Instability, Values, and Social Payments in the Modern History of West African Communities*. Portsmouth, NH: Heinemann Press.

Gwako, Edwins Laban Moogi. 1998. "Widow Inheritance among the Maragoli of Western Kenya." *Journal of Anthropological Research* 54, no. 2: 173–98.

Hamilton, R. W. 1909. "Native Laws and Customs." *East Africa Protectorate Law Reports*, 141–48.

Hamm, Thomas D. 1988. *The Transformation of American Quakerism: Orthodox Friends, 1800–1907*. Bloomington: Indiana University Press.

Hansen, Karen Tranberg, ed. 1992. *African Encounters with Domesticity*. New Brunswick, NJ: Rutgers University Press.

Haugerud, Angelique. 1989. "Land Tenure and Agrarian Change in Kenya." *Africa* 19, no. 1: 61–90.

———. 1995. *The Culture of Politics in Modern Kenya*. Cambridge: Cambridge University Press.

Hay, Margaret Jean. 1976. "Luo Women and Economic Change during the Colonial Period." In *Women in Africa: Studies in Social and Economic Change*, edited by Nancy J. Hafkin and Edna G. Bay. Stanford, CA: Stanford University Press.

Hill, Martin J. D. 1991. *The Harambee Movement in Kenya: Self-Help, Development, and Education among the Kamba of Kitui District*. Atlantic Highlands, NJ: Athlone Press.

Hirsch, Susan. 1998. *Pronouncing and Persevering: Gender and the Discourses of Disputing in an African Islamic Court*. Chicago: University of Chicago Press.

Hobley, C. W. 1902. "Eastern Uganda: An Ethnological Survey." *Journal of the Anthropological Institute* 31:234–45.

———. 1903. "Anthropological Studies in Kavirondo and Nandi." *Journal of the Royal Anthropological Institute* 1, no. 2: 325–59.

———. 1903. "British East Africa: Anthropological Studies in Kavirondo and Nandi." *Journal of the Anthropological Institute* 33:325–59.

———. 1910. *The Ethnology of the A-kamba and Other East African Tribes.* London: Frank Cass.

———. 1922. *Bantu Beliefs and Magic.* London: Frank Cass.

———. 1970. *Kenya, from Chartered Company to Crown Colony: Thirty Years of Exploration and Administration in British East Africa.* 2d ed. (1st ed. 1929.) London: Frank Cass.

Hodgson, Dorothy, and S. McCurdy, eds. 2001. *"Wicked" Women and the Reconfiguration of Gender in Africa.* Portsmouth, NH: Heinemann Press.

Hoehler-Fatton, Cynthia. 1996. *Women of Fire and Spirit: History, Faith, and Gender in Roho Religion in Western Kenya.* New York: Oxford University Press.

Hofmeyr, Isabel. 1994. *We Spend Our Years as a Tale That Is Told: Oral Historical Narrative in a South African Chiefdom.* Portsmouth, NH: Heinemann Press.

Hotchkiss, Willis. 1901. *Sketches from the Dark Continent.* Cleveland: Friends Bible Institute.

———. 1937. *Then and Now in Kenya Colony: Forty Adventurous Years in East Africa.* New York: Fleming H. Revell.

Hoyt, Alta. 1951. *Bantu Folklore Tales of Long Ago.* Wichita, KS: Day's Print Shop.

———. 1971. *We Were Pioneers.* Wichita, KS: privately printed.

Hunt, Nancy Rose. 1990. "'Single Ladies on the Congo': Protestant Missionary Tensions and Voices." *Women Studies International Forum* 13, no. 4: 370–97.

———. 1999. *A Colonial Lexicon of Birth Ritual, Medicalization, and Mobility in the Congo.* Durham, NC: Duke University Press.

Huntingford, George. 1944. *The Eastern Tribes of the Bantu Kavirondo.* People of Kenya Series 15. Nairobi: Government Printer.

Jeater, Diana. 1993. *Marriage, Perversion, and Power: The Construction of Moral Discourse in Southern Rhodesia, 1894–1930.* Oxford: Oxford University Press.

Johnston, Harry. 1902. *The Uganda Protectorate.* 2 vols. London: Hutchinson.

Jones, Jesse. 1928. *Negro Schools in the Southern States.* New York: Oxford University Press.

Jowitt, Harold. 1954. *The Principles of Education for African Teachers in Training.* Toronto: Longmans, Green.

Kahn, Freud. 1969. "Law Reform in Kenya." *East African Law Journal* 5, no. 2: 54–87.

Kakooza, J. M. N. 1969. "Changes in Family Law." *East African Law Journal* 4, no. 1: 1–13.

Kanogo, Tabitha. 1987. *Squatters and the Roots of Mau Mau, 1905–63.* London: James Currey.

Karp, Ivan. 1978. *Fields of Change among the Iteso of Kenya.* London and Boston: Routledge and Kegan Paul.

Kay, S. 1973. "The Southern Abaluyia: The Friends Africa Mission and the Development of Education in Western Kenya, 1902–1965." PhD diss., University of Wisconsin.

Kerber, Linda. 1997. "The Meanings of Citizenship." *Journal of American History* 84, no. 3: 833–54.

Kershaw, Greet. 1997. *Mau Mau from Below*. Oxford: James Currey.

King, Kenneth. 1971. *Pan-Africanism and Education: A Study of Race Philanthropy and Education in the Southern States of America and East Africa*. Oxford: Oxford University Press.

Kirwen, Michael. 1979. *African Widows: An Empirical Study of the Problems of Adapting Western Christian Teachings on Marriage to the Leviratic Custom for the Care of Widows in Four Rural African Societies*. Maryknoll, NY: Orbis Books.

Kitching, Gavin. 1980. *Class and Economic Change in Kenya: The Making of an African Petite Bourgeoisie, 1905–1970*. New Haven, CT: Yale University Press.

Landau, Paul. 1995. *The Realm of the Word: Language, Gender, and Christianity in a Southern African Kingdom*. Portsmouth, NH: Heinemann Press.

Lawler, Nancy Ellen. 1992. *Soldiers of Misfortune: Ivoirien Tirailleurs of World War II*. Athens, OH: Ohio University Press.

Le Roy Ladurie, Emmanuel. 1978. *Montaillou: The Promised Land of Error*. Translated by Barbara Bray. New York: G. Braziller.

Leys, C. 1975. *Underdevelopment in Kenya: The Political Economy of Neocolonialism, 1964–1971*. Berkeley: University of California Press.

Leys, Norman. 1925. *Kenya*. London: Hogarth Press.

Ligale, A. N. 1966. "Some Factors Influencing the Pattern of Rural Settlement in Maragoli, Western Kenya." *East African Geographical Review* 1:65–68.

Lijembe, Joseph. 1967. "The Valley Between: A Muluyia's Story." In *East African Childhood: Three Versions*, edited by L. K. Fox. New York: Oxford University Press.

Lindsay, Lisa. 2003. *Working with Gender: Wage Labor and Social Change in Southwestern Nigeria*. Portsmouth, NH: Heinemann Press.

Lindsay, Lisa, and Stephan F. Miescher, eds. 2003. *Men and Masculinities in Modern Africa*. Portsmouth, NH: Heinemann Press.

Lisingu, Simion J. 1946. *Kitabu Kya Mulogoli Na Vana Veve*. Nairobi: n.p.

Lonsdale, John. 1970. "Political Associations in Western Kenya." In *Protest and Power in Black Africa*, edited by R. I. Rotberg and A. Mazrui. New York: Oxford University Press.

———. 2003. "Authority, Gender, and Violence: The War within Mau Mau's Fight for Land and Freedom." In *Mau Mau and Nationhood: Arms, Authority, and Narration*, edited by E. S. Atieno Odhiambo and J. Lonsdale. Athens, OH: Ohio University Press.

Lovett, Margot. 1994. "On Power and Powerlessness: Marriage as a Political Metaphor in Colonial Western Tanzania." *International Journal of African Historical Studies* 27, no. 2: 42–59.

Lutz, Catherine. 1988. *Unnatural Emotions: Everyday Sentiments on a Micronesian Atoll and Their Challenge to Western Theory*. Chicago: University of Chicago Press.

Lutz, Catherine, and Lila Abu-Lughod, eds. 1990. *Language and the Politics of Emotion.* Studies in Emotion and Social Interaction. Cambridge: Cambridge University Press.

Mackenzie, Fiona. 1991. "Political Economy of the Environment, Gender, and Resistance under Colonialism: Murang'a District, Kenya, 1910–1950." *Canadian Journal of African Studies* 25, no. 2: 226–56.

Mamdani, Mahmood. 1996. *Citizen and Subject: Contemporary Africa and the Legacy of Late Colonialism.* Princeton, NJ: Princeton University Press.

Mandala, Elias. 1990. *Work and Control in a Peasant Economy: A History of the Lower Tchiri Valley in Malawi, 1859–1960.* Madison: University of Wisconsin Press.

Mangat, J. S. 1969. *A History of the Asians in East Africa, 1886–1945.* Oxford: Oxford University Press.

Mann, Kristin. 1985. *Marrying Well: Marriage, Status, and Social Change among the Educated Elite in Colonial Lagos.* Cambridge: Cambridge University Press.

Mann, Kristin, and Richard L. Roberts. 1991. "Law in Colonial Africa." In *Law in Colonial Africa,* edited by K. Mann and R. L. Roberts. Portsmouth, NH: Heinemann Press.

Martin, C. J. 1985. "The Agrarian Question and Migrant Labor: The Case of Western Kenya." *Journal of African Studies* 2:164–74.

Matson, A. T. 1968. "Suicide Pacts among the Kalenjin of Western Kenya." *East African Journal* 5, no. 8: 25–34.

———. 1972. *Nandi Resistance to British Rule, 1890–1906.* Nairobi: East African Publishing House.

Matsuda, Motoji. 1998. *Urbanisation from Below: Creativity and Soft Resistance in the Everyday Life of Maragoli Migrants in Nairobi.* Kyoto, Japan: Kyoto University Press.

Maxon, Robert. 2003. *Going Their Separate Ways: Agrarian Transformation in Kenya, 1930–50.* Cranbury, NJ: Associated University Presses.

Mayer, Philip. 1932. *Bridewealth Limitation among the Gusii.* Nairobi: Government Printer.

———. 1950. *Gusii Bridewealth Law and Custom.* Oxford: Livingstone Institute.

Mbembe, Achille. 2001. *On the Postcolony.* Berkeley: University of California Press.

Mbembe, Achille, and Janet Roitman. 1995. "Figures of the Subject in Times of Crisis." *Public Culture* 7:323–52.

Mbilinyi, Marjorie. 1988. "Runaway Wives in Colonial Tanganyika: Forced Labor and Forced Marriages in Rungwe District, 1919–1961." *International Journal of the Sociology of Law* 16, no. 1: 1–29.

Mboya, Tom. 1979. *The Challenge of Nationhood: A Collection of Speeches and Writings.* London: Heinemann Press.

McCaskie, T. C. 2000. *Asante Identities: History and Modernity in an African Village, 1850–1950.* Edinburgh: Edinburgh University Press.

McKittrick, Meredith. 2002. *To Dwell Secure: Generation, Christianity, and Colonialism in Ovamboland.* Portsmouth, NH: Heinemann Press.

Meinertzhagen, R. 1957. *Kenya Diary, 1902–1906.* London: Longmans.

Miescher, Stephan. 2005. *Making Men in Ghana.* Bloomington: Indiana University Press.

Mitchell, Timothy. 1988. *Colonizing Egypt.* Cambridge: Cambridge University Press.

Mmbulika, L. M. E. 1971. "Resistance and Reaction to Agricultural Change and Development in Maragoli, 1946–1962." BA thesis, University of Nairobi.

Moock, Joyce Lewinger. 1975. "The Migration Process and Differential Economic Behavior in South Maragoli, Western Kenya." PhD diss., Columbia University.

———. 1978–79. "The Content and Maintenance of Social Ties between Urban Migrants and Their Home-Based Support Groups: The Maragoli Case." *African Urban Studies* 3:15–31.

Moock, Peter. 1973. "Managerial Ability in Small Farm Production: An Analysis of Maize Yields in Vihiga Division of Kenya." PhD diss., Columbia University.

Moore, Henrietta, and Megan Vaughan. 1994. *Cutting down Trees: Gender, Nutrition, and Agricultural Change in the Northern Province of Zambia, 1890–1990.* Portsmouth, NH: Heinemann Press.

Moore, Sally Falk. 1978. *Law as Process: An Anthropological Approach.* London: Routledge and Kegan Paul.

Munday, Elizabeth. 1983. "Birth and Death and In-Between: Children in Wanga Society." Institute of African Studies Paper 151. Nairobi: University of Nairobi.

Mungeam, G. H. 1966. *British Rule in Kenya, 1895–1912.* Oxford: Clarendon Press.

———. 1970. Introduction to *Kenya, from a Chartered Company to Crown Colony,* by C. W. Hobley. 2d ed. London: Frank Cass.

———. 1976. *Kenya: Select Historical Documents, 1884–1923.* Nairobi: East African Publishing House.

Munro, Forbes. 1975. *Colonial Rule and the Kamba: Social Change in the Kenya Highlands, 1889–1939.* Oxford: Clarendon Press.

Muriuki, Godfrey. 1974. *A History of the Kikuyu, 1500–1900.* Nairobi: East African Publishing House.

Mutongi, Kenda. 1999. "'Worries of the Heart': Widowed Mothers, Daughters, and Masculinities in Maragoli, Western Kenya, 1940–60." *Journal of African History* 40, no. 1: 67–86. Reprinted in *Readings in Gender in Africa,* edited by Andrea Cornwall. Oxford: James Currey, 2005.

———. 2006. "Thugs or Entrepreneurs? Perceptions of *Matatu* Operators in Nairobi, 1970 to the Present." *Africa* 76, no. 4.

Mutoro, Basilida Anyona. 1997. *Women Working Wonders: Small-Scale Farming and the Role of Women in Vihiga District, Kenya; A Case Study of North Maragoli.* Amsterdam: Thela Publishers.

Mwelesa, Gideon. 1971. Chart: Amita Ga Vaguga Ne Vikevo Mulogoli. Private records, Nairobi.

Mwenesi, Janet. 1980. "Yohanna Amugune of Maragoli, 1878–1960." In *Biographical Essays on Imperialism and Collaboration in Colonial Kenya*, edited by B. E. Kipkorir. Nairobi: Kenya Literature Bureau.

Ndangarembga, Tsitsi. 1988. *Nervous Conditions*. New York: Seal.

Ngau, Peter M. 1987. "Tensions in Empowerment: The Experience of the Harambee (Self-Help) Movement in Kenya." *Economic Development and Cultural Change* 35:523–56.

Norden, Hermann. 1924. *White and Black in East Africa: A Record of Travel and Observation in Two African Crown Colonies*. Boston: S. Maynard.

Oboler, Regina. 1985. *Women, Power, and Economic Change: The Nandi of Kenya*. Stanford, CA: Stanford University Press.

Ogede, S. Ode. 1995. "Context, Form, and Poetic Expression in Igede Funeral Dirges." *African Affairs* 65, no. 1: 79–98.

Ogot, Bethwell A. 1967. *A History of the Southern Luo*. Peoples of East Africa. Nairobi: East African Publishing House.

Ogot, Bethwell A., and W. R. Ochieng, eds. 1995. *Decolonization and Independence in Kenya, 1940–93*. Athens, OH: Ohio University Press.

Ogutu, M. A. 1985. "The Changing Role of Women in Commercial History of Busia District in Kenya, 1900–1983." In *Women and Development in Africa*, edited by G. S. Were. Nairobi: East African Publishing House.

Ominde, S. H. 1965. *The Ethnic Map of the Republic of Kenya*. Nairobi: Department of Geography, University College.

———. 1971. "Rural Economy in Western Kenya." In *Studies in East African Geography and Development*, edited by S. H. Ominde. Berkeley: University of California Press.

Omnia, Shakry. 1998. "Schooled Mothers and Structured Play: Child Rearing in Turn-of-the-Century Egypt." In *Remaking Women: Feminism and Modernity in the Middle East*, edited by L. Abu-Lughod. Princeton, NJ: Princeton University Press.

Osogo, John. 1965. *The Abaluyia: Life in Kenya in the Olden Days*. Nairobi: East African Publishing House.

Otiende, J. D. 1949. *Habari za Baluyia*. Nairobi: n.p.

Owen, W. E. 1932. "The Bantu of Kavirondo." *Journal of East Africa and Uganda Natural History Society* 45, no. 46: 67–77.

Oyeronke, Oyewumi. 1997. *The Invention of Women: Making an African Sense of Western Gender Discourses*. Minneapolis: University of Minnesota Press.

Painter, Levinas. 1966. *The Hill of Vision: The Story of the Quaker Movement in East Africa, 1902–1965*. Kaimosi: East African Yearly Meeting of Friends.

Parkin, David. 1980. "Kind Bridewealth and Hard Cash: Eventing a Structure." In *The Meaning of Marriage Payments*, edited by John L. Comaroff. London: Academic Press.

Parkin, David, and David Nyamwaya, eds. 1987. *Transformations of African Marriages*. Manchester: Manchester University Press.

Parsons, Timothy. 1999. *The African Rank-and-File: Social Implications of Colonial Military Service in the King's African Rifles, 1902–1964*. Portsmouth, NH: Heinemann Press.

Paterson, Derek. 2003. *Creative Writing: Language and Political Imagination in Colonial Central Kenya*. Portsmouth, NH: Heinemann Press.

Phillips, Arthur. 1945. *Report on Native Tribunals*. Nairobi: Government Printer.

———. 1952. "The African Court System in Kenya." *Journal of African Administration* 4:135–38.

———. 1953. *A Survey of African Marriage and Family*. London and New York: Oxford University Press.

Potash, Betty, ed. 1986. *Widows in African Societies: Choices and Constraints*. Stanford, CA: Stanford University Press.

Presley, Cora Ann. 1992. *Kikuyu Women, the Mau Mau Rebellion, and Social Change in Kenya*. Boulder, CO: Westview Press.

Ranger, Terence. 1986. "Religious Movements and Politics in Sub-Saharan Africa." *African Studies Review* 29, no. 2: 1–69.

Rasmussen, Ane Marie Bak. 1995. *A History of the Quaker Movement in Africa*. London: British Academic Press.

Richards, Charlotte. 1947. *Archdeacon Owen of Kavirondo: A Memoir*. Nairobi: Highway Press.

Riley, Denise. 1988. *Am I That Name? Feminism and the Category of "Women" in History*. Minneapolis: University of Minnesota Press.

Roberts, A. D. 1986. "The Gold Boom of the 1930s in East Africa." *African Affairs* 85:32–45.

Roberts, Richard. 1999. "Representation, Structure, and Agency: Divorce in the French Soudan during the Early Twentieth Century." *Journal of African History* 40:389–410.

Robertson, Claire. 1997. *Trouble Showed the Way: Women, Men, and Trade in the Nairobi Area, 1890–1990*. Bloomington: Indiana University Press.

Roper, Michael, and John Tosh. 1991. *Manful Assertions: Masculinities in Britain since 1800*. London: Routledge.

Roscoe, John. 1924. *The Bagesu and Other Tribes of the Uganda Protectorate*. Cambridge: Cambridge University Press.

Ross, Ellen. 1994. "New Thoughts on 'the Oldest Vocation': Mothers and Motherhood in Recent Feminist Scholarship." *Signs* 20, no. 2: 396–413.

Rotberg, Robert I. 1968. Introduction to *Through Masai Land*, by Joseph Thomson. 3d ed. London: Frank Cass.

———. 1971. *Joseph Thomson and the Exploration of Africa*. London: Chatto and Windus.

———. 1983. Introduction to *Imperialism, Colonialism, and Hunger: East and Central Africa*, edited by R. I. Rotberg. Lexington: University of Kentucky Press.

Rowe, John. 1958. "Kaimosi: An Essay in Mission History." Master's thesis, University of Wisconsin, Madison.

Sangree, Walter H. 1966. *Age, Prayer, and Politics in Tiriki, Kenya*. New York: Oxford University Press.

Schmidt, Elizabeth. 1992. *Peasants, Traders, and Wives: Shona Women in the History of Zimbabwe, 1870–1939*. Portsmouth, NH: Heinemann Press.

Scott, James C. 1985. *Weapons of the Weak: Everyday Forms of Peasant Resistance*. New Haven, CT: Yale University Press.

———. 1990. *Domination and the Arts of Resistance: Hidden Transcripts*. New Haven, CT: Yale University Press.

Sewell, William, Jr. 1996. "Three Temporalities: Toward an Eventful Sociology." In *The Historic Turn in the Human Sciences*, edited by T. J. McDonald. Ann Arbor: University of Michigan Press.

Shadle, Brett. 1999. "'Changing Traditions to Meet Current Altering Conditions': Customary Law, African Courts, and the Rejection of Codification in Kenya, 1930–1960." *Journal of African History* 40, no. 3: 411–31.

———. 2000. "'Girl Cases': Runaway Wives, Eloped Daughters, and Abducted Women in Gusiiland, Kenya, c. 1900–1965." PhD diss., Northwestern University.

———. 2003. "Bridewealth and Female Consent: Marriage Disputes in African Courts, Gusiiland, Kenya." *Journal of African History* 44:241–62.

Shipton, Parker. 1989. *Bitter Money: Cultural Economy and Some African Meanings of Forbidden Commodities*. Washington, DC: American Anthropological Association.

Silber, Cathy. Forthcoming. *Writing from the Useless Branch: Text and Practice in Nushu Culture*.

Sorrenson, M. P. K. 1967. *Land Reform in the Kikuyu Country: A Study in Government Policy*. London: Oxford University Press.

Spear, Thomas. 1981. *Kenya's Past: An Introduction to Historical Method in Africa*. London: Longman.

Ssennyonga, Joseph. 1978. "The Maragoli Population Trends: Experiential Perceptions of the Maragoli Themselves." Institute of African Studies Paper 107. Nairobi: University of Nairobi.

———. 1978. "Maragoli's Exceptional Population Dynamics: A Demographic Portrayal." Institute of African Studies Paper 108. Nairobi: University of Nairobi.

———. 1978. "Population Growth and Cultural Inventory: The Maragoli Case." PhD diss., University of Sussex.

Stam, Nicholas. 1929. *The Bahanga*. Washington, DC: Catholic Anthropological Conference.

Stamp, Patricia. 1991. "Burying SM: The Politics of Gender and Ethnicity in Kenya." *Signs* 16, no. 4: 808–45.

Starr, June, and Jane Fishburne Collier. 1989. *History and Power in the Study of Law: New Directions in Legal Anthropology*. Ithaca, NY: Cornell University Press.

Stichter, Sharon. 1982. *Migrant Labour in Kenya: Capitalism and African Response, 1895–1975*. London: Longman.

Stone, Lawrence. 1977. *The Family, Sex, and Marriage in England, 1500–1800.* New York: Harper and Row.

Stranahan, Edgar H. 1905. *Friends African Industrial Mission.* Plainfield, NJ: Quaker Press.

Summers, Carol. 2002. *Africans' Education in Southern Rhodesia, 1918–1940.* Portsmouth, NH: Heinemann Press.

Thiong'o, Ngugi wa. 1967. *A Grain of Wheat.* Nairobi: Heinemann Press.

———. 1977. *Petals of Blood.* Nairobi: Heinemann Press.

Thomas, Lynn. 1989. "Contestation, Construction, and Reconstitution: Public Debates over Marriage Law and Women's Status in Kenya, 1964–1979." MA thesis, Johns Hopkins University.

———. 2003. *The Politics of the Womb: Women, Reproduction, and the State in Kenya.* Berkeley: University of California Press.

Thomas, Samuel. 2000. "Transforming the Gospel of Domesticity: Luhya Girls and the Friends African Mission, 1917–1926." *African Studies Review* 43, no. 2: 1–26.

———. 2001. "Gender and Religion on the Mission Station: Roxie Reeve and the Friends African Mission." *Quaker History* 90, no. 2: 24–46.

Thomas-Slayter, Barbara. 1987. "Development through *Harambee:* Who Wins and Who Loses?" *World Development* 15:463–81.

Thomson, J. B. 1897. *Joseph Thomson: African Explorer.* London: Sampson Low, Marston.

Thomson, Joseph. 1968. *Through Masai Land.* 3d ed. (1st ed. 1885.) London: Frank Cass.

Throup, David. 1987. *Economic and Social Origins of Mau Mau, 1945–53.* London: James Currey.

Thuku, Harry. 1970. *Harry Thuku: An Autobiography.* Nairobi: Oxford University Press.

Tignor, Robert. 1976. *The Colonial Transformation of Kenya: The Kamba, Kikuyu, and Masai from 1900–1939.* Princeton, NJ: Princeton University Press.

Timaeus, Ian, and Angela Reynar. 2003. "Polygynists and Their Wives in Sub-Saharan Africa: An Analysis of Five Demographic and Health Surveys." *Population Studies* 52, no. 1: 145–62.

Trueblood, Elton. 1966. *The People Called Quakers.* New York: Harper and Row.

Turshen, Meredith. 1994. "Population Growth and the Deterioration of Health, Mainland Tanzania, 1920–1960." In *African Population and Capitalism: Historical Perspectives,* edited by Dennis D. Cordell and Joel W. Gregory. Madison: University of Wisconsin Press.

Van Zwanenberg, R. M. 1975. *Colonial Capitalism and Labour in Kenya, 1919–1939.* Kampala, Uganda: East African Literature Bureau.

Vassanji, M. G. 2004. *The In-Between World of Vikram Lall.* New York: Alfred A. Knopf.

Wagner, Günter. 1970. *The Bantu of Western Kenya*. 2 vols. in 1. London: Oxford
  University Press. (Originally published as *The Bantu of North Kavirondo*. 2 vols.
  London: Oxford University Press, 1949–56.)

Were, Gideon S. 1967. *A History of the Abaluyia of Western Kenya, 1500–1930*.
  Nairobi: East African Publishing House.

West, Michael O. 2002. *The Rise of an African Middle Class: Colonial Zimbabwe,
  1898–1965*. Bloomington: Indiana University Press.

White, Landeg. 1987. *Magomero: Portrait of an African Village*. Cambridge:
  Cambridge University Press.

White, Luise. 1990. *The Comforts of Home: Prostitution in Colonial Nairobi*.
  Chicago: University of Chicago Press.

———. 2000. *Speaking with Vampires: Rumor and History in Colonial Africa*.
  Berkeley: University of California Press.

Whyte, Susan Reynolds. 1990. "The Widow's Dream: Sex and Death in Western
  Kenya." In *Personhood and Agency: The Experience of Self and Other in
  African Cultures*, edited by M. Jackson and I. Karp. Washington, DC:
  Smithsonian Institution Press.

———. 1997. *Questioning Misfortune: The Pragmatics of Uncertainty in Eastern
  Uganda*. Cambridge: Cambridge University Press.

Willis, Justin. 2002. *Potent Brew: A Social History of Alcohol in East Africa,
  1850–1999*. Athens, OH: Ohio University Press.

Wilson, L. S. 1992. "The Harambee Movement and Efficient Public Good Provision
  in Kenya." *Journal of Public Economics* 48, no. 1: 1–19.

Wipper, Audrey. 1971. "Equal Rights for Women in Kenya?" *Journal of Modern
  African Studies* 9, no. 3: 429–42.

———. 1975. "The Maendeleo ya Wanawake Movement: Some Paradoxes and
  Contradictions." *African Studies Review* 18, no. 3: 99–120.

———. 1975–76. "The Maendeleo ya Wanawake Movement in the Colonial Period:
  The Canadian Connection, Mau Mau, Embroidery, and Agriculture." *Rural
  Africana* 29:195–214.

———. 1977. "Kikuyu Women and the Harry Thuku Disturbances: Some
  Uniformities of Female Militancy." *Africa* 56, no. 2: 23–35.

———. 1977. *Rural Rebels: A Study of Two Protest Movements in Kenya*. Oxford:
  Oxford University Press.

Wright, Marcia. 1993. *Strategies of Slaves and Women: Life-Stories from
  East/Central Africa*. London: James Currey.

INDEX

Note: Page numbers in italic denote a photograph.

Abunza, Alfred, 168–69
adultery: accusations against military wives, 150, 152, 153; legal status of, 182; succession of property and, 184–86
Advancement of Women, 134, 166
Afandi, Erika, 172–73
Affiliation Act, 182
African culture, 3, 181. *See also* burial customs
Aggrey, James, 100–101
agriculture: cash crops, 83, 129–30, 164, 176; disruption by Hobley's punitive measures, 21; government loans for, 129–30; land consolidation and registration, 9, 164, 169–77, 222n5; of Luyia, 16–17; string bean production, 109; widows' experimentation with, 105; as women's work, 62–63, 135
Agufwa, Jafeti, 149, 150, 151
Ahmed (MP), 179, 180
Ahonya, James: adherence to practical Christianity, 67–68; conversion of, 41–42; resistance to African practices, 49–50; visits to the mission, 30, 33
AIDS, 4, 194
Ajema, Ronika, 104, 109–13
Akamba women, 112–13
Allen, Roberta, 136
Amin, Idi, 3, 195
Amugune: adherence to practical Christianity, 67; mission work of, 54–55; resistance to

African practices, 49–50; visits to the mission, 30, 33
Amugune, Yohana, 80
Angiro, Hezron, 146, 147–48
Appiah, Kwame Anthony, 10, 196
Arab/Swahili slave trade, 16–17, 38–39
Arthur, J. W., 99–100, 214n15
Avugwi, Kezia, 103–4
Avugwi, Mariko, 80
Avugwi, Peter, 103–4, 107–9
Azigare, Petero, 102

backsliding, 52–53, 79
"Back to the Land" speech, 163
Bantu Kavirondo, 15
Bantu of North Kavirondo, The (Wagner), 72–75
Beeson, Wilbur, 136
Beywa, Mariko, 92
Beywa, Marita, 39–40
bicycles, 74, 113–14
Blackburn, Elisha, 27, 53
Blackburn, Virginia, 26, 47–48
black leaders: citizenship rhetoric of, 9, 163–66, 171–72, 174, 177; corruption among, 173–74; idea of land consolidation, 222n5; inherited problems of, 197; Maragoli people's ambivalence toward, 2, 193–98; methods of, 164; promises of, 5, 165
Boit, Priscilla, 185, 186, 187–88

Bond, Mira, 51
boys: assistance to widowed mothers, 105; conversions of, 35–36, 39–42; education of, 61, 64, 97–106; life at the training center, 45; life in *iliini*, 63–64; mothers' fear for at missions, 34–44; Quaker converts, 59, 63–64; success of Quakers and, 68
bridewealth: Amugune's refusal of, 67; benefits to widows, 119; colonial officials' knowledge of, 217n33; divorce and, 154; education and, 119–21, 128, 134, 137–38; legitimacy of marriage and, 187, 190; orphans' lack of, 30; regulation of, 121–26; wartime inflation of, 118–19; widows' remarriage and, 66
burial customs: Christian converts' continued practice of, 65; colonial postmortem and, 30–32; graves and, *49*; irreverence for burial grounds, 59; land consolidation and, 170–71; *lisara* (remembrance ceremony), 66; of Maragoli, 47–49, *49*; *olovego* (hair-shaving ceremony), 66; skull incident and, 32–33, 36–37
bursary scheme for education, 103–4
Butere Girls High School, 3

Cambridge Overseas School Certificate, 102
Cameroon, 197
cannibalism scare, 30–36, 43
cash crops, 83, 129–30, 164, 176
cattle herder tale, 63–64
Chahonyo; Rachel, 65
chai (sweet tea), 110
changaa (alcoholic beverage), 114
Chavulimu, Belisi, 75, 77
Chavulimu, Joshua, 75
chiefs: British negotiations with, 19; demand for education, 97, 100–101, 213n1; on land arbitration committees, 169–70, 171–72; local court system and, 88–90, 92; repatriation of women and, 142–44
children: assistance to widowed mothers, 105, 214n38; legitimacy of, 187, 190. *See also* boys; girls
Chilson, Arthur B., 23–28, *24*, 30–32
Chilson, Edna, 47
Chore, Truphena, 137
Christians, *137*, 170. *See also* Quaker converts; Quaker missionaries
Christmas, 110–11, *111*

circumcision, *48*, 53, 65, 67
citizenship: citizens' view of, 193; government rhetoric, 9, 163–66, 171–72, 174, 177; people's response to, 165–66; succession of property cases and, 186–87; widows' appeal to, 9, 167–69, 172–73, 174–75, 176–77
civilization: education as a means to, 106, 129–30, 135; practical Christianity and, 45–46
civilizing mission, 99
clan rivalries, 89–90
class division, 79–80
clothing, 25–26, 47
Colonial Office, 17–18
colonial officials: allegations of prostitution and, 140, 141; bridewealth issues and, 122, 123–24; concerns about venereal disease, 144, 145; consideration of education for Africans, 99; control of bursaries, 104; gossip concerning, 5–6; interest in Quaker defections, 79; methods of, 164; native land tenure system and, 88; paradox of experiences under, 4, 6–7; reforms in court system, 88–90; study of land tenure system, 83; support of Girls Boarding School, 128; Ugandan exiles' view of, 3; view of educated Africans, 106, 116–17, 193; view of in post-colonial Maragoli, 2–3, 193–98; violent encounters with Africans, 18–20; on women's rights, 182. *See also* District Coordinator; Hobley, Charles W.; Provincial Commissioner of Nyanza; Provincial Commissioner of Nyeri
colonial policies: concerning wills, 189; court reforms, 157–58; moral surveillance of women, 7, 140, 144–46, 163, 191; punitive tactics, 18–20, 30, 44, 163, 193; widows as barometer of impact of, 4–5
colonial warfare, 18–20, 30, 44
Commission on Marriage and Divorce, 224n1
Commission on the Law of Succession, 178, 180
communities: care of widows and orphans, 7–9; disruption from land conflicts, 93–94; national unity movement and, 171–72
confession, 51
corruption: court reforms and, 157; land consolidation and registration and, 9,

168–69, 171–76; in local court system, 89–90, 93–94; Maragoli people's ambivalence toward, 2, 194, 196
councilors, 172
courts: colonial reforms, 88–90, 157–58, 222n29; succession of property and, 178–79, 183–86; trials for spread of venereal disease, 145; widows' land claims and, 90–93; wife-beating cases in, 151, 152, 153, 154, 155, 155–58
cowidows, 183–88, 189
currency: cash for bridewealth and, 118–24; introduction of money, 74, 76; items used as, 20, 203n13; used as bridewealth, 118–19
curse of the dog, 62

Davidson, Basil, 197
Demesi, Maria, 59
diet, 82–83
Dini ya Israel Church, 77–78
diplomacy, 19
disease: African people's cry for remedies, 27–28; AIDS, 4, 194; Maragoli cure for, 49–50; missionaries and, 26, 27; as result of Hobley's punitive actions, 20–22; sacrifices to ancestors and, 49–50, 53; sexually transmitted diseases, 144–46, 150, 151, 152, 153; sleeping sickness, 21; small pox epidemic, 29, 30; small pox epidemics, 21
District Coordinator: appointment of court officials, 88–89; bridewealth issues and, 124, 126; on local courts, 89–90; Maragoli demands for education and, 97–98, 101; position on land conflicts, 85
District Coordinator of North Kavirondo, 139
District Coordinator of Uasin Gishu, 140
Divine Church, 77–78
divorce: stigma of, 154; wife beating and, 151, 152, 153–54
domestic education, 120, 131–32, 134–38
Doresi, Maria, 36
Dougall, J. W. C., 99
drought, 32, 70
drunkenness, 114–15, 116
dukas (stores), 73–74

Ebeywa, Tafroza, 145, 195, 197
education: African questioning of validity of, 100–102; black government's promises of,

165; bridewealth and, 118–21; citizens' contributions to, 166; of girls, 61, 128–38; in iliini, 61, 64; of Maragoli boys, 97–106; Maragoli people's nostalgia for, 2, 194; Phelps-Stokes Commission and, 99
Egendi, Jane, 118, 150–51
elders: cannibalism scare and, 32; local court system and, 88–90; repatriation of women and, 142–44
Eldoret, 21
Emema, Mary, 144
employment, 71–72, 75–76, 116–17. See also King's African Rifle (KAR)
enamel cups, 76–77, 110
entrepreneurship, 73–74, 80
ethnic unification, 168
ethnic warfare, 19–20
European paternalism, 27, 104

Family Provision Act of 1938 (Great Britain), 178
famine, 20–22, 32
farmers' cooperatives, 170
fatherless boys. See orphans
fathers, 64–65
Fearn, Hugh, 85–86
fecundity, 82–83
fires of hell, 50, 52
flag of Kenya, 163
Ford, Jefferson, 78
Friends Industrial Missions, 23–28. See also Kaimosi
funerals: demands on progressive sons, 112; of Maragoli people, 47–49; missionaries barred from, 31; modern attitudes toward, 136–37. See also burial customs

GBS. See Girls Boarding School (GBS)
Gecaga, Mrs. (MP), 182–83
gender codes: court officials and, 158; government promises and, 171–72; plight of progressive sons and, 116–17; role of males, 40, 41, 42–44, 43; wife beating and, 158–59; worries of the heart strategy and, 7–8, 34, 35, 38, 90–91, 130–31
Ghana, 196
girls: assistance to, 105; assistance to widowed mothers, 105; education of, 118–21, 128–38; life at GBS, 131–34; life in an iliini, 60–62; vigilance over, 63

Girls Boarding School (GBS): bridewealth of students of, 118–21; competition for place in, 128–29; government funding of, 128; hardships for student of, 130–34; students of, *133*

gold mining: discovery of gold, 69–70; impact on economy of Maragoli, 72–75; land conflicts and, 83–85; Maragoli workers in, 71–72, 75–76

gossip, 5–6, 129

graves: converted sons' abandonment of, 59; customs concerning, 30, 48–49, *49*; land conflicts and, 89, 91–92; land consolidation and, 170–71; worries of the heart and, 38, 91–92

Great Depression, 70, 83, 105

guns, feuds over, 18

Harambee (cooperation), 165–66

Harambee school, 166

Haviland, Elizabeth, 131–32

health care, 2, 27–28, 29, 165, 194

Hobley, Charles W.: appointment as head of Mumias administration center, 17–19; imposition of tax system, 20; punitive tactics of, 18–20, 30, 44; reception of Quaker missionaries, 25; on use of *Kavirondo*, 202n2; views of his administration, 21–22

Hole, Adelaide, 47

Hole, Edgar T.: agenda for western Kenya, 23–28, *24*; description of Luyia, 25–26; on effects of postmortem, 31; incident with the skull, 32–33, 36, 37; view of burial customs, 48–49

homecraft education, 134

homesickness, 133

Hotchkiss, Willis R., 23–28, *24*, 69, 80

housing: Christian disapproval of round houses, 77; construction of *iliini*, 58, 59–60; of educated young men, 107; of families of progressive sons, 108, 109, 113; of *iliini*, 60; of Maragoli people, 2, 46; of modern couples, 136; of newly arrived missionaries, 27; of practical Christianity, 27, 46–47; of progressive sons, 110, 113, 114

Hoyt, Alta, 70, 78–79, 137

Hoyt, Fred, 70, 78–79

hunger remedy, 32, 40

iliini (villages): acquisition of land for, 56, 57–58; construction of, 58, 59–60; converts' moves to, 54–55; education and training in, 61–62; end of, 79, 93–94; land conflicts in, 86, 90–91, 92, 93; life in, 60–65; practice of widow inheritance in, 66; schools of, 98; structure of, 46, 60

Imbayi, Simion, 155–56

Imbuhira, Mary, 133, 137

Imperial British East African Company (IBEAC), 17

independence, 5, 163, 190

infertility, 150, 151

Inyangala, Sabeti, 169, 171, 172

Iramema, Elisi, 174, 175, 176

Iravoga, Janet, 90, 115

Irihema, Grace, 153

Isha, Grace, 118, 120–21

Isigi, Torkas, 92

Jemo, Maria, 172–73

Jendeka, Mary, 129, 130, 146

jigger worms, 21, 27

Jones, Jesse, 99, 213n10

Jumba, Jonesi, 91

Jumba, Matayo: on abandonment by converted sons, 59; on motives for helping widows, 131; polygamy of, 153, 154, 158; wife abuse by, 153

Jumba, Peter, 122–23, 126

Jumhuri Day, 163

Kagai, John, 156

Kaimosi: boys school in, 102, 104, 109; concerns about gold mining at, 70; defection of Quaker converts, 78–79; education of girls of, 119–20; missionary establishment in, 26; trip into, 27

Kaimosi Boys School, 102, 104, 109

Kakamega, 69–70, 72, 84–86, 102, 103–4, 106

Kakamega Government School, 102, 103–4, 106

Kamba, 18–19

KAR. *See* King's African Rifle (KAR)

Karani, Jedida, 174, 175, 176

Karia, Florence, 184

Kasaya, Berita, 39–42, *40–42*, 43

Kasaya, Nora, 158

Kase (MP), 179

Kavaya, Matayo, 2

Kavaya, Shem, 106

Kavirondo, 15–17, 202n2. *See also* Maragoli/
Maragoli people; North Kavirondo
Kavirondo Welfare Association, 139
Kazira, James, 113
Kaziva, Berita, 93
Kefa, John, 34–36
kehenda mwoyo. *See* worries of the heart
Kellum (headmaster), 104, 109
Kenderi, Erika, 185, 185–86, 187–88
Kenya: ambivalence toward black government
of, 2–3, 193–98; demand for education,
98; improved education in, 102;
independence, 5, 163, 190; land
consolidation and registration, 164–77;
land seizure in, 83; moral panic in,
139–48; rinderpest epidemics, 21;
unification efforts, 168, 177, 178, 181,
182; violent encounters with colonialism,
18–20. *See also* North Nyanza District;
specific town or village
Kenyan Sessional Papers of 1965, 165
Kenyatta, Jomo, 163, 174, 178
Keverenge, James, 58
Keya, Mariko, 114
Keya, Matayo, 114–15
Kibisu (MP), 182
Kibisu, Peter, 165, 174–75
Kikuyu, 18–19, 98
Kikuyu Central Association, 85
Kikuyu Mercy Union, 141
Kilivia, Henry, 120, 121
Kilivia, Petero, 76
King's African Rifle (KAR): apprehensions
about leaving wives, 147–48; competition
for wives and, 118–19, 121–22; marriages
of soldiers, 7, 149–53, 156, 158; rumors of
wayward women and, 146; soldiers of,
216n1
Kinziri, James, 135
Kisala, Petero, 92
Kisia, Petero, 143
Kisiru, Erika, 91
Kisivura, Edith, 138
Kisivura, Meshak, 93
Kisumu, 25, 30–32, 36, 105
Kitigala, 167
Kitosh, 18, 19
kokola buvira (witchcraft), 79

lamentations, 34, 38, 92, 105, 115, 170–71
Lamming, George, 3

land arbitration committees, 169–70,
171–76
land conflicts: acquisition of land for *iliinis*,
57–58, 86, 93; demand for education and,
98; gold mining and, 83–86; graves and,
91–92; litigation over, 87–93; population
density and, 82–83; Quaker scenarios of,
86–87; widows and, 90–93
land consolidation committee, 175–76
land reforms: consolidation and registration,
9, 164, 166–77, 222n5; impact on widows,
5; process of consolidation, 169–70;
widows' response to corruption in, 9
land tenure system, 83, 87–88
Law of Succession, 5, 183–84
Law of Succession Bill, 179–83
Legislative Council, 84
legitimacy, 187, 187–91
leso (cotton cloth), 56, 208n2
levirate/widow remarriage rituals, 9–10, 66,
168–69, 169
Liavuli, Saisi, 153, 154
Libese, Katarina, 90, 114–15
Lidzanga, Rachel, 136–37
Lidzanga, Simeon, 136
Lineiri, Caitano, 139
lisara (remembrance ceremony), 66, 170
Lisimbu, Erika, 158
living standards, 194–97
Local Native Councils (LNCs): allegations of
prostitution and, 139–40; attitudes about
wayward women in 1930s, 147;
bridewealth issues and, 122, 124, 126;
education issues and, 134; repatriation of
women and, 141–44. *See also* North
Kavirondo Local Native Council (LNC)
locust infestations, 9, 70–71, 71
Lotodo (MP), 179
Lubang, Hezron, 139
Lumadede, James, 53
Lusiola, Mary, 41–42
Luvusi, Mark, 38–39
Luyia groups: Bantu speaking people, 15; curse
of the dog and, 62; dress of, 25–26;
Hobley's subjection of, 18–20; Quakers'
view of, 25–26, 45–46; taxes imposed on,
20; Thomson's view of, 16–17. *See also*
Maragoli/Maragoli people

Madegwa, Debra, 136
Mademba, Elima, 167–68, 171, 172

Maendeleo ya Wanawake (Advancement of
    Women), 134, 166
Majani, John, 68
Makadara Magistrate Court, 184–86
male relatives: help with school tuition,
    130–31; violent intervention with boys at
    missions, 39–44; worries of the heart and,
    34, 35, 38. *See also* men
Mamdani, Mahmood, 10, 196
Mandala, Elias, 214n38
Maragoli/Maragoli people: ambivalence
    toward black government, 2–3, 193;
    burial rituals, 47–49; clothing of, 47;
    curse of the dog and, 62; defection of
    Quaker converts, 78; description of, 1;
    dress of, 25–26; education of girls of,
    119–20, 128; effects of gold mining on,
    72–81; expectations for progressive sons,
    107–17; fear of being transformed into a
    mermaid, 37; fear of loss of land, 85–86;
    fear of white cannibalism, 30–37; first
    years of colonial rule and, 17–22;
    Hobley's subjection of, 18–20; houses of,
    2, 46; impact of gold mining on economy
    of, 69–75; interpretations of practical
    Christian teachings, 50–52; land conflicts
    and, 57–58, 82–93; land consolidation and
    registration, 9, 164, 166–77, 222n5;
    legitimacy of children in, 187; locust
    plague, 70–71, 71; Luyia group, 15; male
    migration from during World War II, 119;
    missionaries' view of, 25–26, 45–46;
    mortality rate of men of, 4; population
    density, 25, 82–83, 201n1; response to
    arrival of missionaries, 29; sacrifices to
    ancestors, 49–50, 53, 65–66, 67, 68;
    stereotypes of other tribes, 112; struggle
    for education of boys, 97–106; tattooing
    rituals, 47; taxes imposed on, 20;
    Thomson's description of, 15–17; view of
    white people in, 2–3; warfare rituals of,
    66–67; widow inheritance and, 67; wife
    beating in, 150–59
Maragoli Welfare Association, 139
marriage: of KAR recruits, 149–53; legitimacy
    of, 187, 187–91; respectability of, 154–55
Marriage and Divorce Bill, 182
Masai, 16, 203n8
masculinity: care of the defenseless and, 42; of
    court officers, 158–59; disparagement of
    Christian sons, 68; government

responsibility for needy and, 171–72;
    inflated bridewealth and, 121; Maragoli
    and Christian concepts of, 64–65; wife
    beating and, 155; worries of the heart
    strategy and, 7–8, 43, 90–91, 130–31
Maseno Boys School, 98, 102, 213n2
materialism: demand for education and, 98;
    jealousy of Quaker converts and, 79–80;
    symbols of, 74; as tenet of practical
    Christianity, 45, 52; of unconverted mine
    workers, 76–77
Mbale, 72–73, 98
Mbecha, Stella, 129–30, 131
Mbembe, Achille, 10, 197
Mboya, Tom, 165, 166
medical treatment, 2, 27–28, 29, 29, 194
men: desire for educated wives, 121, 135; help
    with school tuition, 130–31;
    relinquishment of care of widows,
    171–72; responsibility for widows, 7–9;
    rumors about prostitution, 139–40;
    violent intervention with boys at
    missions, 39–44; wife beating, 7, 150–59;
    worries of the heart and, 34, 35, 38, 68.
    See also fathers; masculinity; patriarchy
mermaids, 37–39
metaphorical misunderstandings, 52
Migitsu, Mary, 155–56, *156*
Ministry of Land and Settlements, 164, 168,
    169, 170, 173
Miremu, Musa, 78
Mirimu, Jane, 32
Mise, Elima, 175, *176*
missionaries, 2–3, 6, 7. *See also* Quaker
    missionaries
Mnubi (local chief), 97
modernity: education as a means to, 118–19,
    120–21, 129, 135; election rhetoric and,
    181; inflated bridewealth and, 122–23.
    See also progressive sons
Mombasa, 107–9
moral panic, 7, 9, 139–48, 195
mortality rate, 4, 35
Mphalele, Ezekiel, 3
Mudaki, John: conversion of, 35–36; life in the
    mission, 45; mission work of, 54;
    mother's fears for, 35; sacrifice to
    ancestors, 53; visits to the mission, 30,
    33, 34
Mukiri, Mariko, 93
Muliru, James, 113–14

Mumias administration center, 17–18
Munene (MP), 183
Mungore, Respah, 156
Muse, Petero, 93
Musimbi, Elisi, 106
Musimbi, Mary, 118, 121, 149–51
Musimbi, Respah, 77
Musira, Belisi, 144, 146
Musira, Christopher, 196
Musira, Shem, 122, 126
Muslims, 182
Muteve, Mariko, 93
Muteve, Marita, 186
Muthembi, Jedida, 168–69, 171, 172
Muthoni, 141
Mutiso (MP), 179–80
Mutiva, Belisi, 65
Mutiva, Mariko, 113
Mutiva, Petero, 152–53
Mutiva, Shem, 92
Mutongi, Kenda, 156
Mwamzandi (MP), 180–81
Mwanika, Erika, 110, 112–13
Mwariru, Berita, 186
Mwenesi, Zakayo, 169
Mwenwai, Rose, 121

Nandi, 20
National Assembly, 175–76, 179–83
National Radio broadcasts, 223n12
Native Industrial Training School, 98
Native Land Trust Ordinance, 83–85
Ndangarembga, Tsitsi, 197
Ndanyi, Yohana, 104, 109–11
nepotism: court reforms and, 157; in education, 103–4; land consolidation and registration and, 9, 171; in local court system, 89–90, 92
Njonjo, Charles, 179–81
NKCA. See North Kavirondo Central Association (NKCA)
Nolega, Shem, 136
North Kavirondo, 15–17. See also Maragoli/Maragoli people
North Kavirondo Central Association (NKCA), 85
North Kavirondo Chamber of Commerce, 80
North Kavirondo District, 15. See also North Nyanza District

North Kavirondo Local Native Council (LNC): bridewealth issues and, 126–27; bursary scheme for education, 103; demand for education for boys, 98; land seizure for mining and, 85–86; responsibility for land transfers, 83–84; rumors of prostitution and, 139–40; trials concerning venereal disease, 145
North Kavirondo Taxpayers Welfare Association, 100–102
North Nyanza District, 15–17. See also Maragoli/Maragoli people
Nyangori, 19–20

oath, 157, 158, 222n29
Obusi, Peter, 53
Odanga, Matayo, 91
Odhiambo, Atieno, 223n17
Odiaga, 105–6
offerings, 65
Oliech, Jotham, 146
olovego (hair-shaving ceremony), 66, 170
Olovoga, Inyanza, 56–57
Olovoga, Shem, 56, 57–58
Onyango, Mrs. (MP), 179
Onzere, Shem, 185, 187–88
orphans: definition of, 30, 214n31; education of boys, 102–6; Girls Boarding School for, 119–20, 121; at Maragoli mission, 29; as Quaker converts, 4; success of Quaker missionaries and, 24, 30
Otiende (government councilor), 172–74
Otiende, Melissa, 119, 121, 143, 152–53
Otieno, Mary, 196
Ousmane, Sembene, 3
Owour, Mrs. (Vihiga Homecraft Training Center supervisor), 134
Oyuki, Charles, 122, 126

patriarchy: Christian women and, 63; male authority and, 40–43; role of women and, 62–63; widows' authority and, 141; wife beating and, 155; women in court and, 90–92; worries of the heart strategy and, 7–8, 39–42
p'Bitek, Okot, 3
Pentecostal Church, 77–78
Phelps-Stokes Commission, 99–100
Phillips, Arthur, 89, 157
Pitman, Dorothy, 135–36

polygamy: inflated bridewealth and, 125;
   newly arrived Christian sects and, 78; of
   progressive sons, 112, 114; as
   repercussion of divorce threats, 153, 154,
   158; succession of property and, 179, 180,
   187–88, 189; wives' view of, 187–88
poor people, 93, 121–22
postcolonial period, 163–66, 223n17. *See also*
   black leaders; citizenship; land reforms;
   Law of Succession; Law of Succession Bill
postmortem incident, 30–32, 36–37
practical Christianity, 45–47, 50–54
prayer, 53–54
progressive sons: colonial officials' attitudes
   toward, 106, 116–17, 193; financial
   burden of, 107–13; moral burden of,
   113–17
prostitution rumors: community response to,
   9; inflated bridewealth and, 125; panic
   over, 139–48; wife beating and, 150–52,
   153, 158
protests, 101
Provincial Commissioner of Nyanza, 100,
   122, 123–27, 146, 147–48
Provincial Commissioner of Nyeri, 146–47
Public Trustee's office, 178

Quaker converts: acquisition of land for
   iliinis, 56, 57–58; adherence to African
   customs, 65–67; adherence to practical
   Christianity and, 67–68; attitude toward
   parents, 59; backsliding of, 52–53, 79;
   boys' role, 63–64; changes in burial
   customs, 170; demand for better
   education, 100–102; girls' lives, 61–62;
   hungry lads, 35–36, 39–42; land conflicts
   of 1930s and, 86–87, 90–91, 92–93; life of
   women, 62–63; mockery of non-converts,
   77, 79–80; practice of widow inheritance,
   66; response to new sects, 78;
   responsibilities of men, 64–65; success of,
   68; Sunday services, 65; training of girls,
   60–62; view of unbelievers, 65. *See also*
   Christians
Quaker missionaries: agenda for western
   Kenya, 23–25, 46; arrival in Maragoli, 29;
   basis of success of, 24; cannibalism scare
   and, 30–37, 43; concerns about gold
   mining, 70; converts of, 4, 35–36, 39–42;
   description of Kaimosi, 26; desertions of
   converts and, 78–79; drought and famine

and, 32; education of boys, 4, 45;
   education of girls, 119–20, 121;
   establishment of Industrial Mission in
   Kaimosi, 23–28; fear of technology of,
   37–39; incident with the skull, 32–33;
   LNC bashing of, 101; post-colonial
   Maragoli's view of, 2–3; responses to
   backsliding and misunderstandings,
   53–54, 65–66; rift among, 78; schools of,
   98, 119–20; tenets of practical
   Christianity, 45–47; view of burial
   customs, 47–49; view of Maragolis,
   45–46; view of sacrificing to ancestors,
   49–50; view of tattooing, 47; view of
   widow inheritance, 66

Rees, Deborah Gorman: arrival in Kaimosi,
   28–29; lessons on practical Christianity,
   47; photograph of, *28*; relocation to
   Maragoli, 29; translation of hymns, 65
Rees, Emory: arrival in Kaimosi, 28–29; on
   converts at Maragoli mission, 54;
   description of trails to Kaimosi, 27;
   discouragement of, 31–32; on effects of
   postmortem, 30–31; photograph of, *28*;
   relocation to Maragoli, 29; on Vyoya's
   misunderstanding of divine punishment,
   50; warfare rituals and, 66–67
Reeve, Roxie, 47, 50, 53–54
remarriage of widows, 9–10, 66, 168–69, 169
repatriation of women, 142–44, 148
reserves, 83
rinderpest epidemics, 21, 30
roads, 194
Rosterman mining company, 84

sacrifices to ancestors, 49–50, 53, 65–66, 67–68
Salvation Army, 77–78
Scott, H. S., 99
secular civilization, 73–81
self-help projects, 166
selfishness teaching, 50–51
Semo, Daina, 153, 154
Semo, Erika, 37–38, 45
sewing machines, 73–74
sexually transmitted diseases. *See* venereal
   disease
Shego, Joshua, 135
Shego, Peter, 184, 187
Shemegi, Marita, 90
sickness. *See* disease

skull incident, 32–33, 36, 37
sleeping sickness, 21
small pox epidemic, 21, 29, 30
South Africa, 196
South Kavirondo, 202n3
Spire (British official), 18
Spoon, Mrs. (girls' teacher), 2
Stalker, Roxie, 50–51, 53–54
Stanley, Henry Morton, 203n8
stealing, 51–54
succession of property: adultery and, 184–85;
    Commission on the Law of Succession,
    178–79; court cases over, 183–86;
    indigenous laws concerning, 189–90; Law
    of Succession and, 179–83
Sunday routine, 65
Swahili: need for fluency in courts, 183–84,
    185–86, 191; use of by wives suing
    husbands for wife beating, 150; use of in
    letters to black leaders, 169, 174
swearing, 157, 158, 222n29

tailors' union, 73–74
tattooing, 47
taxes: imposed by Hobley, 20; imposed under
    black rule, 165; for schools, 102
tea, 77
technology, Margoli fear of, 37–39
theft, 50–51, 53–54
Thiongo, Ngugi wa, 3
Thomson, Joseph, 15–17, 22, 25, 80
Thuku, Harry, 101
tithes, 65
tribal warfare, 4
turnboys, 185, 225n17

Uganda, 196
Ugandan exiles, 3, 195
United States, education in South, 99
unmarried female missionaries, 50–51, 207n21

Vaseline, 76, 77
venereal disease: concerns of colonial
    officials, 144–46; infection from military
    husbands, 152, 153; infertility associated
    with, 150, 151
Vihiga Homecraft Training Center, 134
Visero, Berita, 36–37
Visero, James, 102
Visiru, Jane, 153, 157–58
Vugutsa, Esteri, 66, 138, 172

Vugutsa, Marita, 143
Vusha, Beatrice, 184–86, 185–86, 187
Vusha, Keran, 130, 131, 132–33
Vusha, Ronika, 92
Vyoya, Elisi, 113
Vyoya, Shem: conversion of, 39–40, 41–42;
    mission work of, 55; misunderstanding of
    divine punishment, 50, 52; visits to the
    mission, 30, 33

wages: in 1940s, 130; of clerical workers and
    teachers, 107, 116, 193; in factory and
    mining during Great Depression, 72; of
    KAR men, 119
Wagner, Günter, 72–75, 80
Wangare, 141
warfare rituals, 66–67
Waroho Church, 77–78
Webb, G. E., 103–04
weddings, 135–36, 137–38, 145
Weller, H. O., 97, 102
Westernization, 181
white people: care of widows and orphans,
    104; Maragoli fear of being transformed
    by, 37; Maragoli fear of cannibalism of,
    30–37; view of in post-colonial Maragoli,
    2–3, 194. See also colonial officials;
    missionaries; Quaker missionaries
widow inheritance, 9–10, 66, 168–69
widows: allegations of prostitution and, 141,
    144; appeal to citizenship, 9, 167–69,
    172–73, 174–75, 176–77; as barometer of
    impact of colonial and post colonial rule
    on, 4–5; benefits of increased bridewealth,
    118–19; care of, 6–9, 64–65; education of
    daughters and, 130–31, 134; education of
    sons of, 102–6; enlistment of help from
    male relatives, 7–8, 39, 40–44; fear of
    being transformed into a mermaid, 37–39;
    fear of white cannibalism, 32, 34, 35, 40;
    financial expectations for progressive
    sons, 7, 107–17; importance of husband's
    grave, 91–92, 170–71; land consolidation
    and registration and, 5, 9, 166–69, 170–77;
    Law of Succession and, 5; litigation over
    land, 87, 90–93; moral expectations of
    progressive sons, 113–17; percentage of
    African population, 4; reliance upon
    elected officials, 172; reliance upon the
    courts, 151, 152, 153–59; succession of
    property and, 178–79, 183–86;

widows (cont.)
   success of Quaker missionaries and, 24,
      30; suffering of, 6–7; view of Christian
      sons, 32, 59, 67, 68; view of marriage,
      155; violation of rights under black rule,
      164–65; widow inheritance and, 66. See
      also worries of the heart
widows' support group, 129
wife beating, 7, 150–59
Williams (colonial official), 2
Williams, C. H., 134
wills: colonial policy on, 189; commission
      study on, 178–79; execution of, 187;
      indigenous laws concerning, 189; Law of
      Succession Bill and, 182, 183; litigation
      over, 184–85; questions of legitimacy of,
      188
women: access to court system, 157–59;
      considered a source of venereal disease,
      144–45; contributions to independent
      Kenya, 166; curse of the dog and, 62–63;
      homecraft education for, 134; Law of
      Succession Bill and, 178–79; life in an
      iliini, 62–63; marriage to KAR men,
      149–53; moral surveillance of women,
      144–48; prevailing attitudes about in
      1930s, 146–47; proper behavior in court,
      90–91; repatriation of, 142–44, 148;
      response to allegations of prostitution,
      140–41; rumors of prostitution and,

138–48; spousal abuse of, 150–59. See
      also widows
World War II: allegations of prostitution
      during, 139–40; emigration of males
      from rural areas, 119; KAR marriages
      and, 149; moral panic during, 7, 9,
      139–48, 195
worries of the heart: abandonment by
      converted sons and, 59; adherence to
      practical Christianity and, 67–68; appeals
      to the courts for land rights and, 167–68;
      black rule and, 197; daughters' divorces
      and, 151, 155–58; effectiveness of, 40–43;
      expression of, 7–8, 8; fear of being
      transformed into a mermaid, 37–39; fear
      of white cannibalism and, 34, 35; as
      immunization from colonial rule, 196;
      importance of husband's grave, 91–92,
      170–71; land conflicts and, 93; land
      consolidation and registration and,
      171–73, 175; means of showing, 43; of
      mothers of migrant sons, 108–9, 111, 117;
      procuring education for sons and, 103;
      school tuition for girls and, 130–31; of
      shamed mothers, 115–16; succession of
      property and, 189; success of, 177;
      women in court and, 90–92

Zilika, Janet, 155–56
Zimbabwe, 197